The Global Free Trade Error

The doctrine of "free trade" is second only to that of "free markets" in undergirding ideological support for our current global economic structures and rules. From David Ricardo's "comparative advantage principle" to James Meade's Neoclassical or mainstream economics proof of self-adjusting free trade equilibrium, the free trade doctrine has had a lasting and destructive hold on Neoclassical economic thinking since its inception.

The Global Free Trade Error provides a detailed analysis of these foundational models and counter-poses these to alternative Neo-Marxist "unequal exchange" models of global trade and finance. In the first part of the book the three core free trade models alluded to above are respectively demonstrated to be: overdetermined, inapplicable, and infeasible. In particular, Ricardo's parable is shown to support managed trade rather than free trade as Ricardo and two centuries of economic texts have claimed. In the second part of the book, unequal exchange analyses of global trade are shown to provide logically coherent and useful insights into global trade and finance. In the third and final part of the book, this unequal exchange perspective is used, within a general "demand and cost" setting, to develop a set of global managed trade principles for a more equitable and sustainable world trade regime.

This book will be of great interest to those who study political economy, history of economic thought, and international trade, including trade agreements and tariffs.

Ron Baiman teaches economics in the MBA program at Benedictine University, U.S. He has written numerous academic and policy papers, served for many years on the Editorial Board of the *Review of Radical Political Economics*, and is the author of *The Morality of Radical Economics: Ghost Curve Ideology and the Value Neutral Aspect of Neoclassical Economics*, and co-author and co-editor of the Choice award winning collection: *Political Economy and Contemporary Capitalism*.

Routledge Frontiers of Political Economy

The Global Free Trade Error

The Infeasibility of Ricardo's Comparative Advantage Theory

Ron Baiman

LONDON AND NEW YORK

First published 2017 by Routledge

2 Park Square, Milton Park, Abingdon, Oxfordshire OX14 4RN
52 Vanderbilt Avenue, New York, NY 10017

Routledge is an imprint of the Taylor & Francis Group, an informa business

First issued in paperback 2019

British Library Cataloguing in Publication Data
A catalogue record for this book is available from the British Library

Library of Congress Cataloging in Publication Data
Names: Baiman, Ron, 1951- author.
Title: The global free trade error : the infeasibility of Ricardo's comparative
    advantage theory / Ron Baiman.
Description: Abingdon, Oxon ; New York, NY : Routledge, [2017]
Identifiers: LCCN 2016044546| ISBN 9781138852952 (hardback) |
    ISBN 9781315723129 (ebook)
Subjects: LCSH: Free trade. | Comparative advantage (International trade)
Classification: LCC HF1713 .B26 2017 | DDC 382/.7101—dc23
LC record available at https://lccn.loc.gov/2016044546

ISBN: 978-1-138-85295-2 (hbk)
ISBN: 978-0-367-87235-9 (pbk)

Typeset in Times New Roman
by Swales & Willis Ltd, Exeter, Devon, UK

To my life partner Michelle, and my children, Jeremy, Rachel, and Rebecca, without whom this book would not have been possible.

Contents

PART III
Globalization that supports human and planetary
well-being   123

Figures

Tables

Acknowledgements

This book has been many years in the making. Over this period I have received help and encouragement from many colleagues, friends, and students. These have included present and past Chicago Political Economy Group (CPEG) comrades and friends: Joe Persky, Mel Rothenberg, Haydar Kurban, Bill Barclay, Sidney Hollander, Luis Diaz-Perez, Bruce Parry, Paul Sakol Sharon Post, Meherene Larudee, Peter Dorman, John Weeks, Bruce Parry, Fran Tobin, Steve Balkin, Elce Redmond, Samuel Rosenberg, Yasir Abu Zayd, John Weeks, Curtis Black, Bill Bianci, and Peter Dorman; present and former *Review of Radical Political Economics* editorial board comrades: Gary Mangiovi, John Willoughby, Cirus Bina, Gil Skillman, and David Barkin; work colleagues: Waleed Almousa; Chicago Ethical Humanist Society Men's Group comrades: Oliver Pergams, Alan Kimmel, Tom Hoeppner, Steve Julstrom, and Ken Novak; Democratic Socialists of America comrades: Bob Roman, Peg Strobel, Tom Broderick, and Jan Sansone; Committee for New Priorities (now disbanded) board members: Carl Rosen and Terry Davis; my Benedictine students: Yalin Wong and Caitlin Prosapio; and last but not least, my radical post-Keynesian economic friends and colleagues: Dean Baker, Robert Blecker, Robin Hahnel, Lance Taylor, Ed Nell, and Steve Pressman. My apologies for all of my other numerous "helpers" whose names I have forgotten over the years!

I owe a special thanks to William Greider and Ian Fletcher whose supportive feedback on an earlier draft of Chapter 1 came at particularly despairing moments after numerous rejections over many years from multiple mainstream and hetero- dox journals; and to the anonymous referees of the *Review of Political Economy* who took the submission of that chapter seriously and helped improve it. Likewise I am indebted to my Editors, especially Andy Humphries for taking my proposal seriously and helping me shepherd it through the peer review process, and Laura Johnson, Sally Evans-Darby, Alaina Christensen, and Sarah Sleath for editing and production. I am also indebted to the students of the "Neoliberalism and Globalization 'Big Problems' 2000–2007" senior seminar co-taught with Mel Rothenberg at the University of Chicago where Chapters 1 and 5 were conceived and especially to Adam Kalafarski for his insightful critique of the Hahnel "fair trade" solution that induced me to write the essay that comprises Chapter 5. May dogmatic barriers in political economy someday come tumbling down!

1 Introduction

The doctrine of free trade (FT) is second only to that of "free markets" in undergirding ideological support for our current global economic structures and rules. The central place that FT thinking occupies within mainstream Neoclassical (NC) economics is critically important to justifying FT policies, regardless of real motives. From David Ricardo's "comparative advantage principle" to James Meade's NC proof of self-adjusting FT equilibrium, to the broadly disseminated general introductory economics textbook version of FT accepted by most elite policy and business leaders, FT doctrine has had a lasting and destructive hold on economic policy for almost 200 years. In an earlier book I have attempted to make a case for a *moral radical economics* that roundly rejects the free market ideals and the presumption of "objective scientific" neutrality that lies at the heart of the NC self-conception of itself as "The Science" of economics (Baiman, 2016). This book is an attempt to apply moral radical economic thinking to global trade and finance.

The purpose of this book is not to develop precise mathematical models that describe, predict, and generate detailed policy options for world trade and finance. Rather its goal is to analyze in detail the foundational story doctrines, or "memes," that inform the FT global economic ideal and counter-pose this to an alternative (revised) Marxist unequal exchange (UE) radical economic foundational story of global trade and finance. The idea is to show how these in many ways very simple and basic models, or memes, inform *and misinform* global economic policy.

The objective is to set economic guide posts and ideals that conform to widely shared universal *moral economic goals* for global trade and finance without an "objective scientific" pretense that any simple trade or finance model (and especially not the models disseminated in introductory economics textbooks that have the most impact on policy makers and policy) can realistically describe, not to mention predict, real current or future global trade and financial outcomes. Rather, models are posed as *ideals* or *goals* toward which policy should strive.

Because of their ultimate influence on policy, these fundamental doctrines are critical subject matter of a desperately needed *value-based* radical economics that seeks to improve the human condition and avoid planetary disaster (Baiman, 2016) as applied to global trade and finance.

In Part I, Chapters 2–4, the NC FT doctrine, in its various forms, is shown to be mathematically *inconsistent, inapplicable, and infeasible.*

We begin in Chapter 2 by demonstrating that David Ricardo's theory of "comparative advantage," the foundational justification for FT in most introductory economics and general political economy texts, does *not* in fact provide a justification for free trade. Rather, careful analysis shows that Ricardo's original free trade version of comparative advantage is *mathematically overdetermined* and *inconsistent*, and that, under Ricardo's *classical* assumptions, gains from comparative advantage and (relative) specialization can only be realized through *managed trade, not free trade.*

Similarly, Chapter 3 finds that James Meade's proof of the existence of free trade equilibrium is *only applicable if trading partners have relatively similar factor costs.* This implies that under the stringent *Neoclassical* assumptions of Meade's proof, free trade equilibria will not exist for broad categories of trade, for example between countries with highly unequal labor compensation levels. Though often not covered in modern Neoclassical international trade texts, the major Neoclassical international trade theorems, such as the Heckscher-Ohlin, Stolper-Samuelson, and Rybczynski theorems, all presume the existence of a free trade equilibrium based on Meade's proof.[1]

Finally, in Chapter 4 we show that *under any set of assumptions* trade models that assume exchange-rate clearing of global trade will be mathematically unstable and thus economically *infeasible.*

In Part II, Chapters 5–6, alternative "unequal exchange" (UE) models, or "memes," are developed and applied to "north–south" and more recent "rentier"-based international trade and capital flow. As noted above, though these models (just like the FT doctrine) are highly abstract and simplified, they elucidate key underlying relationships that are fundamental to establishing policy goals for a sustainable international trade and finance regime that would benefit humankind and our planet.

Chapter 5 formulates and applies an "analytical Marxist" UE international trade model that draws on modern formulations of Marxist theory that do not depend on a precise "labor theory of value" or algorithm linking prices to "labor values." The model thus constructed is applied to hypothetical "north–south" or "developed/developing" country and "fair trade" (FT) or "managed trade" (MT) situations, and "global Marshall Plan" and "solidarity trading regime" solutions are proposed to support long-term equitable and sustainable global economic development.

Chapter 6 defines and characterizes the modern U.S. economy as a prime example of a "rentier" economy. It then extends the UE model of Chapter 5 to a three-country trading situation that includes "rentier" (U.S.), "unequal exchange" (Germany), and "developing country" (China) economies, elucidating the kind of trade policy changes that would be necessary to change this type of unsustainable and destructive modern trading regime to an MT international trade and finance regime that would benefit all three countries.

Part III, Chapters 7–8, concludes the book by addressing both practical and longer-term international trade and finance MT policy proposals with a specific focus on the U.S. (Chapter 7) and the global economy (Chapter 8).

Chapter 7 analyzes the post-2008 economic condition of the U.S. in a general developed country context that takes into account the impacts of both FT and manufacturing productivity growth, and outlines jobs, trade, and industrial policies that would be necessary to revive the U.S. economy and redirect it toward supporting sustainable and equitable broad-based prosperity.

The concluding Chapter 8 applies the models developed in Parts 1 and 2 to global trade policy and shows how a UE and "demand and cost model" (DCM) perspective, as opposed to a mainstream NC economics FT and "supply and demand model" (SDM) view, leads to an improved understanding of world trade and finance, and national and global policy, goals, and shorter-term practical policy measures, that are necessary to restore a measure of justice and sustainable global prosperity to the world economy.

More detailed abstracts of the various chapters are presented in the introductions to the three parts of the book.

Needless to say, my hope is that this text will contribute to a better world for my children, for all humans, and for our planet in the years to come. I believe that we face a growing existential crisis which a moral radical economics can help resolve by offering critical ideological insight and policy direction (Baiman, 2016). My hope is that this book will serve as a useful example of the value of a radical economic approach to international trade and finance that is unapologetically morally driven toward the goal of improving global human well-being.

Note

1 See, for example, Findlay (1995).

References

Baiman, R. (2016) *The Morality of Radical Economics: Ghost Curve Ideology and the Value Neutral Aspect of Neoclassical Economics* (New York: Palgrave Macmillan).
Findlay, R. (1995) *Factor Proportions, Trade, and Growth* (Cambridge, MA: MIT Press).

Part I

The illogical foundations of free trade ideology

The fact that international trade does not follow textbook models, and that efforts to apply these models in practice often end up causing more harm than good to national economies, and to the global economy and planetary sustainability, is no secret. The following three chapters include numerous references to empirical and practical critiques of the effects of "free trade" policy on individual countries and on world development. The weight of the evidence is abundantly clear. The global push toward ever "freer" trade and capital flows has subverted democracy and led to an unsustainable world economy with historically unprecedented and unimaginable levels of inequality and stagnant growth that appears to be careening toward global environmental catastrophe.

Mainstream Neoclassical (NC) economics has played an outsize role in legitimating the ideology of "free trade" that has so distorted the world economy and undermined democratic ideals. Regardless of the abundant empirical and historical data to the contrary, NC textbook theories and ideologies endure in the minds of world political and business leaders, mainstream media, elite academic and educational curricula, legal practice, and mainstream civil society leaders. There is no question that free trade thinking serves the interests of the wealthiest and most powerful individuals and transnational corporations that increasingly dominate global economics and politics. But a key factor in maintaining the ideological dominance of free trade in support of the "inverted tyranny" (Wolin, 2008) that characterizes modern capitalist democracies is the perceived *ideological power of the free trade doctrine*.

The following three chapters address the *ideological foundations* of free trade thinking and show that even under the most idealistic textbook assumptions, the doctrine is *mathematically infeasible*.

In the first chapter, "The infeasibility of free trade in classical theory: Ricardo's comparative advantage parable has no solution," formal models of Ricardo's comparative advantage parable that include general forms of consumer price-response behavior are constructed from a detailed textual exegesis of Ricardo's story. Using these models, the comparative advantage parable is shown to be mathematically overdetermined and therefore generally unsolvable. To reinforce this conclusion, a numerical solution is derived for a constant elasticity version of the model. A necessary condition for the existence of a solution to the constant elasticity model is that two price elasticities of demand must be functions of the other two price elasticities of demand. General formulas are derived expressing this dependency. When realistic elasticities for wine are set, the model can only be solved if Portuguese demand for English cloth is unrealistically elastic. This demonstrates that sustainable and mutually beneficial trade between England and Portugal can only be realized through managed trade. Thus, contrary to Ricardo's belief, and to the statements of almost every textbook and academic treatise on international trade for the last two centuries, *the parable of comparative advantage supports managed rather than free trade.*

The second chapter, "The limits of free trade in Neoclassical theory: from Heckscher-Ohlin to unequal exchange," addresses the NC version of free trade ideology. This chapter first summarizes the conditions underlying the "modern" algebraic Heckscher-Ohlin model (AHO) and points out that this model does not prove that free trade will generate a balanced and mutually beneficial international trade equilibrium, and that its assumptions of identical technologies, and perfectly competitive marginal product returns and consequent "factor price equalization," are so restrictive that they render the AHO largely irrelevant even within the context of already highly idealized NC trade theory.

The chapter next reviews the older but more theoretically grounded and less restrictive NC international trade models of Meade and Haberler, who, using graphical techniques in a two-country example, demonstrated that: a) free trade will produce a unique stable, sustainable, and mutually beneficial equilibrium; and b) "production possibility frontiers" reflecting comparative advantages likely to result from unequal factor endowments will lead to exports of goods produced with the relatively abundant factor and imports of goods produced with the relative scarce factor in both countries. Finally, the chapter demonstrates that: c) when trading partners have "highly unequal factor costs," as is likely in "north–south" trade, the Meade-Haberler geometric Heckscher-Ohlin (GHO) model will produce imbalanced, and probably not mutually beneficial, "unequal exchange" that can only be sustained through active "trade management."

This shows that even in the most general version of basic NC trade theory, free trade is inconsistent with comparative advantage and partial specialization when wage levels are highly unequal, as they are in most north–south trade.

Finally, the third chapter, "Globally sustainable and balanced international trade based on exchange-rate adjustment is mathematically unstable and therefore economically infeasible," shows that textbook exchange-rate-based "free trade" is mathematically unstable and economically infeasible even under the most idealistic assumptions. Even if: a) Marshall-Lerner conditions are universally satisfied, b) bilateral trade universally responds effectively and efficiently to exchange-rate fluctuations, and c) freely floating or (individual country) administered exchange rates react quickly and in a "normal" direction to trade imbalances, exchange-rate "price signals" cannot be expected to produce globally balanced international trade. Since trade that is not balanced or moving into balance by means of exchange-rate changes after taking into account the impact of other "shift-factors" cannot be viewed as obeying underlying exchange-rate-based "fundamentals," a global free trade regime is not feasible. The chapter shows this by proving under these assumptions that: a) if there is a globally balanced exchange-rate solution to an international trading system, this solution must be unique, and b) the unique solution to this kind of exchange-rate-based trading system will be mathematically unstable. Since the solution is unstable, there is no mechanism driving the system toward this solution. If it exists, this solution is therefore economically infeasible. *The principal theoretical issue addressed in this chapter is whether "normal" exchange-rate responses to trade deficits, whether market-driven or administered, can, under the most ideal assumptions, move global trade toward a more balanced position than would otherwise occur. If this is not possible, the free trade doctrine has no theoretical legitimacy.*

Reference

Wolin, S. S. (2008) *Democracy Incorporated: Managed Democracy and the Specter of Inverted Totalitarianism* (Princeton, NJ: Princeton University Press).

2 The infeasibility of free trade in classical theory

Ricardo's comparative advantage parable has no solution[1]

1 Introduction

David Ricardo's (1817, Ch. 7) perceived demonstration of a market-based, mutually beneficial, "comparative advantage" trade equilibrium between countries with different domestic factor-cost ratios has been part of the intellectual justification for free trade since its publication in 1817. Even economists critical of Neoclassical trade theory contend that the insights of Ricardo and Hume are among the most important principles that need to be taught to undergraduates and to students who get formal training in economics (Krugman, 1996, pp. 117–126). These doctrines – that the benefits of trade are not limited to absolute advantages in production and that trade deficits self-correct – are essential components of the argument for free trade. Ricardo's parable encapsulates both ideas clearly, succinctly, and when the assumptions of the model are satisfied, irrefutably.

Well-known critiques of Ricardo's parable show that his assumptions do not hold in the real world. Some of these assumptions are full employment, current account-based price adjustments between countries, quick and continuous within-country substitutions of production, and widespread distribution of benefits from trade. These critiques note that when these assumptions are violated, free trade may cause rising unemployment, slower growth, and increasing inequality. Such negative consequences of free trade can more than offset any gains from comparative advantages (Prasch, 1996; Blecker, 1999; MacEwan, 1999; Eatwell & Taylor, 2000; Vernengo, 2000). However, the textbook stories endure and generally ignore these critiques.

This chapter takes a different approach. It accepts the assumptions of the basic classical model, and shows that its free trade conclusion is logically inconsistent. This interpretation of Ricardo's parable recognizes that while trade has the *potential* to be mutually beneficial, there is no theoretical basis for the claim that free market forces will lead to a sustainable *realization* of these benefits.[2]

Section 2 begins by constructing simple formal models of Ricardo's parable that include the workings of Hume's specie flow mechanism. This is an essential element of the story often left out of simple barter descriptions of comparative advantage.[3] Using these models, we show that the parable is mathematically overdetermined and therefore unsolvable. Ricardo's free trade solution, which provides: (i) complete specialization, (ii) full employment, (iii) balanced trade, and

(iv) balanced aggregate supply and demand (although not explicitly addressed by Ricardo, this condition is satisfied by his model) will generally not exist.[4] I explore this point further by showing that, under plausible demand conditions, partial benefits of international trade based on comparative advantage in Ricardo's model can only be realized if trade between countries *is* actively managed. Unmanaged free trade will generally result in unsustainable long-term deficits and surpluses between countries.

Thus, even when all the assumptions of Ricardo's model are satisfied, there is no theoretical argument that *free* trade between countries will be mutually beneficial in the absence of policy intervention.

2 A simple own-price formalization of Ricardo's comparative advantage parable

The comparative advantage parable is based on roughly twenty paragraphs (7.13 to 7.32) from Chapter 7 of *On the Principles of Political Economy and Taxation* (Ricardo, 1817).[5] I will cite the first ten, and through detailed exegesis construct a formalization that I call "Model S." As the later ten paragraphs illustrate the same points, their reproduction is not necessary. This formalization assumes no cross-price effects. Section 3 constructs a second formalization, Model G, which includes cross-price effects.

> If Portugal had no commercial connexion with other countries, instead of employing a great part of her capital and industry in the production of wines, with which she purchases for her own use the cloth and hardware of other countries, she would be obliged to devote a part of that capital to the manufacture of those commodities, which she would thus obtain probably inferior in quality as well as quantity.
>
> 7.13

7.13 describes the fact that if Portugal was in a state of autarky and had no commercial connection with other countries, she would be obliged to produce the cloth that she needed herself rather than trading wine for it.

> The quantity of wine which she shall give in exchange for the cloth of England, is not determined by the respective quantities of labour devoted to the production of each, as it would be, if both commodities were manufactured in England, or both in Portugal.
>
> 7.14

In paragraph 7.14 Ricardo notes that if both countries are opened up to trade, the exchange ratio between wine and cloth will not be determined by their relative labor requirements as it would under autarky. Under autarky Ricardo believed that relative prices, or exchange values, were primarily determined by direct labor costs of production.

England may be so circumstanced, that to produce the cloth may require the labour of 100 men for one year; and if she attempted to make the wine, it might require the labour of 120 men for the same time. England would therefore find it in her interest to import wine, and to purchase it by the exportation of cloth.

7.15

Paragraph 7.15 states the basic assumptions of the parable for England. She would need the labor of 100 men for a year "to produce the cloth" or to satisfy England's domestic (autarkic) total domestic demand for cloth, and 120 men for "the same time" (a year) to "make the wine" or to satisfy England's domestic (autarkic) demand for wine. We can therefore assign relative "labor value" prices of 100 for cloth and 120 for wine for England's autarkic total domestic demand for cloth and wine respectively. As described below, the *international* exchange ratio between these two goods will *not* be based on relative labor requirements, as it will be influenced by specie flow between the countries.

The paragraph goes on to state that England will want to export cloth and import wine since she's a more efficient producer of cloth. As explained below, this assumes that Portuguese wine is less costly in (international) gold prices in England than English wine. This is an easy assumption to make, as wine made in Portugal requires *less* labor than wine made in England.

Although Ricardo does not say that England will *completely* specialize in producing cloth, this can be inferred from his statement in the next paragraph (7.16) that Portugal should completely specialize in wine and import all of its cloth from England – even though cloth made in England requires *more* labor than cloth made in Portugal. This can also be inferred from a later example regarding the consequences of the discovery of a more productive wine-making process in England, where Ricardo notes that in this case: "it might become profitable for the two countries to exchange employments; for England to make *all* the wine, and Portugal *all* the cloth consumed by them" (7.21, emphasis added).[6]

Note that Ricardo does not specify units of measurement for England's total domestic wine and cloth demands in this paragraph. The only references Ricardo makes to units of measurement in the parable are in paragraph 7.22, where (in the context of another example) he assumes a price of wine in England of £50 "per pipe" and a price of £45 for "a certain quantity" of cloth. Let's assume that England's total domestic demand for wine is "A" "pipes," and that "a certain quantity" is square yards; so England's total domestic demand for cloth is "B" square yards of cloth. Ricardo is then assuming that in England the price of B square yards of cloth and A pipes of wine is 100 and 120 respectively.

To produce the wine in Portugal, might require only the labour of 80 men for one year, and to produce the cloth in the same country, might require the labour of 90 men for the same time. It would therefore be advantageous for her to export wine in exchange for cloth. This exchange might even take place, notwithstanding that the commodity imported by Portugal could be produced there with less labour than in England. Though she could make the cloth with the labour of 90 men, she would import it from a country where it required the labour of 100 men to produce it, because it would be advantageous to her rather to employ her capital in the production of wine, for which she would obtain more cloth from England, than she could produce by diverting a portion of her capital from the cultivation of vines to the manufacture of cloth.

7.16

Paragraph 7.16 states the basic assumptions of the parable for Portugal. In Portugal it requires the labor of eighty men for one year to produce Portugal's (autarkic) total domestic demand for wine and ninety men for one year to produce her total autarkic domestic demand for cloth. Again, Ricardo does not specify quantities, or units of measurement.

Ricardo then goes on to state that, just as with England for wine in 7.15, "it would be advantageous" for Portugal to import her domestic demand for cloth that she makes with ninety men "from a country where it required the labor of 100 men to produce it" because it "would be advantageous to her rather to employ her capital in the production of wine, for which she could obtain more cloth from England, than she could by diverting a portion of her capital from the cultivation of vines to the manufacture of cloth" (7.16).

This makes clear that Portugal's autarkic total domestic demand for cloth that can be produced in Portugal with ninety men is *equal* to England's autarkic domestic demand that requires 100 men for its production in England or, based on our assumption from paragraph 7.15, "B" square yards. In addition, Ricardo claims that "it would be advantageous" for Portugal to *completely specialize* in wine production, as she could obtain more cloth this way than by "diverting [*even*] *a portion* of her capital from the cultivation of vines to the manufacture of cloth" (emphasis added).

Since 100 men in England can produce "B" square yards of cloth, if England employed all of the $100 + 120 = 220$ men that were engaged in cloth and wine production under autarky just in cloth production, she would be able to produce $220/100 = 2.2B$ square yards of cloth. As Portugal's autarkic domestic demand for cloth was also "B," for England to be able to fully employ these 220 men after complete specialization, "free trade" must increase Portuguese demand for cloth by 0.2B so that: $2B + \Delta Q_{PC} B = 2.2B$ or, canceling the B's:

$$2 + \Delta Q_{PC} = 2.2 \tag{1}$$

must hold, where ΔQ_{PC} is the proportional *increase* over B of free trade-induced Portuguese demand for English cloth that is greater than the initial autarkic Portuguese and English demand for cloth of 2B.

Thus England would give the produce of the labour of 100 men, for the produce of the labour of 80. Such an exchange could not take place between the individuals of the same country. The labour of 100 Englishmen cannot be given for that of 80 Englishmen, but the produce of the labour of 100 Englishmen may be given for the produce of the labour of 80 Portuguese, 60 Russians, or 120 East Indians. The difference in this respect, between a single country and many, is easily accounted for, by considering the difficulty with which capital moves from one country to another, to seek a more profitable employment, and the activity with which it invariably passes from one province to another in the same country.

7.17

Similarly, paragraph 7.17 states: "Thus England would give the produce of the labour of 100 men [English cloth makers] for the produce of the labour of 80 [Portuguese wine makers]." From paragraph 7.15 we can assume that England will fully specialize in cloth production and import from Portugal all of the wine that she previously consumed under autarky. The produce of 100 English men working in cloth production, "B" square yards, is thus going to be exchanged for the produce of eighty Portuguese men working in wine production, and these wine imports from Portugal will fully satisfy English demand for wine (assumed to be "A" pipes). This implies that autarkic Portuguese production and demand for wine is also "A" pipes.

Thus, if Portugal specializes in wine production and imports all of her cloth ("B" square yards of cloth produced by 100 English cloth workers), Portugal will produce $(80+90)/80 = 2.125A$ pipes of wine. This implies that for full employment to be maintained under free trade, or for all of the Portuguese cloth workers to be redirected to wine production, Portugal must produce and sell: $2A + \Delta Q_{EW} A = 2.125A$ pipes of wine, so that after canceling the A's, the condition:

$$2 + \Delta Q_{EW} = 2.125 \tag{2}$$

must hold, where ΔQ_{EW} is additional free trade-induced English demand for wine that is greater than existing English and Portuguese autarkic demand for wine of $2A$.

It would undoubtedly be advantageous to the capitalists of England, and to the consumers in both countries, that under such circumstances, the wine and the cloth should both be made in Portugal, and therefore that the capital and labour of England employed in making cloth, should be removed to Portugal for that purpose. In that case, the relative value of these commodities would be regulated by the same principle, as if one were the produce of Yorkshire, and the other of London: and in every other case, if capital freely flowed towards those countries where it could be most profitably employed, there could be no difference in the rate of profit, and no other difference in the real or labour price of commodities, than the additional quantity of labour required to convey them to the various markets where they were to be sold.

7.18

Experience, however, shews, that the fancied or real insecurity of capital, when not under the immediate control of its owner, together with the natural disinclination which every man has to quit the country of his birth and connexions, and intrust himself with all his habits fixed, to a strange government and new laws, check the emigration of capital. These feelings, which I should be sorry to see weakened, induce most men of property to be satisfied with a low rate of profits in their own country, rather than seek a more advantageous employment for their wealth in foreign nations.

7.19

In 7.18 and 7.19 Ricardo explains why the parable assumes that there will be no capital flow or investment between countries, so commercial arbitrage of productivity and cost differences between countries will take the form of international trade rather than reallocation of investment as it would in one country – as between Yorkshire and London in England.

Gold and silver having been chosen for the general medium of circulation, they are, by the competition of commerce, distributed in such proportions amongst the different countries of the world, as to accommodate themselves to the natural traffic which would take place if no such metals existed, and the trade between countries were purely a trade of barter.

7.20

In 7.20 Ricardo asserts that although trade between England and Portugal will be conducted through a "medium of circulation" such as "gold and silver," the end result will be the same as if it had been conducted through barter. Portugal will specialize in wine production and import all of the cloth that she consumes from England; England will do the opposite.

Thus, cloth cannot be imported into Portugal, unless it sell there for more gold than it cost in the country from which it was imported; and wine cannot be imported into England, unless it will sell for more there than it cost in Portugal. If the trade were purely a trade of barter, it could only continue whilst England could make cloth so cheap as to obtain a greater quantity of wine with a given quantity of labour, by manufacturing cloth than by growing vines; and also whilst the industry of Portugal were attended by the reverse effects. Now suppose England to discover a process for making wine, so that it should become her interest rather to grow it than import it; she would naturally divert a portion of her capital from the foreign trade to the home trade; she would cease to manufacture cloth for exportation, and would grow wine for herself. The money price of these commodities would be regulated accordingly; wine would fall here while cloth continued at its former price, and in Portugal no alteration would take place in the price of either commodity. Cloth would continue for some time to be exported from this country, because its price would continue to be higher in Portugal than here; but money instead of wine would be given in exchange for it, till the accumulation of money here, and its diminution abroad, should so operate on the relative value of cloth in the two countries, that it would cease to be profitable to export it. If the improvement in making wine were of a very important description, it might become profitable for the two countries to exchange employments; for England to make all the wine, and Portugal all the cloth consumed by them; but this could be effected only by a new distribution of the precious metals, which should raise the price of cloth in England, and lower it in Portugal. The relative price of wine would fall in England in consequence of the real advantage from the improvement of its manufacture; that is to say, its natural price would fall; the relative price of cloth would rise there from the accumulation of money.

7.21

In 7.21, Ricardo further explains that "cloth cannot be imported into Portugal, unless it sells there for more gold than it cost in the country from which it was imported," and similarly for wine. Thus, Ricardo makes clear that comparative advantage operates through gold, and that international gold prices for English cloth in Portugal and Portuguese wine in England have to be lower than their respective domestic gold prices for there to be trade.

Trade will thus be conducted through market mechanisms based on gold (or international currency) prices. Any increases or declines in demand for cloth or wine from their initial autarkic equilibrium demands of A pipes of wine or B square yards of cloth will be a function of gold price reductions.

7.20 and 7.21 also make clear that for purposes of international trade, the operative price is not the labor-value price but the international exchange or "gold price" that will, following Hume's specie flow mechanism, rise or fall depending on the inflow or outflow of gold into the domestic economy. This inflow or outflow, in turn, is based on the existence of trade surpluses or deficits, respectively.

Ricardo notes that if England were to discover a wine-making process that would make it cheaper for her to produce wine domestically than to import it from Portugal, she would cease to trade cloth for wine and would export cloth to Portugal for money. In this case: "Cloth would continue for some time to be exported from this country [England], because its price would be continue to be higher in Portugal than here [in England]; but money instead of wine would be given in exchange for it, till the accumulation of money here [in England], and its diminution abroad [in Portugal], should so operate on the relative value of cloth in the two countries, that it would cease to be profitable to export it" [when the gold price of cloth in England again becomes higher than the gold price of cloth in Portugal]. So: "If the improvement in making wine were of a very important description, it might become profitable for the two countries to exchange employments; for England to make all the wine, and Portugal all the cloth consumed by them; but this could be effected only by a new distribution of the precious metals, which should raise the price of cloth in England, and lower it in Portugal."

This example explains Ricardo's pricing principles: (i) relative domestic prices reflect labor productivity, but (ii) the *overall* domestic price level will be tied to the level of the "accumulation of money" and (iii) this accumulation or withdrawal of gold will be determined by international trade surpluses or deficits.

We can therefore assume that in Ricardo's initial configuration of the comparative advantage parable, before trade, the gold price values of the domestic currencies reflect labor values, as he writes in 7.18 that in this initial situation: "The wine and cloth shall both be made in Portugal," indicating that the Portuguese labor-value prices of eighty and ninety "person years" for B square yards of cloth and A pipes of wine are less expensive *in terms of gold* than the English labor value prices of 100 and ninety person years for the same quantities of wine and cloth. We can also assume that Portugal's initial trade surplus will result in an accumulation of gold in Portugal that will drive up Portuguese gold prices until specialization and trade based on comparative advantage becomes feasible. Ricardo's parable relates to this equilibrium position, described in 7.20, whereby gold will be "distributed in such proportions . . . so as to accommodate itself to the natural traffic that would take place . . . and the trade between countries were purely a matter of barter."

For cloth to be made in England, its gold price has to be relatively lower than the gold price of Portuguese cloth and, conversely, the gold price of Portuguese wine has to be lower than the gold price of wine produced in England. Therefore, if E>1 represents the increase in overall gold prices in Portugal relative to gold prices in England that results from the initial accumulation of gold in Portugal and withdrawal of gold from England, at the equilibrium comparative advantage trading solution described above the gold price of Portuguese cloth must be greater than that of cloth produced in England (E90>100) and the gold price of Portuguese wine must be lower than that of wine produced in England (E80<120).

The price-based *increase* in English demand for wine over autarkic demand for A pipes will therefore be a function of the reduction in the gold price, E80, of Portuguese wine relative to the gold price of wine in England of 100, so that:

$$\Delta Q_{EW} = D_{EW}\left(E80\right) \tag{3}$$

where D_{EW} is a general demand function that gives the relative increase in English demand for wine as a function of the gold price of Portuguese wine relative to its English price of 100, and ΔQ_{EW} is a ratio increase over A pipes. A value of $\Delta Q_{EW} = 0.2$ would mean that English consumers are buying 0.2A more wine at this reduced Portuguese import price.

Similarly, the price-based increase in Portuguese demand for imported English cloth will be a function of the reduction in the gold price in Portugal for imported English cloth, 100/E, relative to the gold price of cloth in Portugal of 90 (recall that 90>100/E). Note that gold prices in Portugal have all risen by E times their original value relative to gold prices in England, so that relative to the new after-trade gold prices in Portugal, the English gold price of 100 becomes 100/E. 100/E thus becomes the relative and operative price that induces increased demand for English cloth in Portugal.

$$\Delta Q_{PC} = D_{PC}\left(\frac{100}{E}\right) \tag{4}$$

Conditions (2) and (4) presume that all of Portugal's additional wine production of $A + \Delta Q_{EW}A = 1.125A$ pipes, beyond that needed for domestic consumption A, is exported and consumed in England. Likewise, from (1) and (3) above, all of England's additional cloth production of $B + \Delta Q_{PC}B = 1.2B$ square yards is exported and consumed in Portugal. These rather restrictive conditions on the gains from specialization can be relaxed if cross-price effects are included (see below).

Ricardo assumed that under these conditions, market forces will generate a solution for the equations above.

Finally, for Ricardo's model to work, trade must be balanced. A trade imbalance would cause gold to accumulate in one country and be withdrawn from the other, leading to gold price increases in the first and gold price reductions in the second. Unbalanced trade would eventually make specialization and comparative advantage-based trade unprofitable, and not economically viable. So Ricardo's parable must also include a (gold-price denominated) balanced trade condition:

$$E80(1 + \Delta Q_{EW}) = 100(1 + \Delta Q_{PC}) \tag{5}$$

Here $E80(1 + \Delta Q_{EW})$ is the value of Portuguese wine exports to England in terms of labor-value price per unit of $E80$ in Portuguese gold, and $100(1 + \Delta Q_{PC})$ is the value of English cloth imports to Portugal in English gold prices.

Assuming that all revenue from sales is spent on wine and cloth, these last three equations also ensure that aggregate demand equals aggregate supply in each country, as by multiplying (1) by $E80$, (2) by 100, and using (5) we get:

$$80 + \frac{100}{E}(1 + \Delta Q_{PC}) = 80 \times 2.125 \tag{6}$$

This shows that the additional income received by workers and/or capitalists in Portugal matches their additional expenditure on less expensive English cloth, and:

$$100 + E80(1 + \Delta Q_{EW}) = 100 \times 2.2 \tag{7}$$

which shows that the same is true for English workers and capitalists.[7]

This gives us a simple system (which we call "Model S") that does not take into account cross-price effects. Model S has five independent equations, (1) to (5), and three unknowns: ΔQ_{EW}, ΔQ_{PC}, and E. They set out conditions for: a) complete specialization, b) full employment, c) balanced trade, and d) balanced aggregate supply and demand, for each country. Ricardo claims that market forces will generate a solution to this system. However, this is clearly not the case, as *the system is missing two degrees of freedom and is thus overdetermined and not generally solvable.*

Moreover, as mentioned in note 2, from 7.16 and 7.17 it is clear that though Ricardo based his parable on *complete* specialization, *partial* specialization would also result in an overdetermined and unsolvable mathematical outcome as it would remove one of the full-employment constraints – (1) or (2) above – but still be missing one degree of freedom.

Cross-price and N-country formalizations are also overdetermined

To see if the overdetermination problem results from not taking cross-price effects into account, or if it is an artifact of the two-country model, we construct an own-price *and* cross-price interpretation of Ricardo's parable (Appendix B expands this to an N-country model).

We start by including cross-price effects. Classical political economists have generally focused on the cost-based determinates of equilibrium "natural prices" (see 7.21 above) and thought of "market prices" as relatively uninteresting transitory prices that were not fruitful objects of analysis. They also understood that demand was affected by *real* price changes *relative* to other prices, as opposed to nominal overall price changes that do not change relative prices or incomes (Ricardo, 1817, Ch. 7). They therefore realized that a nominal price change in one good would affect the real prices of the other goods. This effect would be particularly strong in a two-good model and this might have led them to consider cross-price as well as own-price effects.

To allow for this possibility, Model G includes cross-price effects. This implies the following system of four demand equations:

$$\Delta Q_{EW} = D_{EW}\left(E80\right) \tag{8}$$

$$\Delta Q_{PW} = D_{PW}\left(\frac{100}{E}\right) \tag{9}$$

$$\Delta Q_{PC} = D_{PC}\left(\frac{100}{E}\right) \tag{10}$$

$$\Delta Q_{EC} = D_{EC}\left(E80\right) \tag{11}$$

where $\Delta Q_{EW}, \Delta Q_{PW}, \Delta Q_{PC}$, and ΔQ_{EC} are the proportional changes, from autarkic demand of unity, in English demand for wine, Portuguese demand for wine, Portuguese demand for cloth, and English demand for cloth, and D_{EW}, D_{PW}, D_{PC}, and D_{EC} are their respective demand functions, as in Model S.

To these equations we must add, as in Model S, two full-employment equations that assume complete specialization:

$$1 + \Delta Q_{PW} + 1 + \Delta Q_{EW} = 2.125 \tag{12}$$

$$1 + \Delta Q_{EC} + 1 + \Delta Q_{PC} = 2.2 \tag{13}$$

and one balanced trade condition:

$$E80(1 + \Delta Q_{EW}) = 100(1 + \Delta Q_{PC}) \tag{14}$$

We assume "normal" responses to price changes and "normal" specie flow international exchange rate effects so that $\Delta Q_{PW} \leq 0$ and $\Delta Q_{EC} \leq 0$, all other variables are greater or equal to zero, and $E90 > 100$ and $120 > 80E$. These inequality conditions assume that some Portuguese wine consumers, and some English cloth consumers, substitute consumption of cloth for wine, and wine for cloth, in response to lower relative prices of each, and that the equilibrium exchange rate E sets terms of trade between the relative price ratios of the two countries (as in Model S).

Finally, as with Model S, post-trade aggregate income and expenditure for both countries will be balanced in this system, as from (12) we have:

$$E80(1 + \Delta Q_{PW}) + E80(1 + \Delta Q_{EW}) = E80 \times 2.125$$

and from (13) we have:

$$100 \times (1 + \Delta Q_{EC}) + 100 \times (1 + \Delta Q_{PC}) = 100 \times 2.2$$

But from (14) these imply that:

$$80(1 + \Delta Q_{PW}) + \frac{100}{E} \times (1 + \Delta Q_{PC}) = 80 \times 2.125 \tag{15}$$

demonstrating that Portuguese consumers spend all the extra export income they make by specializing in wine production on (relatively inexpensive) English cloth imports and (relatively more expensive) domestically produced wine, and:

$$100 \times (1 + \Delta Q_{EC}) + E80 \times (1 + \Delta Q_{EW}) = 100 \times 2.2 \tag{16}$$

which gives a similar result for English consumers.

We now have a more general formalization of Ricardo's parable. It again provides for: a) complete specialization, b) full employment, c) balanced trade, and d) balanced aggregate supply and demand, for each country. However, this more complete model has five unknowns: ΔQ_{PW}, ΔQ_{EW}, ΔQ_{PC}, ΔQ_{EC}, and E, and seven equations; it is again missing two degrees of freedom and is thus overdetermined and not solvable. Again, partial rather than complete specialization will result in the deficit of one degree of freedom, and the model will still be overdetermined.

Appendix B generalizes the constant elasticity version of this model (see Section 4) to N countries and shows that this general model is also overdetermined and not solvable. As this "degrees of freedom" calculation is independent of the precise specification of the model (with constant elasticities), this demonstration shows that the general N-country, N-good, Ricardian model with cross-price effects is overdetermined.

We conclude that regardless of whether Ricardo's story is interpreted more restrictively (as in Model S) or more generously (as in Model G), and regardless of the number of trading partners to which it is applied (see Appendix B), it is fundamentally overdetermined and not generally solvable.

3 A fully specified constant elasticity model of Ricardo's parable

It is instructive to work out the policy implications of the overdetermination problem by specifying and solving a constant elasticity version of Model G that we call "Model E." In Model E, behavioral demand decisions are assumed to be captured by fixed consumer elasticities of demand for wine and cloth in England and Portugal respectively.

Let E_{EW} be the English price elasticity of demand for wine, E_{PW} the Portuguese price elasticity of demand for wine, E_{PC} the Portuguese price elasticity of demand for cloth, and E_{EC} the English price elasticity of demand for cloth. All other notation will follow that of Model G.

Note that these cross-price models take into account the fact that when the price of an imported good is lower than the domestic price of the same good, the relative price of the other (non-imported) good rises. Thus, for example, if cloth can be bought in England at a price (in Portuguese currency) that is lower than the price of Portuguese cloth, Portuguese wine becomes relatively more expensive than cloth for Portuguese consumers. This implies that the Portuguese will purchase less wine and more cloth than they used to, in response to an appreciation of (the international value of) Portuguese prices and a reduction in English prices.

Equations (17) and (19) model the increased demand for imports resulting from the reduced "own prices" of imported goods, while equations (18) and (20) model the induced decline in demand for domestically produced goods resulting from their relative (domestic) price appreciation. These equations explicitly substitute own-price for cross-price elasticities – a procedure that will only work in the two-good case. (See Appendix A for the derivations of these equations, and Appendix B for N-good and N-country models with standard cross-elasticity formulations, which also demonstrate that the results below are not an artifact of the two-good model.)

In Model E we can fully specify 1b through 4b as the following four price elasticity of demand equations:

$$120\Delta Q_{EW} = E_{EW}(120 - E80) \tag{17}$$

$$100\Delta Q_{PW} = -E_{PW}(E90 - 100) \tag{18}$$

$$E90\Delta Q_{PC} = E_{PC}(E90 - 100) \tag{19}$$

$$E80\Delta Q_{EC} = -E_{EC}(120 - E80) \tag{20}$$

To these we can add the full-employment equations assuming complete specialization:

$$1 + \Delta Q_{PW} + 1 + \Delta Q_{EW} = 2.125 \tag{21}$$

$$1 + \Delta Q_{EC} + 1 + \Delta Q_{PC} = 2.2 \tag{22}$$

and the balanced trade condition:

$$E80(1 + \Delta Q_{EW}) = 100(1 + \Delta Q_{PC}) \tag{23}$$

whereas with the general model, for feasibility and specialization: $\Delta Q_{PW} \leq 0$ and $\Delta Q_{EC} \leq 0$ and all other variables are greater or equal to zero; and $E90 > 100$ and $120 > 80E$. Finally, as the post-trade aggregate income and expenditure balances for both countries derived in Model G depend only on (21), (22), and (23), versions of aggregate demand balance equations (13) and (14) will hold in Model E.

Because consumer demand behavior in Model E is presumed to be captured by fixed price elasticities of demand, the general overdetermination problem of Model G becomes a condition on possible elasticities of demand. Since Model E has nine variables (the four changes in quantity demanded, the four elasticities, and the exchange rate) and seven equations, only two of the elasticities can be freely specified. Overdetermination implies that for there to be a solution to Ricardo's parable (or feasible "natural prices," an exchange rate, and quantities demanded that satisfy all of Ricardo's conditions), two of the demand elasticities must be precise functions of the other two.

For example, if we set $E_{EW} = a$, $E_{PW} = b$, and solve for E_{PC} and E_{EC}, we get the following general solution with two degrees of freedom to Ricardo's parable (after excluding degenerative solutions with one degree of freedom with negative elasticities):

$$E_{EC} = 93750.0 \frac{225.0a + 1600.0a^3 - 3530.0ab + 4480.0a^3b}{(20.0a + 3.125 \times 10^5 + 8.7503 \times 10^5 b)(20.0a + 27.0b)^2}$$
$$+ 93750.0 \frac{8960.0a^2b^2 + 270.0b - 6048.0b^3 - 1404.0b^2 - 2400.0a^2b + 4480.0ab^3 - 2000.0a^2 - 10048.ab^2}{(20.0a + 3.125 \times 10^5 + 8.7503 \times 10^5 b)(20.0a + 27.0b)^2}$$

$$E_{PC} = .05 \frac{1.26 \times 10^9 a^3b + 1.05 \times 10^9 a^3 + 2.52 \times 10^9 a^2b^2 - 6.375 \times 10^8 a^2 + 1.545 \times 10^9 a^2b - 1.1953 \times 10^9 ab}{(97220.0a - 46875. - 3.0b)(20.0a + 27.0b)^2}$$
$$+ .05 \frac{6.3281 \times 10^7 a - 1.125 \times 10^8 ab^2 + 1.26 \times 10^9 ab^3 - 6.075 \times 10^8 b^3 - 5.3156 \times 10^8 b^2 + 7.5938 \times 10^7 b}{(97220.0a - 46875. - 3.0b)(20.0a + 27.0b)^2}$$

$$E_{EW} = a$$
$$E_{PW} = b$$

Similarly, we can solve for ΔQ_{PW}, ΔQ_{EW}, ΔQ_{PC}, ΔQ_{EC}, and E based on these elasticity solutions.[8]

For example, if we assume that wine is a price elastic luxury good in both countries and set $E_{EW} = a = 1.5$ and $E_{PW} = b = 1.5$, we get the following unique elasticity solution to Ricardo's example:

$$E_{EW} = a = 1.5, E_{PC} = c = 2.7177, E_{EC} = d = .21864, E_{PW} = b = 1.5 \qquad (24)$$

$$\Delta Q_{PW} = -0.1516, \quad \Delta Q_{EW} = 0.2766, \quad \Delta Q_{PC} = 0.2494, \quad \Delta Q_{EC} = -0.0494$$

$$E = 1.2234$$

It can be verified through substitution that these values solve equations (1) to (5) above. Thus these values are consistent with complete specialization, full employment, balanced trade, and a feasible exchange rate that induces Portugal to specialize in wine and England in cloth. In addition, assuming that workers and capitalists receive and spend all of the revenue from production and that the lower prices on imported products are completely passed on to consumers, aggregate income and expenditure will be equal in both countries.[9]

Although theoretically consistent, this is an extremely unlikely solution as it requires that the Portuguese price elasticity of demand for cloth be inordinately high: $E_{PC} = c = 2.7177$, especially for a good that is usually considered a necessity. Reasonable demand behavior in Model E thus appears to be generally *inconsistent* with the notion that free trade (or automatic market mechanisms) can generate sustainable specialization and comparative advantage. *Rather, to partially realize sustainable benefits from comparative advantage, it appears that England will have to restrict imports of Portuguese wine to maintain balanced trade.*

More specifically, an English tariff or quota on Portuguese wine imports would have to restrict English imports of Portuguese wine to a level consistent with Portuguese demand for English cloth based on $E_{PC} < 2.7177$. This reduction in wine exports would reduce the gold inflow, and lower the gold-price increase in Portugal, so that E<1.2234. However, because of the tariff or quota on Portuguese wine, English demand for less expensive Portuguese wine would still be reduced: $\Delta Q_{EW} < 0.2766$ to a level consistent with Portugal's demand for cheap English cloth: $\Delta Q_{PC} < 0.2494$. This implies that if full employment were to be maintained in both countries, neither Portugal nor England could fully specialize so that only *partial* gains from trade could be realized.

An increase in E (that was non-specie flow-based) could also reduce the trade imbalance. However, any such single variable adjustment, without additional trade or demand management policy measures, would similarly most likely not produce balanced trade *and* full employment in both countries, as the model requires *two* extra degrees of freedom for a general solution.

4 Conclusion

We have found that, with a plausible consumer price response, Ricardo's story is mathematically overdetermined. Therefore, a sustainable and mutually beneficial free trade equilibrium point will generally not exist in Ricardo's model. Even when all of its assumptions are satisfied, Ricardo's parable does *not* demonstrate mutually beneficial *free* trade. Rather, the parable should be interpreted as demonstrating the *potential* for mutually beneficial and sustainable gains from trade based on comparative advantage when this trade is properly *managed* and not exclusively governed by market forces.[10]

Put another way, under plausible demand assumptions, sustainable and mutually beneficial comparative advantage-based trade between England and Portugal can only be realized if England reduces imports of Portuguese wine to a level commensurate with Portuguese demand for English cloth *through a public policy mechanism*. Even if all of the standard assumptions are satisfied, mutual comparative advantage-based gains from free trade will generally *not* be forthcoming as purely market-based trading will generally produce unsustainable, unbalanced trade and unemployment.

The *realization* of gains from comparative advantage-based trade is thus, like the realization of profit in *Marxian* economic modeling, or of full employment in a *Keynesian or Keleckian* macroeconomy, dependent on "demand management," as market-generated demand will often be inadequate for or disproportionate to production depending on demand behavior and price response. Neoclassical theory circumvents this problem by assuming highly responsive (and unrealistic) elasticities of substitution in production. In Ricardo's *classical* comparative advantage model, this general "realization" or "effective demand" problem produces a mathematical inconsistency due to overdetermination.

Notes

1 This is a slightly edited reprint of a paper originally published in the *Review of Political Economy*, July 2010, 22(3) 419–437.
2 I hope that this endogenous theoretical critique contributes to more realistic and beneficial international trade policies. To avoid any misunderstanding regarding the policy implications of this analysis, let me state at the outset that the issue here is not whether trade or globalization is beneficial (I generally favor increased world trade), but rather whether free, or *market-led*, trade is viable. As many of the empirical critiques point out, during the 1950–73 Bretton-Woods "managed trade" regime, world trade grew faster (according to WTO statistics, at almost double the rate) than during the "Neoliberal" 1973–2005 period (WTO, 2006, Chart II.1).
3 Many introductory texts use the simple barter story to demonstrate the advantages of specialization and trade, and jump from this to support free trade by assuming that the international price in gold for Portuguese wine is 100 and Portuguese cloth 112.5; i.e., they assume a 25% inflation of Portuguese prices, or in modern terms, a 25% appreciation of Portugal's currency relative to England's. The better texts explain that either price inflation (with fixed exchange rates via a specie flow mechanism) or exchange-rate devaluation is necessary for Ricardo's comparative advantage story to work. After covering absolute advantage, Colander (1998, p. 134) notes: "The point of the argument is that both developed and developing countries have comparative advantages in different goods. How do I know? Because trade is a two-way street. If one country could produce all the goods at a lower cost, all production would flow to that country, and its exchange rate – the rate at which one country's currency exchanges for another

country's currency – would rise. Then the comparative cost structure would change." Some international economics texts go into more detail (see Salvatore, 2005, Ch. 2).

4 My model also applies to cases of partial specialization and unemployment in one of the trading partners. The major difference, as can be deduced from dropping one of the complete specialization full-employment conditions below, is that one rather than two degrees of freedom will be missing.

5 From the third edition published in London in 1821 by John Murray. See http://www.econlib.org/LIBRARY/Ricardo/ricP.html for the entire book.

6 Although the argument in this chapter does not depend on complete specialization in both countries.

7 As Ricardo, like other classical political economists, believed that real wages were socially determined, most of the benefits of trade in his model will accrue to capitalists – see note 9 below.

8 All calculations have been done with Scientific Workplace, Version 2.5 software, a product of TCI Software Research.

9 One might question whether this outcome is a function of the limitations of the Ricardian, labor-valued pricing, fixed-coefficient model, which does not allow for partial specialization and does not take consumer demand behavior into account. In fact, Ricardo's neglect of demand was recognized by Mill (1848). Based on work by Marshall (1890), Leontief (1933), and Lerner (1934), Meade (1952) perfected a geometric demonstration of a free trade equilibrium that allowed for partial specialization and included demand-side price-response behavior. It is widely believed that Meade's more flexible variable-coefficient story, which explicitly assumes that prices are determined by supply and demand, and that changes in relative prices will affect production techniques, shows that unhindered international market forces will induce beneficial and sustainable trade based on comparative advantage (Chacholiades, 1990, Ch. 4). However, Meade's proof depends on highly unrealistic substitution parameters and full-employment assumptions, particularly for "north–south" trade between countries with highly unequal factor costs. This might be better modeled as "unequal exchange" (Baiman, 2007).

10 In a well-known paper, Dornbusch et al. (1977) substitute a "continuum of goods" (each produced with fixed labor productivity as in the original Ricardian parable) for the two-good model, and then hypothesize "movement along the continuum" as countries specialize in their comparative advantage goods. This allows for continuous labor cost or productivity-based substitution in production, as in the Neoclassical model, while assuming fixed labor productivity for each individual good. Trade is then balanced through real wage adjustments that are inconsistent with Ricardo's belief in socially determined real wages that do not adjust to balance trade.

Using a truly Neoclassical trade model, Meade constructed a proof of the existence of a free trade equilibrium. His proof, which underlies Neoclassical trade theory, assumes variable coefficient production with highly varying diminishing marginal product substitution. Although standard Neoclassical macro models require variable coefficients and highly unrealistic elasticities of substitution in production to work, this is not the case for "variable coefficient" (with more modest and realistic factor price substitution) Neo-Marxian and neo-Keynesian macro models (Marglin, 1984; Taylor, 1990, 2004).

Appendix A

Equations (18) and (20) are derived as follows. By definition:

$$\frac{\dfrac{1+\Delta Q_{PW}-1}{1}}{\dfrac{\dfrac{E\,80}{100}-\dfrac{E\,80}{E\,90}}{\dfrac{E\,80}{E\,90}}} = -E_{PW}$$

which, after canceling the $E80$ terms in the denominator and a little more manipulation, becomes (18). Equation (20) is derived in a similar fashion.

Appendix B

It is instructive to outline a three-good, three-country model, and then extend it to the N-good, N-country case. Assume that we have three countries – England, France, and Portugal – that produce three goods – cloth, beef, and wine, respectively. Assume that each country initially consumes and produces one unit of each good at the following labor productivity levels. In Portugal 70 units of labor can produce a unit of wine, 80 units of labor can produce a unit of beef, and 90 units of labor can produce a unit of cloth. In France the corresponding ratios are: 95, 85, and 105. In England: 120, 110, and 100. With these relative productivity levels, England will specialize in the production of cloth, France in beef, and Portugal in wine.

Looking at England, given two exchange rates, p, which gives the price of Portuguese currency in English currency, and f, which does the same for French currency, and using the notation of Section 3, we have the following set of three equations for English demand for the three goods:

$$\Delta Q_{EW} = E_{EWW}\left(\frac{120-70p}{120}\right) + E_{EWB}\left(\frac{110-85f}{110}\right)$$

$$\Delta Q_{EB} = E_{EBB}\left(\frac{110-85f}{110}\right) + E_{EBW}\left(\frac{120-70p}{120}\right)$$

$$\Delta Q_{EC} = E_{ECW}\left(\frac{120-70p}{120}\right) + E_{ECB}\left(\frac{110-85f}{110}\right)$$

where E_{EWW} and E_{EBB} are own-price elasticities for English demand for wine and beef from Portugal and France, respectively. The other four elasticities are cross-price elasticities reflecting the effects of relative changes in French beef prices (E_{EWB}) on English demand for Portuguese wine, and Portuguese wine prices (E_{EBW}) on English demand for French beef; and of Portuguese wine prices (E_{ECW}) and French beef prices (E_{ECB}) on domestically produced and consumed English cloth. Note that cross-price elasticities *cannot* be converted to own-price elasticities in this case as they can in the two-country case.

Since England has a comparative advantage in cloth, it will specialize in this good. To maintain full employment, England must produce 3 units of cloth which it will consume at home and export to France and Portugal. This results in the following full-employment condition for England:

$$1 + \Delta Q_{EC} + 1 + \Delta Q_{FC} + 1 + \Delta Q_{PC} = 3.3$$

Finally, if England is to have balanced trade with France and Portugal, the following balanced trade condition must be satisfied:

$$(1+\Delta Q_{EW})p70 + (1+\Delta Q_{EB})f85 = (1+\Delta Q_{PC})100 + (1+\Delta Q_{FC})100$$

France or Portugal will have to satisfy a similar set of five equations. The remaining third country will only have to satisfy four independent equations as the third trade balance equation will be dependent on the other two trade balance equations. We will thus get a total of fourteen equations and twenty-nine variables (eighteen elasticities, nine changes in quantity demanded, and two exchange rates) for the three countries. This sums to fifteen degrees of freedom for eighteen exogenous elasticities, leaving three missing degrees of freedom for a general solution.

For n>2, a similar N-country, N-good model will require $n^2 \times (n-1)$ elasticities, n^2 commodities, and $n-1$ exchange rates for a total of $n^3 + n - 1$ variables. However, the model will require n^2 demand equations, n full-employment equations, and n-1 trade balance equations (because world trade must net to zero, any single country's trade balances can be inferred from those of the other n-1 countries), implying that it will have $n^3 + n - 1 - (n^2 + 2n - 1) = n^3 - n^2 - n$ degrees of freedom. But as it needs $n^3 - n^2$, it will be missing n degrees of freedom.

References

Baiman, R. (2007) Unequal exchange without a labor theory of prices: on the need for a global Marshall Plan and a solidarity trading regime, *Review of Radical Political Economics* 38(1), pp. 71–89.

Blecker, R. (1999) *Taming Global Finance* (Washington, D.C.: Economic Policy Institute).

Chacholiades, M. (1990) *International Economics* (New York: McGraw Hill).

Colander, D. (1998) *Macroeconomics*, 3rd Edition (New York: Irwin/McGraw Hill).

Dornbusch, R., Fischer, S. and Samuelson, P. (1977) Comparative advantage, trade, and payments in a Ricardian model with a continuum of goods, *American Economic Review* 67(5), 823–39.

Eatwell, J. and Taylor, L. (2000) *Global Finance at Risk* (New York: New Press).

Krugman, P. (1996) *Pop Internationalism* (Cambridge, MA: MIT Press).

Leontief, W. (1933) The use of indifference curves in the analysis of foreign trade, *Quarterly Journal of Economics* 27, 493–501.

Lerner, A. P. (1934) The diagrammatic representation of cost conditions in international trade, *Economica* 12(1), 319–34.

MacEwan, A. (1999) *Neo-Liberalism or Democracy?* (New York: Zed Books).

Marglin, S. (1984) *Growth, Distribution, and Prices* (Cambridge, MA: Harvard University Press).

Marshall, A. (1890) *Principles of Economics* (London: Macmillan).

Meade, J. E. (1952) *A Geometry of International Trade* (London: George Allen & Unwin).

Mill, J. S. ([1848] 2004) *Principles of Political Economy* (Amherst, NY: Prometheus Books).

Prasch, R. (1996) Reassessing the theory of comparative advantage, *Review of Political Economy* 8(1), 39–56.

Ricardo, D. [1817] (1973) *The Principles of Political Economy and Taxation* (New York: Dutton).

Salvatore, D. (2005) *Introduction to International Economics* (New York: John Wiley).

Smith, A. [1776] (1937) *The Wealth of Nations* (New York: Modern Library).

World Trade Organization (WTO) (2006) *World Trade Developments in 2005* (Geneva: WTO).

Taylor, L. (1990) *Socially Relevant Policy Analysis* (Cambridge, MA: MIT Press).

Taylor, L. (2004) *Reconstructing Macroeconomics: Structuralist Proposals and Critiques of the Mainstream (*Cambridge, MA: Harvard University Press).

Vernengo, M. (2000) What do undergrads *really* need to know about trade and finance, in R. Baiman, H. Boushey, and D. Saunders (eds) *Political Economy and Contemporary Capitalism* (Armonk, NY: M. E. Sharpe).

3 The limits of free trade in Neoclassical theory

From Heckscher-Ohlin to unequal exchange

1 Introduction

Does Neoclassical trade theory generalize the perceived implications of Ricardo's theorem, that free trade between countries based on comparative advantage will produce a unique, stable, balanced, and mutually beneficial equilibrium?

In Chapter 2 we demonstrated that classical Ricardian trade analysis does not prove that free trade (and freely fluctuating exchange rates) will produce balanced and mutually beneficial trade based on comparative advantage and complete specialization. In this follow-up analysis, we find that in at least one critical area of international trade, north–south or developed, developing country, trade, Neoclassical models also generally fail to generate a sustainable and mutually beneficial free trade equilibrium. Rather than mutually beneficial trade based on partial specialization, we find that when wage levels are highly unequal, comparative advantage-based trade is likely to produce unequal exchange that is neither balanced nor mutually beneficial. Neo-Marxist "unequal exchange" models that analyze the relative benefits and losses of domestic and international labor and capital from free trade, rather than classical and Neoclassical models of "comparative advantage" and mutual benefit, would appear to provide a more realistic and useful analysis of north–south trade (see Chapters 5 and 6).

However, before we can analyze the relative merits of standard Neoclassical trade theory, we need to specify the particular Neoclassical theory that we are interested in. Because of its pervasive influence on the kind of basic trade theory that we are here addressing, we will focus on Neoclassical trade theorems that relate to the Heckscher-Ohlin free trade model. It turns out that there are at least two major variants of this model.

In Section 2 of this chapter we summarize the conditions underlying the "modern" algebraic Heckscher-Ohlin model (AHO) and point out that this model does not prove that free trade will generate a balanced and mutually beneficial international trade equilibrium and that its assumptions of identical technologies, and perfectly competitive marginal product returns and consequent "factor price equalization," are so restrictive that they render the AHO largely irrelevant even within the context of already highly idealized Neoclassical trade theory.

In Sections 3–4, we review the older but more theoretically grounded and less restrictive Neoclassical international trade models of Meade and Haberler, who, using graphical techniques in a two-country, two-good example, demonstrated that: a) free trade will produce a unique, stable, sustainable, and mutually beneficial equilibrium; and b) "production possibility frontiers" reflecting comparative advantages likely to result from unequal factor endowments will lead to exports of goods produced with the relatively abundant factor and imports of goods produced with the relative scarce factor, in both countries.[1]

Finally, in Sections 5 and 6 we show that: c) when trading partners have "highly unequal factor costs," as is likely in "north–south" trade, the Meade-Haberler geometric Heckscher-Ohlin (GHO) model will produce imbalanced and probably not mutually beneficial trade. This shows that even in the most general version of Neoclassical trade theory, "free trade" is inconsistent with comparative advantage-based partial specialization when wage levels are highly unequal as they are in most north–south trade.

For the sake of analytical completeness, in Section 7 we demonstrate that a similar problem may occur for trade between countries with "very unequal production capacities." However, in this case individual-choice-based market-led adjustments are likely to mitigate and possibly resolve the trade imbalance, so that these situations, unlike the case of highly unequal production factor costs, do not theoretically contradict the free trade argument – at least in the long run.

We conclude in Section 8 by noting that this analysis of Neoclassical trade theory complements the analysis of classical Ricardian trade theory in Chapter 2 that shows that free trade is also incompatible with comparative advantage based on complete specialization, and suggests that Neo-Marxist models of unequal exchange may provide the most accurate and useful analysis of trade under these circumstances as discussed in Chapters 5 and 6.

2 The irrelevant algebraic Heckscher-Ohlin (AHO) model

Findlay (1995, Chap. 1) provides a concise version of the two-country two-good AHO model. In addition to the standard set of free trade, full employment, no mobility of capital or labor, fixed endowments, identical homothetic tastes based on homogeneous of degree one utility functions, no factor intensity reversals, increasing cost, diminishing marginal utility, and Neoclassical trade theory assumptions, the AHO model adds the following conditions:

a)   Identical technologies of production and identical quality of factors of production for both trading partners.
b)   Perfect competition and constant returns to scale resulting in perfect marginal productivity pricing in normal price ranges. (Note that this also assumes that marginal costs are above average costs for both products in these price ranges.)

These assumptions produce a perfect functional 1-1 correspondence between factor prices, trading prices, and trade volumes ensuring "factor price equalization" (FPE) that is assumed to generate a free trade equilibrium point in which (essentially by assumption) the relatively labor-abundant country will partially specialize in the production of labor-intensive exports in exchange for capital-intensive imports from the relatively capital-abundant trading partner.

It is important to recognize that the AHO is so restrictive that standard critiques of Heckscher-Ohlin – such as whether "community indifference curves" can be defined, the effect of increasing returns to scale production that does not conform to "increasing cost" concave "production possibility frontiers" (Krugman, 1979, 1980), and related spatial "agglomeration of production" issues whereby multinational producers interact with each other, compromising perfect individual firm profit maximization (Markusen, 2002) – are rather beside the point as they address second-order-of-magnitude effects that are likely to have a much smaller impact than the more basic issues of non-identical technologies and imperfect competition that characterize virtually all real trading situations.

Young (1970, Chap. 3) shows in great detail how eliminating the assumptions of perfect competition and identical factor quality so that factor prices exactly reflect factor endowments can easily undermine the Heckscher-Ohlin conclusion in this model. Similarly, varying the "identical" technologies of production between the countries will eliminate the 1-1 correspondence between factor prices, trading prices, and relative output levels that the AHO depends on (ibid.). Young considers the empirical evidence against the "Ohlinian theorem" and concludes with this telling statement:

> In conclusion, once we have considered the empirical evidence against the Ohlinian theory and the defenses put forward to rescue it, it would on balance seem reasonable to say that the Ohlin-Heckscher theorem has not been refuted. However, this is mainly because the assumptions on which it is built are so unreal and restrictive that it would be virtually impossible to devise a real world test of the theory. The theory is for all practical purposes irrefutable and is, therefore, to that extent a bad theory. Empirically, the theory holds up only if definitions and data are twisted and tortured until it finally "explains" the observed data. But the explanation is by then useless, since the supposed theory has become a tautology – a country will export those goods using relative large amounts of those factors used in its exports.
>
> (p. 41)

Even if one were to accept the AHO assumptions, "factor price equilization" (FPE) at the equilibrium implies that there can be no assurance of balanced and mutually beneficial free trade based on comparative advantage and partial specialization. This will be the case as the model provides no guarantee that the nominal wage reduction in the high-wage country (necessary for FPE) will be more than offset by the nominal import price reduction resulting from comparative advantage-based trade. The AHO thus eliminates the most important ideological argument of the Ricardian free trade doctrine. It should thus be no surprise that the standard, widely misunderstood (see Chapter 2) Ricardian story rather than (a simplified version of) the AHO dominates introductory economics courses.

Even more striking is the fact that in spite of these additional highly restrictive conditions, in canonical formulations such as that of Findlay, AHO theory appears to (without explicit acknowledgment) rely on earlier graph-based Neoclassical trade theory for proof of existence of a unique and stable free trade equilibrium – see discussion of "graphical Heckscher-Ohlin" (GHO) tradition in Sections 3–8. The AHO model is constructed through a set of differential conditions (Findlay, 1995, pp. 8–15) that any solution would have to satisfy. The fact that these conditions alone do not ensure that a unique and stable equilibrium solution *exists* is apparent from AHO-derived "supply and demand" constructions, such as Figure 3.1 below based on Findlay's Figure 1.3 (p. 17).

This figure plots two (good X over good Y) supply ratio curves for the two trading countries, and a single identical aggregate relative demand curve against (good X over good Y) relative price ratios that apply to both countries under the assumption of identical preferences (and indistinguishable "consumption" patterns out of wage and profit income). Findlay notes that free trade will produce a single international price ratio p^* that will be between the two pre-trade market-clearing domestic price ratios, but nowhere is there any proof that this international price will cause the two domestic relative supply curves to generate relative quantity ratios q_a and q_b that lead to country a exports of x that precisely offset country b exports of y at the equilibrium terms of trade p^*. If a trading equilibrium $q^* = x/y$ exists, than if m are exports of x from country a to b, and e imports of y from country b to a, for trade to balance: $q_a = (x+m)/(y-e)$ and $q_b = (x-m)/(y+e)$. But as the shape of the supply and demand curves for x/y is almost completely arbitrary, depending on the two countries' respective capital and labor "endowments," the technologies used to produce goods x and y, demand

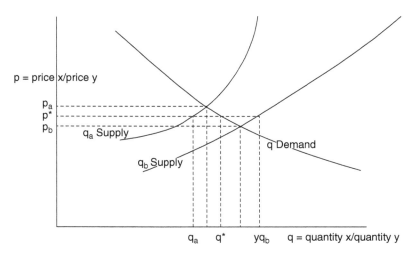

Figure 3.1 Equilibrium in the AHO model

preferences, and price response, there is no obvious reason why an equilibrium q^* should exist. That demonstration is part of what we have labeled the "graphical Heckscher-Ohlin" (GHO) model – see Section 4.

A final important point. AHO theorists recognize that when there is no overlap between the ranges of the domestic price ratios in the trading countries, trade will occur at a single domestic price ratio that is not shared by the other trading partner. In this case complete specialization will occur, in one or both countries, negating the results of the AHO analysis (Findlay, 1995, p. 18). However, rather than simply leading to the balanced trade based on complete specialization that is described (Findlay, 1995, pp. 13–14), and will be discussed below in the context of the more general Meade and Haberler GHO Neoclassical trade theory, these "corner solutions" are likely to produce imbalanced and not mutually beneficial free trade based on "unequal exchange" – see Section 6.

3 Meade's geometric demonstration of a Neoclassical free trade equilibrium

In 1952 James Meade perfected a geometric presentation of a Neoclassical theory of international trade based on earlier work by Hume (1758), Marshall (1890), Leontief (1933), and Lerner (1934). Meade's work forms the core of what we will call the "graphical Heckscher-Ohlin" (GHO) basic Neoclassical free trade theory. By demonstrating the existence of a general, free market comparative advantage-based equilibrium in international trade, without assuming a) and b) above, Meade was able to lay the foundations for subsequent analyses of the characteristics of a free trade equilibrium that culminated in the graphical Heckscher-Ohlin, Stolper-Samuelson, Rybczynski, and other basic Neoclassical trade theorems (Meade, 1952, Chap. 1–3) (Chacholiades, 1990, pp. 47–54, 523–7) (Young, 1970, Chap. 5) (Williams, 1983, Chap. 3).

Assuming diminishing returns in production and diminishing marginal social utility in consumption, Meade constructs a "trade indifference curve" (TIC) for each country by tracing out the combined possibilities of production and trade as depicted in Figure 3.2 below. Curve I_1 is a "social indifference curve" (SIC) for a country which we will call Country A.[2] Curve I^t_1 is Country A's TIC which is constructed by moving the "production possibilities frontier" (PPF) ODEF along the SIC to Q'D'E'F' so that it has one point of contact with I^t_1 (O and Q') and its base remains parallel to the horizontal axis. The slope at each point of tangency with the SIC (E and E') will be equal to the slope of the tangents to the TIC curve at O and Q'. The curve traced out by the point of origin of this moving PPF will be the TIC that corresponds to this SIC. Point E' is obtainable if exports of DQ' can be traded for imports of OD.[3]

Obviously this will depend on the "terms of trade" (TOT) of exports of X for imports of Y. This effect is captured through an "offer curve" (OC) constructed by finding the respective points of intersection of changing TOT rays with different TIC curves, for example with TIC curves I^t_1 and I^t_2 as shown at points O and Q in Figure 3.3 below.

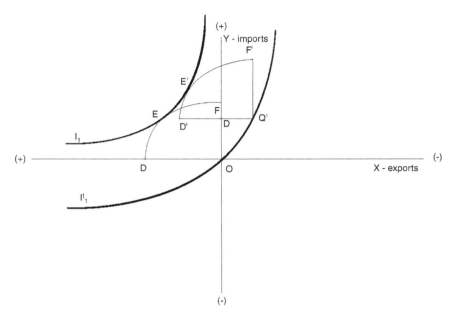

Figure 3.2 Trade indifference curve

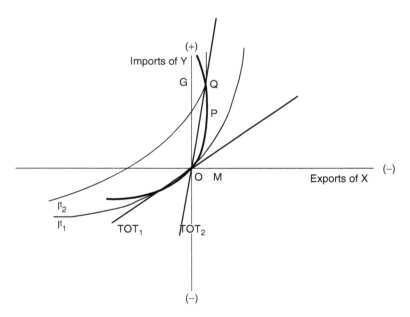

Figure 3.3 Offer curve

I$^t_2$ will provide higher social welfare than I$^t_1$ as it corresponds to a social indifference to the northeast of I$_1$ in Figure 3.2.[4] Point O on the offer curve OPQ reflects the pre-trade equilibrium for Country A of no exports or imports under TOT$_1$. As the relative price of Y declines and the terms of trade ray swings counter-clockwise to TOT$_2$ (for example, if the currency of the country that exports Y depreciates), imports of Y to Country A increase to OG and these are paid for by exports OM. Note that, as shown in Figure 3.3, TIC curves are tangent to TOT lines at each point of intersection of TOT lines with the offer curve. The offer curve (originally constructed by Marshall) thus describes socially optimizing levels of exports and imports at different terms of trade subject to convex PPFs and SICs that reflect diminishing returns in production and diminishing marginal utility in social consumption. The offer curve thus reflects the outcome of Neoclassical supply and demand assumptions.

Meade's demonstration of market-based international trade equilibrium rests on juxtaposing the offer curves of two countries A and B, so that they are facing each other as shown in Figure 3.4 below.

In Meade's model, free trade equilibrium is obtained at point Q, the intersection of B's offer curve (O$_B$) and A's offer curve (O$_A$). Meade assumes that

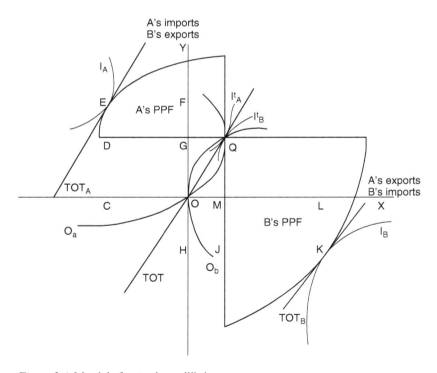

Figure 3.4 Meade's free trade equilibrium

given the indicated slopes and shapes of the offer curves, the terms of trade (TOT) line will adjust until Country A's offer of good X will equal Country B's demand for X and vice versa. Internal relative prices in each country and production bundles adjust to the equilibrium TOT price ratios. In Meade's own words:

> If there is free trade and no surplus or deficit in the balance of trade, then the position of trade equilibrium will be determined at the point Q at which A's and B's offer curves intersect. The point of consumption in A will be at E where the slope of the price line α_2 (TOT$_A$), which is equal to A's consumption-indifference curve and of A's production block, is equal to the terms of international trade α (TOT). Consumers in A will consume OC (or DG) of A-exportables (good X) leaving GQ for export. They will consume OF and produce GF of B-exportables (good Y), requiring OG from imports: GQ will thus be exported and OG imported. In B consumers will consume OH (or MJ) of B-exportables (good Y), leaving MQ (or OG) for export: and they will consume OL of A-exportables (good X), requiring OM (or GQ) from imports. At the consumption point K the slope of B's production block and the consumption indifference curve α_1 (TOT$_B$) is also the same as that of the international terms of trade (α) (TOT).
>
> Figure IV thus shows the final free-trade equilibrium between A and B in the absence of any surplus or deficit in the balance of trade.
>
> (Meade, 1952, p. 22)

Meade's construction clearly includes a production and demand story that shows that a free trade equilibrium would allow for comparative advantage-based, mutually beneficial partial specialization and trade – but does it prove that free trade will generally produce such an equilibrium? In the remainder of the chapter we show that when countries have very unequal factor costs and production capacities, such a free trade equilibrium may fail to exist.[5]

4 Haberler's opportunity cost-based graphical Heckscher-Ohlin (GHO) model

The GHO "Heckscher-Ohlin" model is a straightforward consequence of the different slopes of trading country PPFs at intersections and tangency points with international and domestic equilibrium terms of trade (TOT) in the Meade construction. Figure 3.4 above shows the PPFs of the two trading countries juxtaposed in a manner that reflects Meade's analysis. Figure 3.5 below reproduces these PPFs in similar Meade-like "normal" alignment. Country B is likely to increasingly specialize in Y and Country A in X (when the PPFs are juxtaposed as in Figure 3.5) for almost all Y/X price ratios that will produce a feasible international free trade equilibrium.

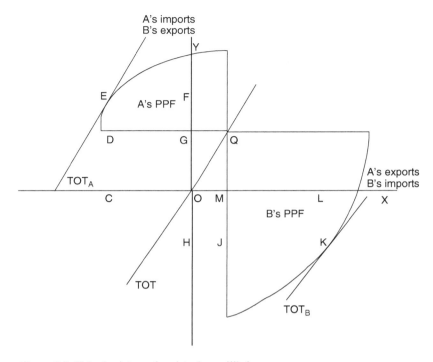

Figure 3.5 Haberler international trade equilibrium

This implies that for most PPFs and feasible price ranges, good X will be relatively cheaper than good Y in Country A compared with Country B, and vice versa for good Y in Country B, for most of their trading ranges. In particular, at the international trading equilibrium production points E and K, Country A specializes in and exports its relatively less costly good X, and imports its relatively more costly good Y, and Country B does the opposite.

This is likely because of the shape of the PPFs and the way in which they need to be juxtaposed to establish a free trade equilibrium, with Country A's "long" commodity X side crossing the Y axis, and Country B's long commodity Y side crossing the X axis. As the "long" sides are likely to reflect the relatively less costly goods, these relative opportunity costs will probably determine the pattern of the free trade equilibrium.

In this "Haberler" generalization of the Heckscher-Ohlin theorem, the only thing that matters are the slopes and shapes of the PPFs of the trading partners, regardless of why they take this form. In cases where countries produce relatively less of a (relatively) costly good and more of a less costly good, as can be seen from Figure 3.5, at an international trade equilibrium point they generally will export their (relatively) expensive product and import the other product. The reasons for these differing slopes and shapes may lie in relative productivity differences, relative factor cost (like real wages) differences, and differences in access to natural resources, or because of other factors, but ultimately they do not impact the Meade-Haberler opportunity cost model.

By adding an assumption of identical constant return-to-scale technologies, equal tastes, and perfect competition, one can "prove" the narrow version of the GHO, which correlates factor abundance with relatively inexpensive production and exports, and relative factor scarcity with more expensive production and imports. Graphical proof of this theorem can be found in Williams (1983, Chap. 3, pp. 42–4). However, as this would require the imposition of the very restrictive Heckscher-Ohlin model assumptions above (see Williams, Chap. 3), we will restrict our attention below to the more general "opportunity cost" Meade-Haberler GHO model described above.

5 The GHO model does not generally apply to countries with highly dissimilar economies

Meade lists seven assumptions for his basic model (Meade, 1952, p. 9). He assumes two countries, two exportable products, and "perfect competition with no external economies or Diseconomies" (assumptions (i)–(iii)). To these he adds standard Neoclassical assumptions: "that price flexibility of one kind or another leads to the full employment of resources" (Meade, 1952, p. 9, assumption (iv)), that marginal utilities and productivities for both goods in both countries are diminishing, and that both tastes and factor supplies are fixed (assumptions (vi) and (vii)).

As we focus on Meade's production assumption (vii), we will cite it in full:

> (vii) that in both of the two countries the total supply of productive factors is fixed so that when the production of one commodity is increased that of the other commodity must be decreased. In addition we shall normally assume increasing costs, i.e. that the greater is the production of the one commodity the greater is the amount of the other which must be sacrificed in order to produce still further increments of the first commodity; but in Chapters IV and V respectively we shall digress in order to say something about the geometrical representation of constant costs and of decreasing costs.
>
> (Meade, 1952, p. 10)

We will address the standard Meade "increasing costs" model presented in most texts (Chacholiades, 1990, Chap. 3). Finally, as we have pointed out, Meade also takes care to ensure that "community indifference curves" can be meaningfully constructed by assuming that each country's citizens have identical tastes and equal endowments (assumption (v)), or in Meade's own words:

> (v) that each country is made up of a set of citizens with identical tastes and factor endowments, so that the indifference map, while it may differ as

between a citizen of A and a citizen of B, is the same for all of the citizens in either of the two countries. In these conditions we can derive community-indifference curves directly from individual indifference curves.[6]

Given these assumptions, and for the "increasing costs" case, Meade shows that a trade equilibrium like that portrayed in Figure 3.4 above is possible (Meade, 1952, Figure IV).

However, Meade's free trade equilibrium is dependent on a TOT equilibrium that generates points of tangency on the PPFs of both countries where the value of the goods X and Y produced equals the value of goods X and Y consumed at the prevailing external and internal exchange rate and at given factor costs and productivity levels in each country (such as K and E in Figure 3.4). These are solution points that ensure full employment and balanced supply and demand at the given TOT in each country.

If the international equilibrium results in a corner solution for a TOT line that is not tangent (such as point K in Figure 3.6 below), the externally determined TOT will not match the internal exchange ratio corresponding to the given production levels for that point. This will result in excess exchange value (more good X per unit of good Y at point K in Figure 3.6 below) that creates an imbalance between resources used and resources produced and obtained through trade for that country (Country B in Figure 3.6).

Similarly, an infeasible point of tangency (such as point K in Figure 3.7 below) means that at the equilibrium TOT, the country will not produce the output levels of goods X and Y necessary to reach the internal equilibrium production and trading point (at point K in Figure 3.7, Country B does not produce enough good Y to trade for that level of consumption of good X).

Both Figures 3.6 and 3.7 satisfy all of the assumptions of Meade's model. This can be verified by using the given PPF "production blocks" of each country to trace trade indifference curves and offer curves, for each country, and arrive at the final free trade equilibrium points and TOT lines shown in the two figures. This is exactly the method used by Meade to demonstrate the existence of the standard free trade equilibrium point. The only difference between these two exceptional cases and Meade's standard case is in the relative sizes and shapes of the PPF blocks and the given indifference curve mappings. Meade's seven basic assumptions above are fully satisfied in these two exceptional cases.

Moreover, neither of these exceptions to Meade's standard equilibrium depends on the existence of an independent medium of exchange, or international currency. Free trade will not result in a sustainable equilibrium in these cases regardless of the numeraire chosen. This numeraire could be one of the commodities in question. Meade's standard equilibrium breaks down in both cases because balanced trade can only continue through "unequal exchange" (either above value as in Figure 3.6, or below value as in Figure 3.7). These kinds of trades will thus create imbalances with any medium of exchange. Only under pure barter conditions resulting in unequal exchanges (for example because ships are forced to offload their entire cargo and exchange whatever they bring for whatever is available in exchange to take home) will these equilibrium points be "free trade equilibrium" points.

However, this clearly stretches the notion of "free trade equilibrium" beyond its usual meaning and results in an international trading model that is implausibly unrealistic even by ideal Neoclassical modeling standards. Most importantly, these cases cannot be considered equilibrium trading positions in Meade's own equal exchange and balanced trade, and supply and demand, usage of the term. As such they represent exceptions to Meade's geometric demonstration of the existence of a free trade equilibrium. With this in mind, without loss of generality, we will generally assume that an international currency is being used as the medium of exchange in many of the hypothetical trading scenarios described below.

We conclude that there are two basic cases in which free trade equilibrium will not obtain even though all of Meade's assumptions hold: a) when countries have such divergent costs (and/or technologies) of production that they have no shared product transformation ratios (as in Figure 3.6), and b) when countries who may have similar factor production cost variation have binding production capacities for the traded goods within international equilibrium trading ranges (as in Figure 3.7). As Meade's equilibrium fails to obtain in these situations, restrictions that would exclude these cases from the scope of the theorem can be seen as missing assumptions in Meade's original presentation of the model.

As at least case a) would appear to be highly relevant to current international trade patterns, these cannot be dismissed as exceptional mathematical curiosities. Case a) would seem to often apply to trade between developed and developing countries for goods with highly unequal labor costs. A prime example of this might be trade between China and the U.S. in labor-intensive, and capital and knowledge-intensive, manufacturing, respectively. Case b) would appear to sometimes apply to trade between developed, or developing, countries of greatly different sizes. For example, trade between the U.S. and Sweden for specialized machine tools that (because of knowledge or embedded capital) can be made for less in Sweden might exhibit case b) characteristics. Many bilateral trading situations may include elements of both cases. Trade between the U.S. and Mexico may be an example of this.

In both case a) and case b) situations, the free trade or free market-determined international terms of trade equilibrium price dictated by the Meade model will correspond to a corner non-tangent, or infeasible, solution for at least one country's domestic product transformation ratio.[7]

6 Possible trading outcomes for countries with very unequal production factor costs

Figure 3.6 below illustrates an international and domestic free trade price equilibrium for case a).

Note that, relative to Country A, in Country B production of good Y is much less costly than production of good X. Moreover, as Country B's PPF has very little (but some!) convexity, for all points along both countries' PPFs:

$$\frac{P_Y^B}{P_X^B} < \frac{P_Y^A}{P_X^A} \text{ for all possible levels of production of X and Y.} \tag{6.1}$$

This implies that there can be no international TOT that moves off the corner solution for Country B at point K. The optimal production/consumption mix for Country A at point E may, or may not, also be a corner solution. We have chosen the relatively simpler and seemingly more relevant case where it is not (see note 8).

As noted above, Country A could be the U.S. importing labor-intensive manu-factured goods (Y) from China (Country B), where they can be produced at much less cost relative to high-end knowledge and capital-intensive products X, because of extraordinarily low (by U.S. standards) labor, environmental, and social costs. Since the domestic U.S. production price for Y is always higher than the Chinese price for Y, the slope of China's PPF has no influence, and the international price (allowing for very high sales and promotion markup over its Chinese cost of pro-duction) is set by the U.S. internal price. This international price allows for some U.S., presumably less profitable, domestic production of Y. The same, however, cannot be said for domestic production of good X in China. Because its produc-tion requires, say, highly expensive (relative to the price of labor in China) capital goods (produced by high-wage U.S. labor), its domestic opportunity cost will

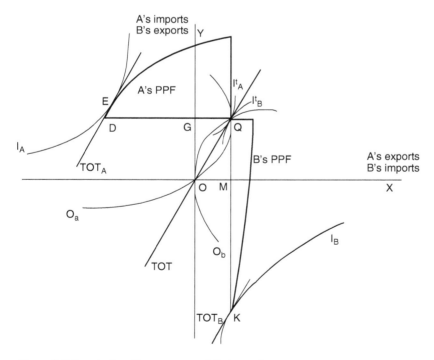

Figure 3.6 Free trade with very unequal factor costs

always be above its international opportunity cost (both in terms of good Y). China will therefore specialize in the production of good Y, and import all of its needs for good X.

By assumption 6.1, the slope of the tangent to point E in Figure 3.6 is greater than the slope of any tangent to Country B's PPF: $\frac{P_Y^B}{P_X^B} < \frac{P_Y^A}{P_X^A}$. At equilibrium the tangent to point E is equal to the slope of the TOT received by Country B at point K for its exports of Y and imports of X. This implies that free trade in this situation will be characterized by "unequal exchange" with Country B receiving "excess income" or "above normal profits" relative to cost of production, for good Y. Moreover, as, unlike the AHO, the GHO does not assume that factor costs converge to each other (PFE), this inequality of costs will not be eliminated through increased wage or capital cost convergence, at least not at a pace fast enough to rebalance trade in a practical time-period. Alternatively, as discussed in Chapter 2, price movements toward "complete specialization" will not resolve the trade balance problem either.

What kind of effects will the excess income generated by exports of Y from Country B cause?

Without active (non-"free market") monetary or fiscal policy, these trade and income imbalances are likely to spill over into current domestic and/or international markets for other goods causing chronic inflation, and/or product or labor market, and/or trade deficits or surpluses. As the model offers no guidance on this, there is no possible way to determine whether these effects will be beneficial or harmful to the citizens of Countries A or B. In particular it is not possible to demonstrate that "free trade" in this situation will necessarily be mutually beneficial to both countries.

For example, if a substantial share of these excess earnings accrue to outsourcing multinational firms from Country A that subcontracts for production of good Y in Country B and then sells this for above normal profits in Country A, much of these extra earnings may accrue to stock owners and upper management in Country A.[8] They may use some of this extra income to purchase more inexpensive products from Country B, causing a chronic deficit in Country A's trade balance. Though this trade imbalance may be offset by profit flows from Country B, producers of good Y in Country A will still lose their jobs, and they are not likely to be the agents benefiting from the increased "offshore" profit flows.

Another possibility is that market forces acting on individual agents will cause a shift in the international TOT that will reduce Country B's, and possibly increase Country A's, social welfare. This may occur if, as a result of the above normal profitability of good Y exports from Country B, competition between firms that control these exports causes a further lowering of the international price of good Y relative to good X. This kind of counter-clockwise swing in the international TOT (further lowering the international price of Y relative to X) may occur, in spite of the fact that it may reduce Country B's social utility (cause it to move to a lower SIC as the TOT line will intersect O_b southwest of point Q in Figure 3.6), because it is individually necessary for the export agents (who control the flow of trade) to do this. These inexpensive imports may cause the remaining producers of good Y in Country A to go out of business, resulting in a situation of complete specialization and fixed-coefficient production for both countries. If this occurs, (see note 8) at least one of the trading countries will experience either a trade deficit or increased unemployment. In the longer run, both countries may suffer unemployment, lower wages, and deteriorating social and environmental conditions because of the ability of agents that control this process of international arbitrage to force workers and citizens in both countries to accept these lower standards.

Of course opposite effects are also possible. Agents in Country B may be able to use the rents from this kind of "unequal exchange" for increased productive investment that will lead to improved wages and social and environmental standards in the long run. Empirical evidence suggests that this can occur in countries such as South Korea and Japan that enjoyed preferred access by domestic firms to markets in countries with (initially) much higher real wage levels, and were able to protect domestic production from imports and actively plan and regulate export earnings to promote long-term development and improve long-run conditions (Amsden, 1989; Stiglitz, 2002; Best, 1990). There is also evidence that countries that are able to leverage their abundant, inexpensive, and educated labor resources, and large internal consumer markets, to increase their bargaining power with foreign direct investors may be able to capture a significant portion of this surplus and use it to acquire new technology and induce substantial foreign capital investment of these domestically obtained earnings (Greider, 1998). A recent International Labor Organization (ILO) report notes that China and India did well (in aggregate terms, though both suffered large increases in relative inequality) in the generally dismal picture of reduced growth, and increased inequality and unemployment, for most countries, during the most recent free trade period from 1990 to 2000 (ILO, 2004).

As we have already noted, the problem would appear to be that in a free trade regime, market incentives acting on individual (multinational) agents produce activity that drives down standards worldwide for the benefit of an elite class of owners and upper managers. Most developing countries do not have the bargaining power to capture a significant share of this surplus from unequal exchange and use it to raise working and living standards. In such a system, trade is not a means of improving productivity as in the standard Ricardian and Meadian stories. Rather, it causes downward pressure on worldwide living standards through the unregulated private control and ownership of footloose investment. This analysis suggests that a Neo-Marxist exploitative "unequal exchange" view of north–south trade may provide a more realistic view of this kind of trade than the standard Ricardian/Meadian, non-corner solution, "comparative advantage" model. This is because in an "unequal exchange" corner solution, the issue becomes not so much what the benefits are, but rather who controls and benefits from their disposition, see Chapters 5 and 6 or (Baiman, 2006, 2014).

7 Possible trading outcomes for countries with very unequal production capacities

Figure 3.7 below shows a free trade equilibrium for case b).

In case b), although Countries A and B have shared product transformation ratios TOT_A and TOT_B equal to the equilibrium international TOT, Country B's production point K for TOT_B is not a feasible trading position. This is because at point K Country B will not produce enough Y exports to pay for the necessary good X imports from Country A at equilibrium international TOT.[9] Formally:

$$\frac{P_Y^B}{P_X^B} = \frac{P_Y^A}{P_X^A} \quad \text{at an infeasible trading point for at least one country.} \quad (7.1)$$

In a formal sense, as with case a), Meade's model does not offer any feasible solution for this situation.

However, one plausible outcome, similar to the possible market-driven change in the international TOT discussed in case a), may be a market-induced raising of the price of Y relative to X. This could occur because of the excess demand for Y imports relative to the initial quantity produced for export at the equilibrium international TOT. This clockwise swing in the international TOT, which could reduce Country A or Country B's overall social welfare, may occur as the result of market forces acting on the individual firms controlling the exports

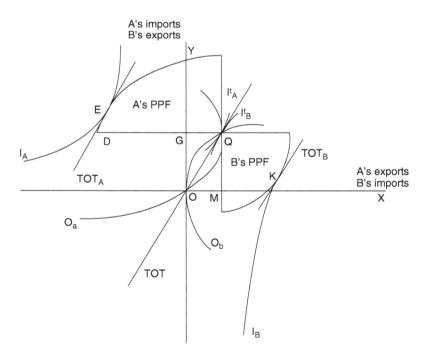

Figure 3.7 Free trade with very unequal production capacities

from Country B. If this occurred, international trade would result in an "unequal exchange" price for good Y that would generate the same kind of surplus income "externality" as in case a).

However, it should be noted that if this occurs in trade between countries with similar production factor-cost ratios (with a similar range of product transformation ratios as in Figure 3.7), market-driven investment in additional capacity (to prevent competitors from capturing the above normal profits) could increase Country B's good Y production capacity (expanding B's PPF downward in Figure 3.7) to where point K could become a feasible trading production point, resulting in a standard (non-corner) Meadian equilibrium.[10]

There would thus seem to be a greater possibility that this kind of longer-term "structural remedy" would occur in case b) between countries at similar levels of development than in case a). This is because a structural remedy for case a), such as raising real wages in Country B to levels comparable to those for producers of good Y in Country A, would require social policies that work against market incentives for individual agents. Such a long-term structural solution for case a) would therefore only be possible through collective action in the face of intense downward pressure on the real wages paid by individual countries and export agents from worldwide competition for export markets and foreign investment.

8 Conclusion

In summary, a standard GHO Meadian free trade equilibrium will produce "unequal exchange" between countries with greatly unequal production factor costs. Moreover, this cannot be seen as an unimportant exceptional situation as it would appear to characterize much of "north–south" trade between developing and developed countries, currently the most controversial type of international trade.

We conclude that the GHO model cannot be cited as theoretical proof that a mutually beneficial GHO free trade equilibrium based on comparative advantage satisfying: a) partial or complete specialization, b) balanced trade, c) full employment, and d) aggregate supply and demand balance will generally exist, especially between countries with very unequal production factor-cost ratios. To the contrary, Meade's and by implication the GHO model suggests that free trade between countries with highly unequal production factor costs will be characterized by "unequal exchange" so that sustainable realization of the benefits of comparative advantage-based trade will require active policy intervention.

This analysis lends support to the notion that hopes for mutually beneficial world trade, particularly between developing and developed countries with very unequal wage levels, as in case a) above, rest not on will-o-the-wisp "free trade" principles, but rather on devising a sustainable world trade regime. It suggests that the key issues in devising such a regime revolve around questions of who should control and benefit from the possibly pervasive "unequal exchange" nature of north–south trade. Policies that directly address this issue, such as tariff systems that level labor costs subject to productivity adjustments and rebate the difference to developing countries, may be a key component of a sustainable international trading system that would raise rather than lower international labor, social, and environmental standards (see Part III of this book and Schweickart, 2002, pp. 76–80; Paley, 1998).

This analysis also suggests that there is a greater likelihood that free trade market failure that is strictly due to capacity constraints, as in case b) above, will be temporary as a remedy in this case is more likely to be aligned with market incentives.

Notes

1 Chacholiades (1990, Chap. 4) is one of the few relatively modern trade texts that acknowledges and devotes considerable attention to Meade's construction as being the basis for the later theorems. An earlier text, Young (1970), also includes an extensive discussion of the Meade model (Chap. 5) and provides a review of the Haberler GHO model (Young, Chaps. 2–3) (Haberler, 1961), and an excellent critical review of the AHO model. In general it should be noted that the early theory addressed in this paper continues to form the core of the international trade curriculum taught in intermediate international trade courses (Chacholiades, 1990). The standard interpretation of Meade's construction (even though it is not generally acknowledged in texts) therefore continues to play a key role in framing policy views on free trade even though its practical applications are limited in the current environment of largely unregulated capital flows and currency exchange speculation (Blecker, 1999). Other well-known basic trade results such as the Heckscher-Ohlin, Stolper-Samuelson, and Rybszynski theorems assume rather than prove that a balanced full-employment free trade equilibrium exists (Chacholiades, 1990, Chap. 4) (Williams, 1983, Chap. 3).
2 Meade assumed that all the citizens in each country had equal tastes and endowments so that such a curve could be constructed (see discussion below of Meade's assumption (v)).
3 In Figures 3.2–3.4 below we try to, more or less, follow Meade's rather confusing notation in his Figures I–IV (Meade, 1952, Appendix).
4 Assuming SICs are meaningful measures of social welfare; see discussion that follows.
5 It should be noted that as Meade, writing in 1952, probably had in mind trade between advanced countries, it is not surprising that he either neglected or did not believe it was necessary to point out that his construction did not apply to trade between countries at very unequal levels of development. Likewise, he may have dismissed trade between countries with greatly unequal production capacities as a special case that did not merit additional analysis.
6 Meade goes on to remark in a footnote that this assumption cannot be replaced by "market behavior curves" that could establish points of market equilibrium as then: "we can no longer say that the community is necessarily better off if it moves from a lower to a higher market behavior curve, since the change may have involved an undesirable redistribution of income" (Meade, 1952, p. 9).
7 For example, Chacholiades (1990, pp. 36–8) goes further than most in including a discussion of the problems related to constructing a "social indifference curve" but then states that: "An important justification for the continued use of social indifference curves is, besides their simplicity, the fact that they give rise to results that are qualitatively similar to those derived more laboriously but with the use of a totally disaggregated model. This is the reason why we use them in this book." (p. 38). However, this is not a well-grounded statement as, for example, free trade can lead to large increases in social welfare, reducing inequality even if the aggregate value of social

consumption rises (Pieper and Taylor, 1998). A "totally disaggregated" model that took this into account should thus arrive a conclusion that could be the opposite of that of an aggregate "social indifference" curve analysis of the same trading situation.

8 In cases where trade results in corner solutions for both countries, the discussion that follows here will apply to the agents exporting out of the country with the net trade (foreign currency) surplus. In this case the terms of trade will settle in-between the corner cost ratios for both countries and, unless trade-generated above normal profit levels are coincidently equal, trade in one commodity will produce a larger surplus than that in the other commodity. In this case, full employment will not be maintained in one of the countries.

This has been demonstrated in the context of analyzing Ricardo's comparative advantage parable. As demonstrated in Chapter 2, balanced trade and full employment in a model with complete specialization, fixed coefficients of production, and intermediate international terms of trade breaks down when plausible market-based demand behavior is introduced. In this kind of model free trade will either produce a trade surplus or fail to provide full employment, in at least one of the trading countries.

9 For example, according to Chinese government data, in 1998 over 40% of China's (then only) $200 billion in exports were produced by multinational firms operating in China (Burke, 2000).

10 Observant readers will notice that there is an apparent "kink" in the curve in Figure 3.7. This is because of the limitations of my graphing software. Viewers should imagine a sharp "curvature" that satisfies Neoclassical continuity assumptions.

References

Amsden, A. H. (1989) *Asia's Next Giant* (New York: Oxford University Press).

Baiman, R. (2006) Unequal exchange without a labor theory of prices: on the need for a global Marshall Plan and a solidarity trading regime, *Review of Radical Political Economics* 38(1), Winter, 71–89.

—— (2014) Unequal exchange and the rentier economy, *Review of Radical Political Economics* 46(4), 536–57.

Best, M. (1990) *The New Competition* (Cambridge, MA: Harvard University Press).

Blecker, R. A. (1999) *Taming Global Finance* (Washington D.C.: The Economic Policy Institute).

Burke, J. (2000) U.S. investment in China worsens trade deficit, Washington D.C.: The Economic Policy Institute. Briefing Paper #93, May.

Chacholiades, M. (1990) *International Economics* (New York: McGraw Hill).

Findlay, R. (1995) *Factor Proportions, Trade, and Growth* (Cambridge, MA: MIT Press).

Greider, W. (1998) *One World Ready or Not: The Manic Logic of Global Capitalism* (New York: Simon & Schuster).

Haberler, G. (1961) *A Survey of International Trade Theory* (Princeton: Princeton University Press).

Hume, D. (1758) *Writings on Economics*, Eugene Rotwein (ed.) 1955 (Madison: University of Wisconsin).

International Labor Organization (2004) *A Fair Globalization – Creating Opportunities for All* (Geneva, Switzerland: International Labor Organization).

Krugman, P. (1979) Increasing returns, monopolistic competition and international trade, *Journal of International Economics* 9(4), 469–79.

—— (1980) Scale economies, product differentiation and the pattern of trade, *American Economic Review* 70(4), 950–9.

Leontief, W. W. (1993) The use of indifference curves in the analysis of foreign trade, *Quarterly Journal of Economics* 27, 493–501.

Lerner, A. P. (1934) The diagrammatic representation of cost conditions in international trade, *Economica* 12, N.S. 1, 319–34.

Markusen, J. (2002) *Multinational Firms and the Theory of International Trade* (Cambridge, MA: MIT Press).

Marglin, S. (1984) *Growth, Distribution, and Prices* (Cambridge, MA: Harvard University Press).

Marshall, A. (1890) *Principles of Economics* (London: Macmillan & Co).

Meade, J. E. (1952) *A Geometry of International Trade* (London: George Allen and Unwin).

Paley, T. (1998) *Plenty of Nothing* (Princeton: Princeton University Press).

Pieper, U. and Taylor, P. (1998) The revival of the liberal creed: the IMF, the World Bank, and inequality in a globalized economy, in *Globalization and Progressive Economic Policy*, Baker, Epstein, and Pollin (eds.). (Cambridge: Cambridge University Press).

Ricardo, D. (1817) *The Principles of Political Economy and Taxation*, 1973 reprint (New York: Dutton)

Schweickart, D. (2002) *After Capitalism* (New York: Rowman & Littlefield).

Smith, A. (1776) *The Wealth of Nations* (New York: Modern Library (1937)).

Stiglitz, J. (2002) *Globalization and Its Discontents* (New York: W.W. Norton & Company).

—— (2004) The broken promise of NAFTA, *New York Times.* January 6.

Taylor, L. (2004) *Reconstructing Macroeconomics: Structuralist Proposals and Critiques of the Mainstream* (Cambridge, MA: Harvard University Press).

Williams, J. (1983) *The Open Economy and the World Economy* (New York: Basic Books).

Young, D. (1970) *International Economics* (Scranton, PA: Intext).

4 Globally sustainable and balanced international trade based on exchange-rate adjustment is mathematically unstable and therefore economically infeasible

1 Introduction

Can international trade be managed through "self-correcting," or individual country-administered, exchange-rate adjustments?

A central theoretical conclusion of the economics profession, going back at least to David Ricardo (1817), holds that, at least under highly idealized conditions, this is possible. However, as demonstrated in Chapter 2, Ricardo's model is in fact mathematically *overdetermined* and thus generally has no feasible solution. Other analyses of international trade similarly refute the notion that freely floating, or individual country-administered, exchange rates can produce balanced, and therefore sustainable, world trade – see for example Blecker (1999), Eatwell and Taylor (2000), Taylor (2004), Fletcher (2009), and Shaikh (1999, 2007).[1]

In this chapter we attempt to add to the cumulative weight of these and other theoretical and empirical critiques of *exchange-rate-based* trade by addressing the purely logical issue of whether *freely floating*, or *administered but not coordinated across multiple countries*, exchange rates can produce a stable, balanced, and sustainable international trade solution *even if all of the standard assumptions are fully satisfied*.[2]

We do this by constructing a simple but completely generalizable partial-equilibrium short-term demand model. This model is based on the standard introductory textbook model of exchange-rate-driven international trade which assumes that if: a) Marshall-Lerner (ML) conditions[3] are universally satisfied, b) bilateral trade universally responds effectively and efficiently to exchange-rate fluctuations, and c) freely floating, or individual country-administered, exchange rates react quickly and in a "normal" direction to trade imbalances, international trade can be balanced, or at least move toward international trade balance, through exchange-rate *price adjustments*, even as other factors that impact trade change over time; see for example Colander (2008).[4] We will show that this idea, which is the *essential story* of the "free trade doctrine," repeated in every introductory economics or political science text on international trade, is mathematically infeasible. Global trade based on *normal* market-driven, or individual country-managed, exchange-rate adjustment will not generally move trade toward greater balance.[5]

The basic problem is that though there is always a unique single internation-ally balanced trade solution under these assumptions, this unique solution will *not* generally be arrived at through *market-driven free trade* adjustment because it will always be mathematically *unstable*.[6] Moreover, for the same reason, administrative efforts by *individual* nations to set their own exchange rates to achieve balanced trade will almost always fail to produce *worldwide* balanced trade, as exchange-rate movements that may improve *bilateral* balance for individual nations are *not* generally consistent with the movements necessary to generate *international* balance.[7] We conclude that sustainable benefits from international trade generally *cannot* be realized through purely market-based *free trade*, or through nationally administered *exchange-rate adjustment* systems that are focused on bilateral trade balances, no matter how perfectly calibrated and responsive these might be.

Our argument proceeds as follows. In Section 2 we offer a simple informal summary of the main argument of the chapter. Readers who find this explana-tion convincing may skip to the conclusion in Section 6 of the chapter. Readers who would like to see a formal exposition should continue to read Sections 3–6. Section 3 provides a demonstration that any solution to a general multiple-country and multiple-good international trading system that satisfies these assumptions must be *unique*. This is shown by analyzing the characteristics that *any* system of exchange-rate-based import demand equations would have to exhibit. In Section 4, a three-country international trade model is constructed and it is shown that if an international balanced trade solution exists, it *cannot* consist of three bilat-eral trade *balances*. Section 5 proves that the alternative possibility of a unique solution with three bilateral trade *imbalances* will be, barring extreme coinci-dence, *unstable* and thus also not a viable *economic* solution.[8] Section 6 shows that the same is true for a general N-country model. If a balanced international trade solution exists, it will be mathematically unstable and thus highly unlikely to be obtained, or maintained, through bilateral exchange-rate adjustments, as in this system *normal bilateral exchange-rate adjustments* will generally *not* move the system toward global balance. Section 7 elaborates on the conclusion, that market-led *freely floating*, or individual country-administered, *exchange-rate* adjustments, even under the most ideal exchange-rate-based international trade assumptions, will generally be unstable and not conducive to more balanced global trade.[9]

The principal theoretical issue addressed by this chapter is whether freely float-ing, or individual country-administered, exchange rates and *normal* exchange-rate response to trade deficits can, in theory (if shift-factors are stable enough), produce a balanced international free trade regime. If this is not possible, self-adjusting *free trade*, and *individual country-administered trade*, exchange-rate-based trade doctrines have no theoretical legitimacy.

2 The simple instability argument

Readers who are already convinced that, if it exists, the global balanced-trade solution to any generic exchange-rate-based international trade model must be unique, may want to skip to Section 3 where the central *instability* arguments begin. Readers who prefer a heuristic argument rather than the detailed formal exposition presented in Sections 3–6 may be satisfied with the following simple explanation of the central instability argument.

The point made in this chapter is extremely simple. In fact I believe that its simplicity is the main obstacle to its not having, as far as I know, been previously pointed out as a *fundamental inconsistency* of the free trade doctrine.

The problem is that the prices, or exchange rates, in any three or more country exchange-rate-based international trading model do not pertain to individual markets as in a domestic economy, but rather directly affect two or more markets, or bilateral trade flow balances between three or more countries, at once.[10] Because of this, exchange-rate fluctuations that might lead to greater trade balance in one market, or bilateral trade flow between two countries, will *directly* change exchange rates that govern other bilateral trade flows with at least one other country. This intrinsic externality effect undermines any possibility that the unique *mathematical* global trade equilibrium will be *stable*, or have any economic *relevance*.[11] This is because the *collateral* exchange-rate changes occurring in other markets, as a result of the exchange-rate fluctuations affecting one bilateral trade flow, generally have no, or negligible, relationship to trade balances in these other markets. Therefore, even if an exchange rate adjustment improves trade balances for bilateral trading between two countries, i.e. *one* bilateral trade flow, there is *no* causal mechanism ensuring that *overall* trade balances move toward the unique global trade equilibrium. This structural feature of international trade, not shared by markets and prices in the domestic economy, renders notions of a stable price-based or *exchange-rate-based* equilibrium in international trade models impossible.

For example, Europe (in late 2007) had a trade surplus with the U.S. but a deficit with China. The Euro's appreciation vis-à-vis the Dollar was expected to eventually reduce Europe's trade surplus with U.S., but the Yuan's relatively slower appreciation vis-à-vis the Dollar led to a Euro appreciation relative to the Yuan that *increased* Europe's deficit with China, leading to an increased *overall* European trade deficit. A larger and more rapid appreciation of the Yuan could have conceivably rebalanced this system, but it appeared unlikely to come about from *free market* forces (Palley, 2007a, 2007b).

This problem and the externality issues that are raised by problems like this have been identified as a theoretical issue for particular cases of linked exchange rates by many economists – see for example Takatoshi and Ogawa (2002), but the general conclusion, that *free trade* or bilateral exchange-rate-based administered trade is a *fundamentally unworkable* economic doctrine, even under the most ideal Neoclassical assumptions, has been ignored.

For a general exposition of this proposition, showing that it is not a special case but a mathematically unavoidable characteristic of any bilateral exchange-rate-based international trade regime, see the formal exposition in Sections 3–6. The chapter's conclusions are presented in Section 7.

3 Exchange-rate-based international trading systems have, at most, one balanced-trade solution

Exchange-rate-based trading theories assume that, under appropriate conditions, exchange-rate adjustment will cause international trade to balance. The implicit assumption here is that if Marshall-Lerner conditions hold, and exchange rates are free to *float*, or are administered or adjusted by means of proactive government policies, to quickly respond to trade *fundamentals* in a "normal" way so that they depreciate in response to trade deficits and appreciate in response to surpluses, there will be price, or exchange-rate, *clearing* of international trade. This implies that exchange-rate adjustment will induce an exchange-rate-based international trading system to move toward an equilibrium position that will be obtained under *ceteris paribus* conditions, or if other non-price *shift-factors* remain constant long enough. In the following we first show that these kind of models can have at most *one* unique balanced exchange-rate solution for every set of non-exchange-rate, or *non-price* parameters.

THEOREM 1: Any linear international trade model that *assumes* that trade flows can be balanced through *exchange-rate* fluctuations can have at most one exchange-rate solution that balances international trade for every set of values of other international trade impacting non-exchange-rate factors. Similarly, any solution to a non-linear international trade model that obeys introductory text-book international trade assumptions in a partially differentiable, or reasonably continuous, way will be locally unique. These assumptions are that: a) Marshall-Lerner conditions are universally satisfied, b) bilateral trade universally responds effectively and efficiently to exchange-rate fluctuations, and c) freely floating, or individual country-administered, exchange rates react quickly and in a *normal* direction to trade imbalances.

Variable count

In international trade one country's imports are the sum of other countries' exports. Trade flows can thus be modeled as either exports or imports or an appropriate combination of either. We choose to model all flows from the import side.

In the general, exchange-rate-based, N-country import demand model, each country will produce, consume, export, and import N_i types of goods and services, of which $M_j =< N_j$ are (at least partially) imported. Any international import-demand model must, for each country i (i = 1, …,N), solve for the value of the imported quantities of each of the goods or services that are (at least partially) imported into country i. The value of M_i is *the number of such unknown import quantities demanded in each country i.* Thus the total number of unknown imported quantities demanded for all N countries will be $\sum_{i=1}^{N} M_i$.

In any general import demand model, for each country i there must be an import demand equation for import quantity m_{ij} (i = 1 … N, j = 1 … M_i) within the different countries. Note that though the goods or services may be the same across countries, the quantity imported m_{ij} will generally be different in different countries.

For each country i, each import demand equation will consist of an import quantity demanded m_{ij} that will be dependent on: the other goods or services that have been imported, the N−1 exchange rates (one country will have a *numeraire* international medium of exchange currency), and on q_{ij} (i = 1 … N, j = 1 … Q_i) independent parameters or "shift-factors" that affect import demand for this good or service in country i but that are independent of the exchange rates, where Q_i *is the number of shift-factor parameters (excluding other import quantities demanded) for each import quantity demanded variable m_{ij} in country i.* Examples of these might include: the levels of domestic goods and services production, non-trade-related capital flows, domestic and international prices of own and related goods and services in local currencies, national monetary and fiscal policy, income, income distribution, taste, price elasticities of imports and exports, and N−1 independent exchange-rate variables (as the Nth exchange rate will be determined by the other N−1 exchange rates). Note that shift-factor parameters that are identical across different goods or services, or countries, should not be counted as *additional* shift-factor parameters in the final tally of unique *shift-factor* parameters for the complete system of import demand equations: $\sum_{i=1}^{Mi} Q_i$.

All told, for all N countries we will then have a system of equations with $\sum_{i=1}^{N} M_i$ import quantities demanded as unknowns, and $\sum_{i=1}^{N} Q_i$ independent parameters along with N−1 independent exchange-rate variables, for a total number of unknown *variables* and independent *parameters* equal to:

$$\sum_{i=1}^{N} M_i + \sum_{i=1}^{N} Q_i + N-1 \qquad (2.1)$$

Equation count

As noted above, each import quantity demanded m_{ij} in each country i will have to satisfy an import demand equation, and each country (except for one – see below) will have to satisfy a trade balance equation with all of its trading partners. Therefore internationally balanced trade will have to satisfy $\sum_{i=1}^{N} M_i$ demand equations and N-1 trade balance equations for a total of independent *equations* equal to:

$$\sum_{i=1}^{N} M_i + N-1 \qquad (2.2)$$

Note that though trade must be balanced for each of the N countries, balanced trade in N−1 countries will cause trade to be balanced in the Nth country. Thus there will be only N−1 *independent* trade balance equations.

Due to the great diversity between products and countries, there is no reason to believe that any commodity import demand equation for any country, including all of its long-term and other non-price-related parameters, can, in a general case, be derived from any other set of commodity import demand equations, including those of other countries. In any case, if by chance imported quantities demanded of different goods or services for the same or different countries are for some reason dependent on each other, a *composite* commodity can be created to ensure that all of the equations in the system are mathematically independent. We can therefore safely assume that in general the equations counted in (2.2) will all be *independent* equations.

Degrees of freedom calculation

As can be readily seen, subtracting (2.2) from (2.1) gives us exactly (but no more than) the $\sum_{i=1}^{N} Q_i$ degrees of freedom that are needed for a general solution to this system that does not constrict the values of the parameters or shift-factors Q_i in any way. Thus for any given set of values for these non-exchange-rate-related, or at least *short-term* non-exchange-rate-related, parameters, we have a system of $\sum_{i=1}^{N} M_i + \text{N}-1$ independent equations and $\sum_{i=1}^{N} M_i + \text{N}-1$ unknowns.

This implies that if a mathematical solution exists, it will be unique, i.e. there will be a single unique vector of exchange rates and import quantities demanded for any given set of shift-factors or non-exchange-rate-independent parameters, that will result in internationally balanced trade. Note if it exists, the solution will be a *mathematical* solution but *not* (as will be shown below) an *economically meaningful* or *feasible* solution as it will be mathematically *unstable*.

This will be true for a linear demand system, as well as for localized solutions for non-linear differentiable demand systems as solutions to these systems will have to satisfy linear systems of partial differential equations to which the same degrees of freedom calculus will apply.

Note that this (rather trivial) point will be true for *any* system of linear, and/ or non-linear but partially differentiable, exchange-rate-based import equations. Any international trade model which assumes price, or exchange-rate, trade clearing, subject to other assumptions (for example regarding domestic and international effective demand, or technology and capital stock, or taste, or monetary and fiscal policy), will satisfy (2.1) and (2.2). Such models include standard Neoclassical (NC) trade models with preferences, technologies, and factor endowments given; "Heckscher-Ohlin" NC trade models which assume equal preferences and technologies but different factor endowments across countries; and "misbehaved" Heckscher-Ohlin-Samuelson NC models that include factors such as "skill" (Findlay, 1995; Amsden, 1983). Following Ricardo, these models explicitly or implicitly presume that *terms of trade* that reflect *comparative advantages* are determined by *free trade*, or bilateral managed trade, based on short-run exchange-rate fluctuations (Baiman, 2010). Any international trade model that assumes that international terms of trade primarily reflect *exchange-rate clearing*, subject to other assumptions (for example regarding technology and preferences;

or technology, skills, and capital and labor stock) and other possible *shift-factors* (like capital flows, monetary or fiscal policy, growth, and inflation), will satisfy (2.1) and (2.2).

In contrast, most heterodox trade models such as Romerian Neo-Marxist "unequal exchange" models which assume highly unequal capital stock endowments, orthodox Marxist labor-value pricing trade models, or Sraffian models with fixed or flexible wages and mobile or immobile capital explicitly or implicitly reject the notion of a *free trade equilibrium*, as they presume that international terms-of-trade (after taking into account the impact of the other factors listed above) are not primarily based on exchange-rate valuation, but rather tend to reflect real productivity differences, or *absolute advantage* rather than *comparative advantage* (Baiman, 2006, 2014; Shaikh, 1980, 1995, 1999; Brewer, 1985).

4 A three-country free trade solution cannot include any bilateral trade balances

The fact that a *unique* possible balanced trading solution may exist does not in itself mean that *market forces*, or individual country-administered exchange rates, will move international trading toward this solution. If the unique solution is not one that *free market* forces, or exchange-rate policies directed toward *individual country* trade balance, would move toward, there is no reason to believe that this unique solution (if it exists) can ever be obtained. In other words, if the unique solution is mathematically *unstable* – or does not include a dynamic process whereby the system will gravitate toward the unique solution – there is no reason to believe that it will be realized, even under the most theoretically ideal conditions.

Assume three countries: Portugal (P) which uses Euros (E), United Kingdom (K) which uses pounds (£), and U.S. (U) which uses Dollars ($). Assume (for now[12]) that the Dollar ($) is the international currency, and that exchange rates are: y = $/E and x = $/£.

Assume the trade flows (all measured in importers' currencies) as shown in Figure 4.1 below.

U imports c from P and d from K

P imports b from U and a from K

K imports e from P and f from U

where, as is noted above, the symbols a, b, c, d, and e represent the financial value of the total bundle of imported goods and services measured in import country currency.

Trade balance equations (converted to $ with importers paying in domestic currency) are then:

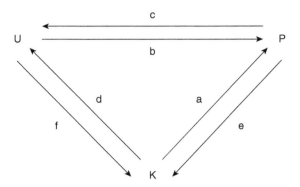

Figure 4.1 Three-country trade flows

U: $yb + xf = d + c$ (4.1)

P: $c + xe = ya + yb$ (4.2)

K: $d + ya = xf + xe$ (4.3)

This confirms the dependence of the trade balance equations as if the balances for U and P are added together and yb + c is subtracted from both sides, the balance for K falls out. (4.1) to (4.3) are purely *static* mathematical constraints that any exchange-rate or price-based solution to world trade must satisfy as long-term *centers of gravity* if international trade is to tend toward balance. Under ideal *free trade*, *normal* conditions (4.1)–(4.3) are supposed to move toward balance based on exchange-rate fluctuations. The exchange-rate adjustments in turn are supposed to be driven by the supply and demand for each currency as determined by the needs of trading partners, so that exchange rates gravitate toward values that equalize bilateral trade between countries.[13] Alternatively, as is detailed below, an individual country's exchange rates may be administratively set so as to achieve balanced trade with one or more of its trading partners. The free trade doctrine assumes that if these individual country-administered exchange rates mimic exchange-rate movements that would be, or should but for some reason are not, induced by market forces affecting similar currency valuations, they will lead to more balanced trade.[14]

More specifically, we assume that under *free trade*, or *standard* exchange-rate administrative measures for achieving *balanced* trade, there will be *normal* exchange-rate effects, i.e. trade deficits will cause currency depreciation and trade surpluses in currency appreciation. In the vastly simplified *market-led* exchange-rate systems that we are addressing, these exchange-rate effects are supposed to be a direct result of trading needs. If country A has a surplus with country B, exporters from A to B will have more of B's currency from sales receipts than exporters from B to A will have of A's currency. As exporters from A to B have to pay producers in country A in A's currency for these goods, and vice versa for exporters from B to A, both sets of exporters need to exchange most of their sales receipts back to the currency of the country in which the goods were produced. Country A's trade surplus with country B will thus result in an excess supply of currency B and demand for currency A, leading to a depreciation of currency B and an appreciation of currency A.

For *administered systems* we assume that governments attempt to set exchange rates with a view to balancing an individual country's trade. Below we show that both free trade and administered trade *in this sense* will not in general move trade toward greater global balance. We sometimes refer to this kind of administered trade as a type of "free trade" though this is not a common usage of the term.

Normal effects imply that currency depreciation will reduce a trade deficit, and currency appreciation will shrink a trade surplus, and that these *free trade*, or individual country-administered, exchange-rate effects will be strong enough and occur quickly enough to induce exchange-rate-based adjustment toward balanced trade. Standard trade texts claim that this *normal* response will occur when Marshall-Lerner conditions are satisfied.

We note in passing that as these conditions do not take into account trade-induced changes in overall output (they implicitly assume Say's law), this is not generally true, especially for smaller developing countries – see Taylor (2004, pp. 253–7). In fact, the *income effects* of exchange fluctuations are empirically well documented, and are at the core of the many Keynesian and post-Keynesian critiques of free trade cited and noted above. However, for the purpose of this chapter we will ignore these *Keynesian* effects of trade imbalance and show that even if the M-L conditions are satisfied so that exchange-rate fluctuations, or administrative settings, produce *normal*, timely, and effective trade responses, movement toward a *free trade*, or *normal* administered exchange-rate, equilibrium will *not* generally occur.

LEMMA 1: In a three-country trading system that satisfies the classical textbook assumptions of Theorem 1, the three bilateral trade relationships cannot generally all be balanced. In other words, the following:

$$yb = c \qquad (4.4)$$

$$d = xf \qquad (4.5)$$

$$ya = xe \qquad (4.6)$$

is not generally feasible.

Proof

The special case of (4.4)–(4.6) is not generally feasible as based on (2.2) we would then have for the three-country case this many independent equations:[15]

$$\sum_{i=1}^{3} M_i + 3 \qquad (4.7)$$

where the *three* free market trade balance equations (4.4)–(4.6) are substituted for N−1 or *two* independent generic trade balance conditions, for example (4.1) and (4.2), as stipulated by (2.2). As has been shown above, (4.3) is a *dependent* equation as it can be derived from (4.1) and (4.2). It thus does not reduce the number of degrees of freedom. In contrast, (4.6) *cannot* be derived from (4.4) and (4.5) and therefore reduces the number of degrees of freedom by one.

Another way to see this is to note that (4.1) implies that there is an arbitrary constant C such that:

$$xf - d = c - yb = C$$

and if this is the case, (4.2) implies that:

$$ya - xe = c - yb = C$$

and therefore from (4.3):

$$xf - d = ya - xe = C$$

But the conditions (4.4–4.6) require that:

$$yb - c = xf - d = ya - xe = 0$$

This enforced equality to zero rather than to an *arbitrary constant* C reduces the degrees of freedom in a three-country balanced bilateral trading system by one.

The number of unknowns, or variables, however, remains as calculated in (2.1). Thus, for the three-country case the number of variables will be:

$$\sum_{i=1}^{3} M_i + \sum_{i=1}^{3} Q_i + 2 \qquad\qquad (4.8)$$

including import quantities demanded, the long-term parameters, and the two exchange rates. This leaves us with one missing degree of freedom as (4.8) minus (4.7) gives:

$\sum_{i=1}^{3} Q_i - 1$. This causes this system to be mathematically overdetermined and not generally solvable as one of the unknowns, or shift-factors, would then have to be dependent on the others, contrary to the assumptions of the general exchange-rate-based model.

Note that Lemma 1 *does not* imply that three countries may not have mutual bilateral trade balances. Rather it states that in exchange-rate-based trading models this can only occur with a *particular* configuration of *shift-factors* and will not be possible with a general set of shift-factors, or non-exchange-rate-related parameters. Specifically, Lemma 1 states that for this kind of trade flow configuration to occur, one shift-factor must be dependent on the others, so that this bilateral balanced trade solution will become *infeasible* if the shift-factors change without preserving the shift-factor dependency relationship, regardless of changes in exchange rates.

COROLLARY 1: As the number of *free trade* bilateral trade balancing constraints like (4.4)–(4.6) increases, degrees of freedom are reduced as additional equations like (4.3) and (4.5) below are set to zero rather than to an arbitrary constant, causing an increasing overdetermination problem for the system.

6 Any feasible three-country free trade solution is generally unstable

We can therefore assume that, if it exists, the general unique equilibrium trade solution includes *imbalanced* bilateral trade flows for at least one of three possible country pairs in a three-country international trading system.

Suppose, without loss of generality, that *the unique* international trade solution is one where U has a trade surplus with P.[16] For (4.1) to remain in balance, this imbalance must be perfectly offset by trade with U's only other partner K, so that (4.1) remains in balance:

$$UP: \quad y°b° > c° \tag{4.1}$$

$$KU: \quad d° > x°f° \tag{4.2}$$

Such that:

$$U: \quad y°b° - c° = d° - x°f° \tag{4.3}$$

where (°) designates the unique balanced trade equilibrium values generated by exchange rates y° and x°, leading to equilibrium import (or export) quantities demanded: b°, c°, d°, and f°.

Moreover, this solution will also determine equilibrium values for a° and e° since for the international system to be in balance, P will then have to have just the right surplus with K:

$$KP: \quad y°a° < x°e° \tag{4.4}$$

Such that:

$$P: \quad x°e° - y°a° = y°b° - c°, \text{ i.e. (a slightly rearranged)}$$
(4.2) will hold. $\tag{4.5}$

(4.3) and (4.5) will then guarantee:

$$K: \quad x°e° - y°a° = d° - x°f° \tag{4.6}$$

so that (4.3) will hold as well. This shows that one bilateral trade imbalance inevitably leads to three bilateral trade imbalances.

THEOREM 2: The solution (4.1)–(4.6) above will be a *mathematically unstable* and therefore *economically infeasible* outcome.

Proof

At the point in time where (4.1)–(4.6) holds (or in *static* terms), the *excess* Euro demand for Dollars generated by (4.1) will equal the excess Dollar demand for Pounds generated by (4.2), and both of these (in Dollar terms) will equal the excess Pound demand for Euros from (4.4) (as in this case P has a surplus with K), so that if the excess Dollars from (4.2) were exchanged for the excess Euros from (4.1), and these were then exchanged for the excess Pounds from (4.4), all parties would be satisfied and exchange rates could remain at levels satisfying (4.1), (4.2), and (4.4).

Problems appear, however, when one looks at the detailed behavioral *dynamics* that might make this work. First note that the holders of the *excess* Euros from (4.1) want Dollars, the holders of the *excess* Dollars from (4.2) want Pounds, and the holders of the *excess* Pounds from (4.4) want Euros, so that *none* of the agents' immediate currency demands and offers match up with any other agents' currency offers and demands as they *would have to* for barter exchange to occur. Demands and offers are equal in dollar value but not in the barter sense of agents with reciprocal offers and demands. Thus a *medium of exchange* like gold (or any other convertible currency) is *necessary* for these currency exchanges to occur.[17]

This implies that for the exchange rates that lead to the system (4.1)–(4.6) to remain constant, or for supply and demand for each currency to match, an *international medium of exchange*, say gold, and an International Currency Trader (ICT) with a stock of gold must be introduced. The ICT will pay the exporters gold for Euros, Dollars, and Pounds, and then sell these currencies back to exporters in Portugal, the U.S., and the U.K., respectively. In this way Euros can be exchanged for gold and then gold for Dollars, Dollars can be exchanged for gold and gold for Pounds, and Pounds for gold and gold for Euros, canceling out all the intermediate gold transactions, balancing supply and demand for exchange currency, and stabilizing the exchange rates maintaining the balanced trade equilibrium (4.3), (4.5), and (4.6).[18]

However, as the exporters are all selling and buying currency from an *intermediary*, they and the identities of their home countries that are the sources of *demand for*, or *supply of*, the currencies are irrelevant. Currency effects that originate from any one of (4.1), (4.2), or (4.4) will thus *spill over* to another of these equations. This is a critical point that is generally overlooked in simple *real barter-based* trade or in *two-country* trade models.

A surplus supply of Euros and excess demand for Dollars that may originate from a surplus of U.S. exports to Portugal does not just depreciate the value of the Euros that *these* importers receive, or appreciate the dollars used to pay the U.S. producers of *these* products. Rather, these currency effects are transmitted to Dollars and Euros in *general*, including those that are used in other international trading transactions. As the direction and rate of change of the currency movements originating from one trade imbalance are more or less independent of other trade imbalances, particularly between countries that have no, or marginal, trading relations with the countries in the original imbalance, these currency adjustments will *not*, except accidentally, be those that would be required to bring the other trading relations that they impact into balance.

Suppose, for example, that for some short-term reason that does not affect the long-term parameters of the system, U's trade surplus with P, that was initially in the state of equilibrium specified in (4.1), *increases*, so that (4.1) becomes:

$$\text{UP:} \quad y^1 b^1 > c^1 \tag{4.7}$$

where:

$$y^1 b^1 - c^1 > y^\circ b^\circ - c^\circ \tag{4.8}$$

This will increase the excess supply of Euros and demand for Dollars relative to that of (4.1). As Pounds are not used in this trade, the demand and supply of Pounds will not be affected. Thus relative to some *constant* (assumed without loss of generality) international currency like *gold*:[19] a) the Dollar will appreciate, b) the Euro will depreciate, and c) the value of the Pound will remain unchanged. Though the decline of y=$/E will be greater, this will cause both y=$/E *and* x=$/£ to *decline*.

The decline in y will, under our *exchange-rate-based* trade assumptions, reduce U's surplus with P, moving (4.7) back toward the equilibrium values of (4.1).

But at the same time, the decline in x, or appreciation of the Dollar vis-à-vis the Pound, will under these same assumptions cause K's surplus with U to *increase* so that (4.2) will change to:

$$\text{KU:} \quad d^1 > x^1 f^1 \tag{4.9}$$

where:

$$d^1 - x^1 f^1 > d^\circ - x^\circ f^\circ \tag{4.10}$$

This will in turn increase the value of the Pound and *reduce* the value of the Dollar, *raising* x=$/£ and moving (4.7) away from (4.1). This increase in x will be greater or smaller than the decline in x from (4.7). Depending on the speed and Dollar magnitudes of the export and import responses in (4.7) and (4.9) to these exchange-rate fluctuations, (4.7) may or may not move closer to (4.1), and (4.9) may or may not move closer to (4.2).[20]

Finally, unless they net-out to zero, the changes in x and y will cause the £/E=y/x ratio to change, leading to an indeterminate change in (4.4).

As there is absolutely no reason why these exchange-rate effects should move the disequilibrium import quantities back to the unique balanced trade position of (4.1), (4.2), and (4.4), we conclude that the unique solution (4.1), (4.2), and (4.4) is unstable. Therefore there generally will be no *free market*, or *normal* administered exchange rates, that will move international trade toward the unique balanced trade position (if it exists), or be able to maintain the system in this balanced position if it is disturbed for any reason that does not involve an existing shift-factor change. If it exists at all, *a three-country balanced exchange-rate-based trade equilibrium will thus be an unstable, and therefore economically unfeasible, outcome.*[21]

7 A balanced N-country "free trade" system is also economically infeasible

THEOREM 3: A balanced N>3 country *exchange-rate-based* free, or individual country-administered, trade solution will be *mathematically unstable* and thus *economically infeasible.*[22]

Proof

In Section 4 we demonstrated that bilateral trade balances between three or more countries are not possible. We have also proved that if one pair of countries has a trade imbalance, at least three countries must have precisely offsetting imbalanced bilateral trade if overall international trade is to be balanced. We have shown that if any one of these bilateral trade inequalities changes, the currency value of the two currencies involved will change (relative to a third currency), and this will necessarily impact the other two bilateral trade relations. Finally, we have pointed out that there is no reason that these currency appreciations and depreciations will lead to the kind of perfectly offsetting trade expansions or contractions between these three countries that would be necessary to move the system to a globally balanced position. To the contrary, as individual country satisfaction of the Marshall-Lerner conditions ensures a *qualitatively* "normal" trade response to exchange-rate fluctuation in the simple textbook model that we are addressing, and does not guarantee that exchange-rate elasticities of imports between three or more countries will have the precise values necessary to re-establish international balance if such a balance were perturbed, there is no reason to assume that a market-led free trading system or exchange-rate-based individual country-administered trading system will ever come back into balance, and if it does, that such a balanced solution will be stable.

But any N-country balanced trade solution must have at least three bilateral trade imbalances and therefore will be mathematically unstable. If, as is likely, the unique balanced trading solution to an N-country trading system includes more than three bilateral imbalances, the above logic will apply to more than three countries. Due to the *inseparability* of the currency impacts of any bilateral trade imbalance, a perturbation (due to short-term non-shift-factor causes) of any bilateral trade relationship from an initial international balanced trade position will cause exchange-rate changes that will affect other bilateral trading relationships in indeterminate ways that will not generally move the system toward the unique international trade balance consistent with the non-exchange-rate-dependent shift-factor parameters of the system.

8 Conclusion

We conclude that there is no reason why purely exchange-rate *price adjustments*, whether *market-led* or *administered by individual countries to balance their own trade*, will produce *globally* balanced free trade. To the contrary, it is reasonable to assume that trade imbalances will induce an arbitrary subset of consistent, or inconsistent, currency adjustments at varying rates with varying impacts on import demands, and that these adjustments will not, except coincidentally, move global trade toward balance. And, if by chance, a unique internationally balanced trade position is obtained, it is not likely to last as it will almost always be mathematically unstable for almost any perturbation. The concrete example described in Section 2 above illustrates this situation.

I should again stress that in practice, in the current environment of largely unregulated capital flows and currency exchange speculation, exchange-rate movements are often de-linked from trade or current account positions for long periods of time – the U.S. is, of course, exhibit "A" of this phenomenon, so that the empirical applications of ideal textbook free trade stability or instability are in some sense beside the point. Textbook trade-based exchange-rate fluctuation, whether stabilizing or not, simply does not apply (Blecker, 1999).

But the central conclusion of this chapter is still highly relevant. Since international trade *cannot* be balanced through individual country-based exchange-rate fluctuations no matter how ideal free trade and currency markets are, active global trade management policies are necessary to sustain a global trading system that moves toward balance. This may involve *global* (not individual country) exchange-rate management. However, as it would appear to be nearly impossible to offset the numerous, persistent, and ongoing trade effects of non-exchange-rate-based "shift-factors" through continuous global exchange-rate adjustments, no matter how well targeted, it is highly likely that exchange-rate management policies would have to be coupled with other non-exchange-rate trade flow management policies to achieve persistent movements toward global trade balance. This was of course the case during the Bretton-Woods "Golden Age," or Keynesian period, of relatively fixed exchange rates and effective domestic capital controls (Stretton, 1999; Marglin & Schor, 1992).

This is not to say that the Bretton-Woods system can be recreated or was sustainable in the long run to begin with. For one thing, the system depended on a continual increase in U.S. dollars as the world reserve currency to support global liquidity. As the U.S. maintained surplus or balanced trade and current accounts through much of this 1944–70 period, the increased dollar injections were based on large and persistent U.S. capital account outflows to finance private investment, overseas military spending, and foreign aid, and to finance U.S. global economic and military expansion. Some of this outflow of dollars was financed through the selling of dwindling gold reserves, but increasingly it was financed by more U.S. dollar liabilities to foreigners. As this was clearly not sustainable over the long term, the system broke down in the 1970s (Meltzer, 1991). However, trade flows and exchange rates were much more stable during this period than they have been since. Though the free trade doctrine has played a key ideological role in sustaining the illusion that balanced international trade does not require global trade management, world trade has been unstable and increasingly out of balance since the Bretton-Woods system collapsed (Stretton, 1999; Eatwell & Taylor, 2000).

Automatic self-adjustment of international trade through free trade responding to freely floating exchange rates is *not* possible over the long run. Similarly administered exchange rates tied to individual country trade deficits or surpluses will *not* lead to a trading system that consistently moves toward greater balance. There is no alternative to *collective action* or *managed trade*. A new global trade management system must be constructed if sustainable domestic and international economic growth is to be restored (Keynes, 1933). The floating exchange rate and free trade-based regime has led to increased global inequality, instability, and environmental destruction (Baiman, 2006, 2014; Klein, 2014). The free trade doctrine held up as an international trading ideal is a nonsensical mirage.

Notes

1 These critiques which point out the assumptions upon which the "free trade" model rests often do not hold, and offer alternative more realistic trade models that are not primarily based on exchange-rate adjustments.
2 Though the standard introductory textbook assumptions of the very simple model addressed in this chapter assume that exchange-rate fluctuations will impact individual country exports and imports in "normal" fashion, these assumptions do not explain how exchange-rate adjustments are supposed to drive a multi-country trading system toward a global balanced trade equilibrium – the only kind of equilibrium that can be sustained over the long term. The discussion that follows shows that because of unavoidable exchange-rate "externality" effects from one bilateral trading situation to another, any "free market" or "bilateral managed" exchange-rate-based international trade model equilibrium (if it exists) will be unstable.
3 The "Marshall-Lerner" (ML) condition (after economists Alfred Marshall and Abba P. Lerner) is that absolute values of a country's exchange rate elasticity of exports, minus the absolute value of exchange rate elasticity of imports, is greater than 1. In standard trade literature this condition is assumed to ensure a "normal" response to exchange-rate devaluation, i.e. that an exchange-rate devaluation will cause exports minus imports, both valued in domestic currency, to increase. Like many other Neoclassical economic results, the presumed effect of the ML condition in ensuring a "normal" response to exchange-rate fluctuation ignores the potential effect of currency devaluation on overall output levels. Post-Keynesian economists have pointed out that, especially in developing countries, devaluation often reduces the trade deficit because of economic contraction regardless of whether the ML conditions hold as in these countries they often do not (Taylor, 2004, pp. 253–7).
4 Many factors can cause trade to be out of balance, under *free trade* or *managed trade* conditions. The textbook free trade doctrine does *not* claim that trade will always be in balance under (the above) ideal conditions. Rather the argument is that under these conditions normal exchange-rate fluctuations will move international trade toward

greater balance than would exist otherwise, i.e. that under proper conditions (the assumptions above) exchange-rate *fundamentals* will move trade flows toward *restoring balance*, regardless of how imbalanced other factors may cause trade to be. The introductory textbook doctrine only postulates theoretical global trade *balance* if shift-factors are stable during the period when exchange-rate adjustments work their magic. This chapter shows that this doctrine is mathematically and logically infeasible, i.e. that even under the most ideal conditions *fundamentals* will (almost always, barring exceptional circumstances) *not* consistently move international trade toward greater balance.

5 Needless to say, actual short-term, and even long-term, exchange-rate adjustments, freely floating or managed, do not generally follow this simple rule. Our concern in this chapter is with how simple free trade and exchange-rate-based trade *doctrine* is justified in introductory economics and public policy courses. Actual current exchange rates are influenced as much, or more, by fiscal and monetary policy, capital movements, and currency speculation. See Blecker (1999) and Taylor (2004) for a critical review of these more sophisticated trade models. For the record, I don't believe that any formal mathematical model can reasonably approximate actual existing international trade relationships, as these are primarily defined by broad political economic policies and practices that go well beyond the parameters included in trade models (Fletcher, 2009; Fingleton, 2009). The point of this chapter is to show that any trade *doctrine* that assumes that in some ideal world, or model, international trade can be *self-regulating*, or *guided* by means of direct or indirect bilateral *exchange-rate* adjustment, is prima facie mathematically invalid. This cannot work, even in theory, even under the most idealistic (and unrealistic) assumptions. The textbook trade story is not based on actual facts about real-world trade but rather on an idealized, and as pointed out in this chapter *internally inconsistent*, doctrine of how international trade would work if all the assumptions were true. Moreover, to the extent that they have any formal training in economics, the economic theory that the vast majority of policy makers, public officials, business people, media spokespersons, and voters are exposed to is *introductory textbook economics*. This theory, or story, or doctrine therefore has *broad public policy impact*. Its critique, which is the topic of this chapter, is thus germane and important.

6 This is true in almost every case. The only exception would be a situation where through sheer coincidence shift-factors are such that by pure happenstance normal exchange-rate changes move the system toward greater balance. As this would be purely accidental and not a general causal outcome, it can be dismissed as theoretical.

7 Though this would appear to, at least in theory, leave open the possibility of *global exchange-rate-based managed trade* through broad-based international diplomacy, in practice to be successful such agreements would have to take non-exchange-rate-based *shift-factors* into account consistent with the major finding of this chapter that global trade balance is only possible through *managed trade* that includes *non-exchange-rate* measures. To work, global trade management would have to include *non-exchange-rate trade management*, as was the case during the Bretton-Woods period. Similarly, as the current Euro Zone difficulties have shown, a *single currency* solution for *world trade* is *not* a realistic option for the foreseeable future.

8 This is not a mathematical *impossibility* theorem. One can conjure up conditions that could produce a stable three-country solution but such conditions are *highly unlikely*. Showing that the free trade doctrine is economically infeasible *in almost all* circumstances is more than adequate for invalidating a doctrine which claims the contrary that if the assumptions hold, *normal exchange-rate* adjustment will *always* lead to more balanced trade.

9 Op. cit.

10 Of course domestic markets often have *cross-price* effects, but these have an *indirect* impact on market prices that can be modeled in demand and cost (or supply) functions. They are not *direct* price effects that render global price clearing of bilateral trade flows impossible.

11 An unstable equilibrium has no economic relevance as the economic system to which it applies will not gravitate toward it, or remain in equilibrium if it is accidently obtained, except by happenstance.

12 In Section 5, without loss of generality, *gold* will be introduced as an *international medium of exchange* to make the exposition symmetrical between the three currencies and thus easier to follow.

13 As noted in earlier notes, this is a doctrine, not a reality. In particular, in this model, international supply and demand of currency are assumed, as in the simple introductory textbook model, to be purely functions of trade – not, for example, of currency speculation and capital flows or any other *non-trade* variables, as these *other* factors are assumed to be *shift-factors* that remain constant, and thus have no influence on exchange rates, during the period that exchange rates are presumed to be moving the system toward equilibrium.

14 As will be shown in what follows, though administrators can conceivably *jump* to whatever exchange rates they deem suitable, as long as their efforts are directed toward balancing their own *individual* country's bilateral trade flows and do not take into account global trade balancing effects, they will generally *not* lead to more balanced global trade.

15 See proof of Theorem 1 above for an explanation as to why the import demand and trade balance equations can be assumed to be independent.

16 The instability demonstration described in the text below would also clearly apply to (4.4)–(4.6), were such a solution mathematically feasible. However, as it is not, for expositional simplification we restrict ourselves to solutions composed of strict inequalities in this section – see discussion that follows.

17 Either Dollars, Pounds, or Euros could also serve but as this would make the explanation asymmetrical between the three currencies, a fourth currency *gold* is, *with no loss of generality*, introduced. The use of gold as an international reserve is irrelevant to the argument. Any internationally convertible currency could be used in its place.

18 As noted in note 17, we could specify that Dollars for example are the *international currency* but this would lead to an asymmetry between the currencies that would complicate the story without adding to it in any substantive way.

19 See note 18.

20 Moreover, per the discussion regarding individually managed exchange rates, the exchange rates do not have to be endogenous or determined by trade deficits or surpluses for this instability to occur. Efforts to administratively set exchange rates to balance bilateral trade will also *not* generally be conducive to global trade balance, and for the same reason. Spill-over exchange-rate effects will impact other trade flows in indeterminate ways that will not generally lead to more globally balanced trade.

21 Note that this global trade solution will not be reached even if a *Walrasian Auctioneer* tallies up offers and bids at different exchange rates and does not allow trading until *equilibrium* exchange rates are obtained; as such a *bilateral balanced* trading solution is, from Corollary 1, generally impossible. The only way an *auctioneer* would be able to guarantee a solution, if one exists, would be by solving the system of trade flow equations described in Theorem 1 and managing trade flows and exchange rates accordingly. But this would be a version of the *globally managed trade* shown to be necessary in this chapter. For this reason, though it may be possible to obtain *individual agent stability* for an idealized Walrasian system even with out-of-equilibrium trading under suitable production factor substitution, utility, and agent strategic behavior assumptions (Gintis and Mandel, 2012), it's hard to imagine how such a result could be obtained for a general global trading model due to the indeterminate *externality* effects of exchange-rate *price signals* that render these signals useless for directing trade flows toward global equilibrium values. The problem in the international trading situation is not just *out-of-equilibrium*

exchanges as in a Walrasian context, but bilateral equilibrium or out-of-equilibrium exchange-rate price fluctuations that have *no relevance* as *price signals* for moving trading toward a *general global* equilibrium.

22 As has been noted in earlier notes, the instability argument that follows clearly also applies to solutions that include one or more bilateral trade balances.

References

Amsden, A. H. (1983) "De-skilling," skilled commodities, and the NICs' emerging competitive advantage, *American Economic Review* 73(2), May, 333–37.

Baiman, R. (2006) Unequal exchange without a labor theory of prices: on the need for a global Marshall Plan and a solidarity trading regime, *Review of Radical Political Economics* 38(1), Winter, 71–89.

—— (2010) The infeasibility of free trade in classical theory: Ricardo's comparative advantage parable has no solution, *Review of Political Economy* 22(3), 419–37.

—— (2014) Unequal exchange and the rentier economy, *Review of Radical Political Economics* 46(4), 536–57.

Blecker, R. A. (1999) *Taming Global Finance* (Washington D.C.: The Economic Policy Institute).

Brewer, A. (1985) Trade with fixed real wages and mobile capital, *Journal of International Economics* 18, 177–86.

Colander, D. (2008) *Economics* (Burr Ridge, IL: McGraw Hill).

Eatwell, J. and Taylor, L. (2000) *Global Finance at Risk* (London: Polity Press).

Findlay, R. (1995) *Factor Proportions, Trade, and Growth* (Cambridge, MA: MIT Press).

Fingleton, E. (2009) *In the Jaws of the Dragon: America's Fate in the Coming Era of Chinese Dominance* (New York: St. Martin's Press).

Fletcher, I. (2009) *Free Trade Doesn't Work* (Washington D. C.: U.S. Business & Industry Council).

Gintis, H. and Mandel, A. (2012) The dynamics of Walrasian general equilibrium: theory and application, Paper for publication in *Complexity Economics*: http://www.umass.edu/preferen/gintis/gestabilityreview.pdf.

Keynes, J. M. (1933) National self-sufficiency, *The Yale Review* 22(4), June, 755–69.

Klein, N. (2014) *This Changes Everything: Capitalism vs. Climate Change* (New York: Simon and Schuster).

Marglin, S. A. (1984) *Growth, Distribution, and Prices* (Cambridge, MA: Harvard University Press).

Marglin, S. and Schor, J. (1992) *The Golden Age of Capitalism: Reinventing the Post-War Experience* (Oxford: Clarendon Press).

Meade, J. E. (1952) *A Geometry of International Trade* (London: George Allen and Unwin).

Meltzer, A. H. (1991) U.S. policy in the Bretton-Woods era, May. St. Louis Federal Reserve Bank Research Publications: https://research.stlouisfed.org/publications/review/91/05/Bretton_May_Jun1991.pdf.

Palley, T. (2007a) Exchange-rates: there is a better way, Oct. 31, posted at www.ThomasPalley.com.

Palley, T. (2007b) Triangular trouble: the Euro, the Dollar, and the Renminbi, Oct. 15, posted at www.ThomasPalley.com.

Ricardo, D. (1817) *The Principles of Political Economy and Taxation*, 1973 reprint (New York: Dutton).

Riddell, T., Shackelford, J., Schneider, G., and Stamos, S. (2011) *Economics: A Tool for Critically Understanding Society*, 9th Ed. (Boston, MA: Addison-Wesley/Pearson).

Shaikh, A. (1980) The laws of international exchange, in *Growth, Profits and Property*, Edward J. Nell (ed.) (Cambridge: Cambridge University Press).

—— (1995) Free trade, unemployment and economic policy, in *Global Unemployment*, John Eatwell (ed.) (Armonk, NY: M.E. Sharpe).

—— (1999) Real exchange-rates and the international mobility of capital, Working Paper No. 265, The Jerome Levy Economics Institute of Bard College.

—— (ed.) (2007) *Globalization and the Myths of Free Trade: History, Theory, and Empirical Evidence* (London: Routledge).

Stretton, H. (1999) *Economics: A New Introduction* (London: Pluto Press).

Takatoshi, I. and Ogawa, E. (2002) On the desirability of a regional basket currency arrangement, *Journal of Japanese and International Economics* 16(3), 317–34.

Taylor, L. (2004) *Reconstructing Macroeconomics* (Cambridge, MA: Harvard University Press).

Part II

The logical (and moral) foundations of unequal exchange trade theory

If Neoclassical free trade models of international trade and finance are logically and mathematically invalid or infeasible, are there other simple models that offer a more realistic conceptualization of global trade and finance?

The following two chapters offer one such alternative based on a generalized "unequal exchange" theory grounded in, but not algorithmically tied to, labor values.[1] These models attempt to uncover the links between global commerce and human impact. These include both labor effort as well as private and public benefits and costs in terms of consumption, income and income inequality, and growth. The underlying question is simple. In what ways can global trade and financial flows improve or worsen human well-being (Baiman, 2016)?

These chapters focus on the production and distribution of goods and services and highlight the ways in which global trade and finance can distort long-term economic development, especially for developing and "rentier" economies. Chapter 7 of Part III offers policy suggestions particularly applicable to the latter via a detailed analysis of trends in the U.S., the leading rentier economy in the world.

Chapter 5, "Unequal exchange without a labor theory of prices: on the need for a global Marshall Plan and solidarity trading regime," employs a modified three-sector, two-good, Roemerian model, first developed by Hahnel (1999), to analyze different international trading regimes. The model shows that free trade leads to "unequal exchange" which produces poverty in the south and unemployment in the north, and though "fair trade" eliminates inequality, it preserves a global division of labor that limits long-term development. The analysis shows that a "global Marshall Plan" and a "solidarity trading regime" are necessary to generate equitable and sustainable long-term development for the south and the north.

Chapter 6, "Unequal exchange and the rentier economy," offers a detailed analysis of Bureau of Economic Analysis (BEA) methodology and data that strongly suggests that U.S. GDP is overvalued on the output side. The chapter shows that the ability to generate income without producing real value-added output is a key characteristic of a "rentier economy." It defines a "rentier economy" as an economy characterized by large increases in "finance, insurance, and real estate" (FIRE), declining manufacturing share, declining real investment in plant and equipment, increased outsourcing of production and rising trade deficits, declining employment and real wage growth, rising profits, growing inequality, and increasing aggregate demand dependency on private (household and business) and public sector debt. Based on these indicators, relative to other advanced countries like Germany, the U.S. has since the mid-1970s increasingly become a "rentier economy." By grafting a schematic "rentier economy" onto the simple "free trade unequal exchange" model of Chapter 6, this chapter highlights the labor exchange, inequality, and efficiency characteristics of rentier (U.S.), unequal exchange (German), and developing country (China) economies. The chapter shows that reviving and restoring full employment in a rentier economy, like the U.S., requires a public policy-induced reallocation of resources away from rentier activity back to productive high-value-added "unequal exchange" production.

Note

1 Shaikh (2016) offers abundant empirical evidence and additional theoretical analysis in support of underlying *absolute* rather than *comparative* cost determinants of exchange rates and trade flows that appears consistent with the unequal exchange global trade memes presented in Chapters 5 and 6 of this book.

References

Baiman, R. (2016) *The Morality of Radical Economics: Ghost Curve Ideology and the Value Neutral Aspect of Neoclassical Economics* (New York: Palgrave Macmillan).
Hahnel, R. (1999) *Panic Rules* (Boston: South End Press).
Shaikh, Anwar. (2016) *Capitalism: Competition, Conflict, Crises* (New York: Oxford University Press).

5 Unequal exchange without a labor theory of prices

On the need for a global Marshall Plan and solidarity trading regime[1]

1 Introduction

Political economists have long argued that international trade can be a means of exploitation and the source of increased global inequality (Hobson, 1902). In more modern times exploitation through trade has most often been associated with the direct exercise of political power under colonialism (Fanon, 1963), or with the indirect exercise of such power within a neocolonialist regime (Nkrumah, 1965). Within the Marxist tradition, "imperialism," which emerges with the development of "monopoly capitalism," is a new form of international exploitation through trade that differs from its mercantilist and precapitalist colonialist forms (Lenin, 1916). In this view, imperialist exploitation, like that of capitalism, is often carried out through economic relationships that are, or at least appear to be, based on voluntary "equal exchange" rather than more directly coercive political mechanisms.

The opacity of this "veil of equal exchange" is a subject of some dispute within Marxist political economy. Some thinkers who draw from this tradition link imperialist, or neoimperialist, "development of underdevelopment" to center monopoly power, transfer of profit, and control over investment flows, coupled with the covert and overt use of military power without colonization (Frank, 1978; Baran, 1968). Others contend that in recent history many of these factors have been a function of internationally mediated political power and ideological hegemony as opposed to the more direct exercise of state power (Pieper and Taylor, 1998). These "market distortion" and "state intervention" factors are sometimes said to be a reflection of "unequal trade."[2]

However, some twenty-four years ago, Arghiri Emmanuel (1972) suggested in an influential book that imperialist exploitation of less developed areas of the world (the periphery) by developed countries (the center) may occur even under conditions of perfect competition and free trade. Emmanuel attempted to show that under conditions of immobile labor but perfectly mobile capital and perfectly competitive free trade, international trade in "specific goods" (produced only in the periphery) will result in a transfer of "social value" (socially necessary embodied labor time) from the periphery to the center.[3]

Emmanuel's contention was that the social value of specific traded periphery goods would be set by the labor used in the periphery to produce them. This "socially necessary labor value" would be above their "price of production," as the price of production would be determined by the lower wage costs that would be sustained by the immobility of labor, but equal profit rates, of periphery producers. Profit rates would be equal worldwide due to the perfect mobility of capital and perfect competition between capitalists. Periphery producers would thus be trading goods of higher social value for goods of lower social value and thus transferring surplus value from the periphery to the center through "unequal exchange" that did not occur because of "unequal trade."

Samir Amin (1976) sought to extend and modify unequal exchange to include trade in "nonspecific" goods (produced in both the center and periphery) when periphery wage levels are relatively lower than productivity levels. He also attempted to extend the theory to noncapitalist countries in the third world by arguing that when their products were traded internationally they would have the value equivalent of like products produced in capitalist countries.

Numerous authors including De Janvery and Kramer (1979) and Kay (1975) have been critical of both versions of unequal exchange, arguing that unequal wages and perfect mobility of capital are incompatible in the long run. They claimed that even with immobile labor, capital mobility will eventually result in an equalization of wages between center and periphery for both specific and nonspecific goods production. This will occur because low wages in the periphery will induce greater investment and job growth that will eventually cause wages to increase compared to wages in the center, where disinvestment and slower job creation will lead to a relative decline in real wages.

These authors acknowledge that because of productivity differences, "exploitation," in the sense of unequal exchange of embodied labor time, may occur in the short run in a perfectly competitive world trading system of the kind envisioned by Emmanuel and Amin. This may occur as lower productivity in the periphery will cause actual embodied labor (as opposed to socially necessary labor time) in goods produced in the periphery to exchange for goods with lower levels of embodied labor from the center. But this will reflect the normal process of incomplete convergence of "individual values" among producers of similar goods to "socially necessary" labor values, and a necessary divergence of value prices from prices of production due to differential rates of "organic composition of capital." Because of this they claim that modern imperialism must by and large rest on "unequal trade" rather than "unequal exchange."[4]

Regardless of the merits of De Janvery and Kramer's theoretical argument, it is now clear that for most developing countries foreign investment has not led to broad-based wage gains as labor force growth has exceeded employment growth, even in highly productive export sectors. Emmanuel and Amin thus appear to have been correct in practice.

However, new developments in Marxist economics that have occurred since this early debate have changed the theoretical framework within which unequal exchange may be valuated. Theorists who reject the validity and usefulness of a specific "labor theory of prices" have developed a form of Marxist analysis that derives "exploitation" (in the sense of the exchange of unequal amounts of embodied labor) from unequal class ownership.[5] In this view the "extraction of surplus value" is not correlated with the exploitation of labor power (Roemer, 1982, 1988).[6]

This methodology has been applied by radical political economists working outside the Marxist tradition to international trade (Hahnel, 1999).[7] Hahnel has used a "Roemerian" model to demonstrate that perfectly competitive "free trade" can exacerbate inequality and exploitation. Though he does not call it "unequal exchange," it can be fairly labeled as such, as it purports to demonstrate that exploitation through international trade can occur under competitive conditions that are not dependent on "unequal trade."

In this chapter, I will analyze and modify the Hahnel unequal exchange model and attempt to show that, after some corrections, it does indeed provide an "analytical Marxist" version of unequal exchange that is not based on the more traditional "specific" labor theory of value that underlies Emmanuel and Amin's original formulations.[8] I will then discuss the implications of this modified Hahnel model for global inequality, underdevelopment, and "fair trade" policy.

2 A modified Hahnel model of international trade

Hahnel (1999, Appendix B) postulates a world divided between north (the center) and south (the periphery) in which there are three technologies of production, two goods, one form of "labor" (L), and a subsistence utility function for both northern and southern populations. The two goods are a consumption good called "corn" (C) and a capital good called "machines" (M).

The three linear fixed-coefficient technologies with single periods of production include: a labor-intensive consumption goods sector, a capital-intensive consumption goods sector, and an even more capital-intensive capital goods sector, defined as follows:

1) 5 units of labor + 0 machines yields 10 units of corn
2) 2 units of labor + 1 machine yields 10 units of corn
3) 1 unit of labor + 2 machines yields 10 machines

Hahnel further postulates that:

a) Each northern and southern country has 1,000 workers who need 1,000 units of C per period. With its 1,000 workers each country can provide up to 1,000 units of "labor" per production cycle.
b) The workers of all countries desire to work as little as possible, or utilize as few units of labor as possible, to produce this subsistence consumption.
c) Northern countries have an initial capital stock of two hundred machines.
d) Southern countries have a capital stock of only fifty machines.
e) These endowments must be replenished in each production cycle for social reproduction to be sustained.

Hahnel's model thus modifies Roemer's "factory" and "farm" technology models by adding a capital goods sector, and by replacing "capitalists" and "workers" with northern and southern countries (Roemer, 1988). Both models envision national economic reproduction as a linear programming problem with an objective function that seeks to use the available technologies to produce 1,000 units of C per period with the least possible labor. Alternatively, these models are modern versions of classical economic reproduction models.[9]

Hahnel makes a further assumption that when goods are traded between countries, this international trade is "perfectly competitive"; that is, it is unrestricted by either state or monopolistic intervention. In this context this means that each worker individually, and each country's workers in aggregate, perfectly minimize the labor time necessary (the cost) for the sustainable production of their *immediate* subsistence consumption needs, subject to their country's given machine stock (capital) and the assumed international trading regime. Deviations from this assumption will be spelled out when they occur.

Another assumption that Hahnel does not explicitly make but that we believe is critical to the workings of the model is that:

f)   There are more southern (capital-poor) countries than northern (capital- rich) countries.

Readers will recognize that this assumption, which ensures an overall "shortage" of machines, is equivalent to Roemer's assumptions of multiple "workers" to few "capitalists" that guarantee a "seller's market" for capital goods (Roemer, 1988, pp. 23–5). As in Roemer's analysis, this means that though the models assume "free and perfectly competitive trade" by *individual* agents (countries), this assumption gives northern countries (or capitalists) a *class* monopoly over capital goods (machines), a key and scarce factor of production.

With these assumptions in place we can proceed to solve the model for different international trading regimes. These solutions are produced in Tables 5.1–5.5 below. "Autarky," as depicted in Table 5.1, and "fair trade," in Table 5.3, replicate Hahnel's (1999, Appendix B) solutions. However, I believe that Hahnel's "free trade" solution is in error and have replaced it with Table 5.2 below. The "global Marshall Plan," described in Table 5.4, and "developmental trade," shown in Table 5.5, attempt to expand the model to address alternative trading policies that would appear to be either more beneficial or more realistic for long-run global development than Hahnel's version of "fair trade."

3 Autarky

In this international regime each nation produces for itself and does not trade with other nations. Northern and southern countries use their own available endowments to produce their subsistence 1,000 units of corn with as little work as possible using the following production schema (see Table 5.1).

Table 5.1 Autarky

		Technology	L	M(input)	C	M(output)
North						
		2	200	100	1000	
		3	12.5	25		125
	Total Production		212.5	125	1000	
	Total Use			125	1000	
	Unused Machines			75		
South						
		1	300	0	600	
		2	80	40	400	
		3	5	10		50
	Total Production			50	1000	
	Total Use		385	50	1000	

Note: a) the available technologies ensure surplus labor in both categories of countries; b) the available technologies ensure a surplus of machines in northern countries; c) the available technologies ensure a shortage of machines in southern countries; d) southern countries have no desire to produce machines to increase their capital stock in the future as their utility function dictates that they work as few hours as possible in the current production cycle.

As can be seen from Table 5.1, autarky is both inefficient and unfair in a global sense. It is inefficient as seventy-five northern machines that could be used to increase the productivity of labor are not being used. The global system (scaled to one northern and one southern country) is using 597.5 units of labor to produce 2,000 units of corn for an overall efficiency ratio (corn over labor) of 0.29875. This represents a level of work effort that could clearly be reduced by using the surplus machines and substituting away from labor-intensive consumer goods production in the south.

It is unfair as the labor/corn ratios are 0.2125 in the north but 0.385 in the south. In this sense there is global "exploitation" or inequality of labor effort that results directly from the different initial endowments. Workers in southern countries have to work $0.385/0.2125=1.81$ more hours than northern country workers for the same amount of corn. This replicates Roemer's notion of "exploitation" through trade that does not require extraction of surplus value through a labor market.

4 Free trade

In a free trade regime all countries will attempt to maximize their gain, or save as much labor time as possible, by producing and trading corn and machines. Northern countries have excess machines to sell. They will clearly gain from selling them for any amount of corn that will cover their opportunity cost (in corn) of replacing them. From technology 3: $0.1L + 0.2M = M$. Solving this for M shows that countries that have 0.2 spare machines can produce an additional M, including replacement of the existing stock of machines used up, by expending 0.125L. Meanwhile, from technology 2: 0.2L + 0.1M = C. Substituting in M = 0.125L and solving for L gives L = (1/0.2125)C, so that every unit of labor used in producing replacement machines instead of corn could have been used to produce 1/0.2125 units of corn – again including replacement of machines used up, this time with a smaller 0.02M stock of initial available machines. This implies that for northern countries each M has an opportunity cost of 0.125 × (1/0.2125), or about 0.5882C. In other words, as long as they retain sufficient machines to reproduce their capital stock of machines and additional needed corn, northern countries will benefit from trading their extra machines for any amount of corn greater than about 0.5882C.

Southern countries have used up all their machines in producing corn and replacement machines and have been forced, under autarky, to produce 600 units of corn using the inefficient labor-intensive technology From technology 3 we have: 2L + 0M = 4C. But with an imported machine that does not need replacement, using technology 2 we have: 2L + 1M = 10C, indicating that it is worthwhile for southern countries to pay up to 6C per imported machine. This therefore becomes the price that southern countries will have to pay for machines imported from northern countries. Given condition (f), southern countries will bid up the price of the scarce machines from the north to a level that is insignificantly (for the purposes of our description of the model) below 6C.

This conclusion differs from that reached by Hahnel (1999, Appendix B). Hahnel points out (pp. 113–14) that without machines, seventeen units of labor will produce only thirty-four units of corn with technology 1. But with ten machines, that same seventeen units of labor can produce eighty units of corn (using 16L, 8M, and technology 2) and reproduce the ten machines (using 1L, the remaining 2M, and technology 3). This implies that each new imported machine is *worth* (80–34)/10 or 4.6 units of corn for countries that have no unused machines. This is clearly true. However, Hahnel then assumes that 4.6 units of C for 1M will be *the price*, or terms of trade, that southern countries will pay for machines from northern countries under perfectly competitive free trade conditions. With this price, by importing machines, southern countries are able to capture some of the benefits of trade in a free trade regime by saving 385–370.37 = 14.63 units of labor (Hahnel, 1999, p. 115).

But this cannot be true in a seller's market, where southern countries will bid up the price to (just about) their *reservation price* of 6C per 1M, as is noted above. Of course Hahnel does not make the seller's market assumption (f). But even so, it is unclear how terms of trade of 4.6 would obtain except by a coincidence of equality of demand and supply of machines at this price. This seems less realistic than our assumption of a northern "seller's market," or excess demand for machines by southern countries, which we derive from assumption (f) above.

In any case, returning to our solution above, given that their opportunity cost for reproducing machines is only about 0.5882C, northern countries will be happy to trade their excess machines for 6C. Labor time minimization and subsistence production therefore lead to the trading and production pattern described in Table 5.2 below.[10]

Table 5.2 Free trade

		Technology	L	M(input)	C	M(output)
North						
		2	20	10	100	
		3	20	40		200
	Exports			150		
	Total Production			200	100	
	Imports				900	
	Total Use		40	50	1000	Price = 6
South						
		2	380	190	1900	
		3	5	10		50
	Exports				900	
	Total Production			50	1900	
	Imports			150		
	Total Use		385	200	1000	Price = 6

Note that no country has the option of increasing its labor input above what is needed for producing subsistence in a current production cycle to reduce future necessary labor time. Under market-driven free trade behavior, southern countries will strive for *immediate* labor-time minimization or immediate "profit maximization." They will not divert some labor to producing more machines in this cycle so that they can produce corn with less labor in the next cycle, as this would require them to increase overall labor time, or costs of production, in this cycle. Countries do not have the option of "long-term" management of trade and/or production. Under a market-driven free trade "individual choice" *short-term profit-maximizing regime*, producers and consumers in all countries will produce and buy goods at the lowest current price from wherever in the world they can get them.

By allowing for full utilization of machines, or capital, free trade has clearly increased the efficiency of the global economy. Using the same two-country normalization, only $40 + 385 = 425$ labor units are necessary to produce 2,000 units for an efficiency ratio of 0.2125 L/C for both countries combined. The free trade regime is thus over 28% more efficient in terms of labor time saved than autarky $(1 - 0.2125/0.29875 = 0.288)$.

However, this increased efficiency comes at a price. Under free trade, northern countries need only forty units of labor to produce 1000C for an efficiency rate of only 0.04 L/C and a saving of 172.5 units of labor. In contrast, *southern countries save no labor at all* as they continue to use 385 units of labor to produce their 1000C at the same L/C rate of 0.5882. "Free trade" in an international capitalist system with a "class monopoly" by the northern countries over the means of production allocates all of the efficiency trading gains to the north, just as "free markets" under domestic capitalism with a class monopoly by capitalists over the means of production allocate all efficiency gains to capital (with surplus labor and in the absence of countervailing power by unions and the state) (Roemer, 1982).

This, of course, results in a dramatic increase in inequality (of work effort) to 0.385/0.04 = 9.625, indicating that southern countries have to work 9.625 times more than northern countries for their 1000C rather than only 1.81 times more under autarky.[11]

Moreover, as Hahnel points out, to the extent that the efficiency of the capital using technologies 2 and 3 improves relative to the labor-intensive technology 1 – a likely occurrence under the normal process of technological change – free trade will *increase* global inequality even as global efficiency improves, and this is true regardless of whether the technological improvement is output-increasing, labor-saving, or machine-saving. This is even clearer in the modified Hahnel model of Table 5.2, as this model implies that any efficiency improvements in technologies 2 and 3 will be completely captured by the northern countries through an increase in the international price of corn relative to machines even as the labor cost of machines may go down.

To recapitulate, "free trade" has little in common with classical benefits of trade relating to specialization and absolute, or comparative, advantage with full employment and "intermediate" terms of trade; or with more realistic "new trade theory" that looks at benefits of trade in terms of absolute advantages such as technological specialization, increasing returns, and agglomeration.[12] Rather, it reflects an *exploitative* relationship of unequal exchange, whereby northern countries are able to use their advantage in capital stock ownership to impose a regime of unequal exchange, by trading goods with less labor for goods with more labor, over the south.

"Free" market-led trade based on short-term profit maximization leads the south to import most of its capital goods from the north, as developing an expanded capital goods sector in the south would require a redirection of labor away from corn production and immediate labor cost minimization or "profit maximization." The south is forever consigned to relatively lower-productivity consumption goods production for the north. Because of this lower productivity, wages for workers in the south will be lower than those of workers in the north. Moreover, as the north has no incentive to save the jobs of workers in its dramatically reduced consumption-goods sector, the high wages and jobs in the north's capital goods industry go to only a small number of workers. The north now employs 172.5 fewer workers than it did under autarky, while employment in the south has stayed at the same level.

Free trade thus does not help the south at all in an absolute sense (as workers in the south have to work just as long as they did under autarky), and positively harms southern countries in a relative sense, in the short run and the long run. They are left more frustrated than ever at the luxurious lifestyle obtained by the workers in northern countries that now seems even less feasible. To the extent that income is linked to employment and productivity, it also leads to a dramatic internal increase in unemployment and inequality in the north, as a small number of workers gain employment and increased wages at the expense of the majority of workers who have no jobs and no income. This will occur even though the overall economy in the north has made large efficiency gains.

This is an extreme example, to be sure, but not so far removed from the claims by Latin American "structuralists" in the 1970s that declining terms of trade for nonindustrial products made "free trade" a losing proposition in the long run for developing countries (Furtado, 1970; Prebisch, 1971). This led to efforts at "import substituting industrialization" (ISI) by Latin American countries that were abandoned with the onset of the international debt crises and neoliberal hegemony in the 1980s. Though by some accounts ISI had some success in Latin America before it was prematurely and unnecessarily dismantled, the Southeast Asian version of competitive export-led ISI has clearly been an economic development success story (Brailovsky, 1981; Stein, 1996). I address this latter version of ISI in Table 5.4.

More generally, Singer (1998) notes that though the 1970s "Prebisch-Singer" ECLA (Economic Commission for Latin America) declining terms-of-trade hypotheses went against the then-prevailing expectations of "convergence" of north–south income levels, it has, with a few exceptions, been confirmed by the third-world debt crises and the increased north–south *divergence* of the last few decades. Moreover, in the north, a trend toward increased efficiency and productivity gains, coupled with greater unemployment and increases in income inequality (in some northern countries), has been a key characteristic of the neoliberal "free trade" regime of the last two decades (Eatwell, 1996). For example, a recent comprehensive review of household tax returns found that 94% of U.S. overall income growth from 1973 to 1998 went to the upper 1% of taxpayers (Piketty and Saez, 2001).

Note also that this free trade "unequal exchange" outcome does not primarily result from an exchange of goods of equal, or differing, "socially necessary labor value" and equal "prices of production" being produced by firms, or countries, with different labor productivities, so that the same, or different, goods have different "individual" or "socially necessary" labor values, as in the Emmanuel, Amin, and Mandel cases. Rather, both sets of countries have access to the same equally productive technologies, but because of their larger initial stock of machines, northern countries are able to specialize in (high labor productivity) machine production and trade for (lower labor productivity) corn production. This trade *composition* effect, rather than differing productivities for the same, or specific, sets of goods, leads to the north–south difference in labor input. This is similar to the Emmanuel and Amin stories, in that low-productivity goods are exchanged for high-productivity goods, but the analysis focuses on the effects of unequal capital stock ownership constraining production and trade choices, rather than on the resulting labor content, or labor *productivity*, differences underlying the traded bundles. Roemerian analysis grounds exploitation in class monopoly and unequal ownership rather than "point of production" surplus extraction. The latter is one, but not the only, manifestation of the former (Roemer, 1988). Moreover, because of its link to the composition of trade, the Roemer/Hahnel analysis more directly inverts the standard "comparative advantage" story by showing that "free trade" and specialization, based on short-term comparative advantage, may only benefit the north and increase global inequality.

5 Policy options

The modified Hahnel/Roemer model can be used to explore policy options for global trade that include versions of: a) "fair trade," b) a "global Marshall Plan," and c) "developmental trade."

Hahnel advocates a "fair trade" regime that would simply set the terms of trade so as to, in effect, compensate the southern countries for their lack of machine capital stock by letting them import machines from the north at a low enough price to equalize work effort in both the north and south. Table 5.3 below describes the Hahnel "fair trade" solution.[13]

This imposed price is high enough to just make it worthwhile for the north to export machines, given their large initial stock and the 0.5882C opportunity cost of machines (see calculation in Section 3). Moreover, as all the machines are being used, the global efficiency for this solution is at 425L/2000C = 0.2125 equal to that of the "free trade" solution, but global inequality in labor time expended by northern and southern countries would be completely eliminated as both northern and southern countries have to expend equal 212.5 units of labor to produce their subsistence.

In terms of the simple assumptions of the model, this is indeed an efficient and fair solution. However, it leaves the "hierarchical" global social division of labor mostly intact as all of the high-productivity and high-wage capital-goods production is done in the north, and the south is consigned to lower productivity and generally lower-wage consumption-goods production. This kind of trade does not, in this sense, allow for full *development* of the economies of the south. Purely market-oriented trade based on short-term labor-cost minimization or profit maximization, even when terms of trade are "fair" in terms of (a short-term) exchange of labor units, leaves intact a global trading system that is based on a hierarchical global division of labor. In the long term this system also does not capture the real potential benefits of trade, enumerated above, between *countries at comparable levels of economic development.*

Table 5.3 Fair trade

		Technology	L	M(input)	C	M(output)
North						
		2	187.5	93.75	937.5	
		3	25	50		250
	Exports			106.25		
	Total Production			250	937.5	
	Imports				62.5	
	Total Use		212.5	143.75	1000	Price = 0.5882
South						
		2	212.5	106.25	1062.5	
	Exports				62.5	
	Total Production				1062.5	
	Imports			106.25		
	Total Use		212.5	106.25	1000	Price = 0.5882

Clearly, what is needed is a policy that eliminates the fundamental inequity in capital stock ownership that lies at the core of both free trade exploitation and fair trade developmental stagnation.

An ideal solution would be a "global Marshall Plan" along the lines of that proposed by the Brandt Commission of the Socialist International some years ago: a commission that included the late U.S. democratic socialist leader Michael Harrington as well as the late Jamaican and third-world socialist leader Michael Manley (Brandt Commission, 1983). Under this regime the north should simply extend grants and long-term credits to the south to allow them to purchase capital goods (machine tools) that the north, given its perennial excess capacity and unemployment problems, could easily produce. In terms of the Hahnel model, this would simply involve transferring the north's "surplus" machine tools to the south, resulting in the system of global production described in Table 5.4 below.

This clearly provides the same global efficiency and equity gains as fair trade. However, it also provides development for the south, and a balanced employment and wage structure in both countries with no hierarchical global social division of labor.

International trade in this system will not be a vehicle for reproducing international unequal exchange and exploitation or stagnant development in the south and unemployment and lower wages in the north. Rather, international trade between countries at comparable levels of economic development will further the benefits of specialization, economies of scale, agglomeration, and real absolute and comparative advantage based on differing mixes of innate or produced "endowments" between nations that enjoy similar overall levels of economic development, including wage structures and social and environmental benefits.

Some might argue that the global Marshall Plan model is unrealistic, but this is clearly not true from a purely economic point of view. For example, in 1998 the additional cost of universal education, health care, reproductive health care, adequate food, clean water, and safe sewers for the entire world would have been about $40 billion a year, a sum that amounted to less than 4% of the combined

Table 5.4 Global Marshall Plan

		Technology	L	M(input)	C	M(output)
North						
		2	200	100	1000	
		3	12.5	25		125
	Total Production			125	1000	
	Total Use		212.5	125	1000	
	Exports			75		Price = 0
South						
		2	200	100	1000	
		3	12.5	25		125
	Total Production			125	1000	
	Total Use		212.5	125	1000	Price = 0
	Imports			75		

wealth of the richest 225 people in the world – presumably mostly residents of the north (Stiglitz, 2004). In other words, with a wealth tax that these 225 people would hardly notice, enough capital could be transferred to satisfy all of the basic needs of southern workers and their families. Though not adequate in itself, this would clearly be a good start to significantly improve productivity, not to mention human decency.

However, political will is another matter. The moral perversity of the current global political economic system is perhaps best captured by a statement from the World Bank, one of global capitalism's key cheerleading institutions. In its 1999 Global Development Finance report, the bank notes that in spite of ever increasing payments, the debt burden of developing countries continues to rise to the point where $13 is spent on debt repayment for every $1 received in grants (World Bank, 1999).

More recently, as a result of the increasing instability of world financial markets brought about by neoliberal "free trade" policies, developing countries have begun to accumulate large holdings of foreign reserves, often in dollars or U.S. Treasury Bills with very low returns. This is another instance of the south sending capital, or lending domestic savings, to the north. This reverse flow is estimated to reduce southern annual GDP growth by over 1.0% per year (Weisbrot and Baker, 2002).

In short, though perfectly "realistic" in terms of real economic costs, an effective global Marshall Plan would require a political restructuring of world trade and capital flows that are currently highly beneficial to northern financial institutions and governments. However, even these institutions may find that a massive, or at least substantial, increase in foreign aid to the south is necessary to mitigate the increasingly violent north–south conflagrations of the last few years. In the longer run, without such a restructuring there may be no sustainable stable political economic future.

In the meantime, an alternative method (more feasible for some countries than for others) of arriving at a similar result may be illustrated by stretching the model's assumptions a bit. Accordingly, let us assume, as I implicitly have in our critique of the fair trade model, that wages for workers in both the north and south are related to their productivity, that northern countries have an interest in maintaining full employment and a more equitable distribution of income, and that southern countries would like to fully develop their economies to achieve northern productivity and income levels.

Moreover, let us assume that either or both of the following policy regimes prevail:

a)   Southern countries have strong states that are able to guide, or direct, domestic capital investment, or democratic socialist governments with worker cooperatives and democratic control over net new investment (see, for example, Schweickart, 2002). These southern states are able, through planned industrialization and technological learning, to sell emerging southern, relatively capital-intensive, "light industrial" technology 2 consumer goods to the north at favorable terms of trade (at northern prices). Moreover, southern development planners are able to induce or force their capitalists, or worker-owners, to use this extra profit to import capital goods from the north that would allow for a long-term expansion of productive capacity in the south. This would essentially be an export-led "import substitution industrialization" (ISI) policy directed at developing higher productivity and value-added industrial capacity. Something like this has in fact occurred in the few current or former southern countries like Japan, South Korea, Taiwan, Singapore, and China that have achieved economic development – though, especially in China, this has been accompanied by severe labor repression (see Conclusions section). These countries have all either obtained cold war—induced preferred access to northern country markets and/or have strong developmental trade-oriented governments and market clout that has enabled them to leverage long-run developmental benefits from trade and/or foreign investment. These options are, unfortunately, not available to most developing countries.

b) In addition, or alternatively, labor unions and "fair trade" activists in the north are able to demand that northern governments enact "solidarity trade agreements" with the south. These would maintain employment of northern workers in technology 2 industries by charging high tariffs on corn from the south (raising the value of corn relative to machines) and, in solidarity with southern labor unions and "fair trade" advocates, mandate that this "extra income" for southern products be used to develop the economies and raise the wages of workers in the south. They therefore are able to prevail over northern governments to turn over these extra tariff receipts to unions, NGOs, or governments in the south, to be used for ISI and wages as well as social and environmental benefits in the south. In other words, these funds would be used for productive reinvestment in private and social infrastructure in the south, and not luxury consumption of northern goods, or other forms of investment, in the north.

This policy would follow the "socialist fair trade" regime spelled out in Schweickart (2002, pp. 76–80), and the "fair trade" regime proposed in Paley (1998), under which social tariffs on international trade would be set to effectively equalize wage, environmental, and social spending differences between countries, subject to productivity adjustments that take into account different levels of national development. The revenue from these tariffs would then be rebated to less-developed countries to support economic development measures that would bring their labor, social, and environmental standards *up* to prevailing developed-country levels. Under these modified assumptions, a dynamic "virtuous cycle" of global development might be initiated by starting with the "developmental trade" regime as shown in Table 5.5 below.[14]

In developmental trading, either southern countries are able to sell consumption goods to the north at inflated northern country prices, or northern countries levy social tariffs on cheap imports from the south and rebate the revenue to the south. This allows southern countries to enjoy beneficial terms of trade in spite of their capital goods deficit and permits northern countries to maintain employment

Table 5.5 Developmental trade

		Technology	L	M (input)	C	M (output)
North						
		2	187.5	93.75	937.5	
		3	25	50		250
	Exports			106.25		
	Total Production			250	937.5	
	Imports				62.5	
	Total Use		212.5	143.75	1000	Price = 0.5882
South						
		1	50		100	
		2	192.5	96.25	962.5	
		3	5	10		50
	Exports				62.5	
	Total Production			50	1062.5	
	Accumulation					50
	Imports			106.25		
	Total Use		247.5	106.25	1000	Price = 0.5882

levels that are similar to those they had achieved under autarky with somewhat higher wages for their workers because of their increased productivity.

Moreover, under developmental trade, southern countries are able to significantly lower their working hours and level of "exploitation" relative to autarky (247.5 instead of 385) and are able to accumulate capital stock (machines) so as to develop their economies and improve their future productive efficiency. Given the high trading price that they receive from the north for their goods, they could simply reduce their labor and not accumulate capital. In fact, as the corn price of machines (0.5882) under developmental trade is equal to the price of machines under fair trade, it is clear that the south is using (247.5 – 212.5 = 35) more units of labor than necessary to simply reproduce its 1000C *in the short term*.

However, southern countries are implementing planned development policies on their own or in collaboration with the north. These will take the form of "export-led import substituting industrialization policies" and/or "solidarity trade agreements" that impose *political constraints* on market-led trading. Trade will no longer be based exclusively on short-term profit maximization or labor minimization and immediate consumption-goods needs. Instead, the south will increase its labor costs to secure extra profit from trade for long-term productive domestic capital investment, leading to future economic development and *higher* labor, social, and environmental standards.

As the south accumulates fifty units of capital during each production cycle, it will be able to fully develop its capital goods sector (technology 3) after at most 125/50 = 2.5 cycles of this kind of trading. Actually, this will occur sooner as the south can use the fifty extra machines accumulated in this cycle to more rapidly develop in the next period.

In the process of development, the south will gradually shift resources away from its "farm" technology 1 to an industrial "factory" technology 2. This shift will follow the historical pattern of "transformational growth" from agriculture to industry (Nell, 1999). Meanwhile, the slightly larger concentration of northern labor in highly capital-intensive capital-goods technology 3 may reflect the next stage of transformational growth to a future economic sectoral balance that is more advanced than that depicted in the "global Marshall Plan" (Table 5.4).[14] If hourly and social incomes are increased in step with productivity increases, this future sectoral balance, toward which southern countries will converge, will require less labor and afford more leisure for all workers.[15]

In terms of the general policy implications of the model, the numeric values in Table 5.5 are not important except insofar as they demonstrate the feasibility of this regime in which:

a) The north is no less efficient (in terms of labor time) than under autarky and retains a fairly balanced industrial structure.
b) The south improves its efficiency position over autarky and is able to rapidly accumulate machines or capital stock.
c) Global production is efficient in the sense that no machines go unused.
d) Terms of trade are still adequate to make it worthwhile for the north to trade with the south (0.5885).
e) Contrary to the free trade regime, *all the benefits of trade go to the south* until productive parity between north and south is reached.

"Developmental trading" employs planned developmental policies that explicitly deviate from short-term profit maximization. This kind of political management of trade offers another, more reformist, path through which the world can reach the optimal outcome shown in Table 5.4. After parity is reached, continued balanced-dynamic accumulation in both the north and south and mutually beneficial global trade will, of course, increase long-run productivity benefits.

6 Conclusions

Though economic development is never as simple a matter as an accumulation of capital stock that leads to seamless sectoral transformation, these models provide pedagogically useful insights into some of the underlying problems with "free trade," and show the analogy between global exploitation and "unequal exchange" through "free trade," and domestic exploitation (and "unequal exchange") through "freely competitive" capitalism. They demonstrate the usefulness of a Roemerian focus on inequalities of wealth as a key factor in supporting unequal power in exchange and long-term global inequity and unequal development among countries. Finally, they elucidate the potential limitations of price, or terms-of-trade adjustments, without politically planned developmental policy for long-term global development. Both the "Marshall Plan" and "developmental trade" regimes require terms-of-trade adjustments and non-market-based politically driven planned-development policies to succeed.

The key here is that these policies ensure that reinvestment in developing countries leads to widespread growth of incomes and improvements in social and environmental standards. Foreign investment by multinational corporations that is not regulated or guided for long-term development purposes with regard to domestic content, technology transfer, and social and environmental standards will not generally lead to diffuse and balanced development. Mexico, for example, has recently been losing "maquila" jobs from re-export plants along the U.S. border, and seen a lowering of wage levels and an increasing wage gap with the United States, as well as reduced per-capita income growth, in the ten years since NAFTA (the North American Free Trade Agreement) was implemented despite large increases in foreign direct and portfolio investment (Stiglitz, 2004; Ros & Lustig, 2000). In contrast, investment in Japan, South Korea, and Taiwan has been led by domestic companies with strong direct or indirect public involvement and preferred access to U.S. markets (Stein, 1996; Amsden, 1989).

More recently, China has been able to leverage its dominant market position to extract developmental concessions from foreign investors (Greider, 1997). However, China also severely represses its labor force and social and natural environment to attract greater foreign investment, and low Chinese standards have exerted downward pressure on labor, social, and environmental conditions in the United States and Mexico (Stiglitz, 2004).[16]

As most developing countries do not have the preferred access of Japan, South Korea, or Taiwan, or the tremendous market power and repressive capacity of China, they cannot establish a developmental trade regime on their own, especially given the current intense neoliberal opposition to such policies by international organizations such as the WTO, World Bank, and IMF (Stretton, 1999; Stiglitz, 2002).[17] A global Marshall Plan and/or "solidarity trading regime" would appear to be essential to broad-based international development in most of the south, and to equitable and sustainable economic prosperity in the north.

In the current "free trade" regime, most international private investment is clearly directed toward exploiting low-cost labor and benefiting from international arbitrage that blocks improvements in wages, labor organizing, social contribution, and environmental standards in the south and in the north. The Roemer and modified Hahnel models show how capitalism, without countervailing social and political forces, can generate ever greater class concentration of power and polarization of income, and how a "free trade" global regime may, without strong political countervailing forces, lead to evermore polarized and unequal global inequality of wealth and power among nations. These models also indicate why in the long run, "last resort" democratic political control or regulation of both domestic and international trade, and investment based on trade, may be necessary for globally widespread, socially and environmentally equitable, sustained development.

Notes

1 This is a slightly edited reprint of a paper originally published in the *Review of Radical Political Economics*, Winter 2006, 38(1), 71–89.
2 Much of this introduction follows an excellent critical summary of the early "unequal exchange" debate in De Janvery and Kramer (1979).
3 See well-known treatments of Marxist economics such as: Foley (1986), Fine and Saad-Filho (1984), Weeks (1982), and Sweezy (1942) for further explanations of these terms.
4 However, not all authors define "unequal exchange" in this way. Mandel (1975), for example, defines "exploitation through trade" resulting from a divergence of "individual value" within countries from "social value" among countries as "unequal exchange." Shaikh (1980) seems to employ a similar use of the term.
5 The distinction between a "specific" labor theory of value that claims that an algorithm exists for calculating prices from values, which I have labeled "a labor theory of prices," and a "general" theory that holds that labor is the source of value but that prices cannot be calculated from values, is made by Nell (1980). This chapter employs a labor theory of value but not a labor theory of prices. This is consistent with the "new interpretation" of the labor theory of value (Foley, 2000). See notes 10 and 12.
6 Needless to say, Roemer's form of "analytical Marxism" has not been universally embraced by all Marxist economists. Rather it has spawned a debate that is beyond the scope of this chapter (Devine and Dymski, 1989). Suffice it to say that though Roemer does not address the source or sustainability of the extreme inequalities in ownership that are characteristic of capitalism, at least in a global trade context it appears that these can be plausibly explained by barriers to technological diffusion and the extension of investment credit from the north, and rapid population growth and massive labor "surplus" in the south. In any case, it appears that Roemer's fundamental insight that capitalism is based on a "class monopoly" holds true.
7 This chapter focuses on developments inspired by John Roemer's work; see note 8. It does not address other versions of the theory of "unequal exchange," such as those that have been produced by Shaikh (1980), Weeks (1982), and Mandel (1975). However, as has been noted in note 5, the models used are fully compatible with another, even more recent "new interpretation" school of Marxist economics (Foley, 2000; Duménil and Lévy, 2000).
8 "Analytical Marxism" is a term that has been applied to work that has drawn upon or been inspired by Roemer's efforts. These have been portrayed as attempts to produce more formal and rigorous forms of Marxist analysis; see the collection of authors in Roemer (1986).
9 Marglin (1984) as well as Shaikh (1974) show that standard Neoclassical growth and production models critically depend on unrealistically large, or unitary, elasticities of technological substitution. Marglin demonstrates that introducing variable production coefficients into "neo-Keynesian" or "Neo-Marxist" models does not substantially alter their policy implications. Taylor (1990) makes a similar point for Kaleckian "structuralist computable general equilibrium" models derived from "social accounting matrices." In short, outside of the world of standard Neoclassical or Walrasian analysis, there is evidence that fixed-coefficient production models may serve as useful rough approximations of actual economic reproduction for policy analysis purposes.
10 The "maximal" number of machines that any northern country can produce for export while still retaining enough machines to replace its stock of 200M is 160M. Given this constraint, there are actually two minimum labor 40L solutions for northern countries. Northern countries may also export all 160M at 6C each and produce their remaining 40C needs using technology 1 with 20L. Since both solutions give the same northern-country efficiency results and the former (the solution described in Table 5.2) allows for a one-to-one southern-country trading match, we have, without loss of generality,

selected it. Even so, as there are more southern than northern countries, some southern countries will be importing fewer than 150 machines.

11 In "new interpretation" terms, the "money equivalent of labor time," or MELI, is $2000/425 = 4.7059$ (Foley, 2000), or conversely, the labor required to produce a unit of corn is $425/2000 = 0.2125$. Since $1L + 2M = 10$ M, the labor required to produce a machine is 0.125. Thus the north exports $0.125 \times 150 = 18.75$ units of labor to the south but receives $0.2125 \times 900 = 191.25$ labor units from the south. Note that $385 - 191.25 + 18.75 = 212.5$.

12 It should be noted that Ricardo's "comparative advantage" story has been roundly critiqued as a plausible doctrine even when international terms of trade are not overtly advantageous to one side, most notably because of its neglect of employment effects from trade (Stretton, 1999; Shaikh, 1995). And, as is pointed out in Chapter 2, even if full employment and all of Ricardo's other assumptions are given, the comparative advantage story is generally overdetermined and unsolvable for all but a very specific set of import and cross-price elasticities of demand.

13 Hahnel points out that under this regime northern countries will only be able to deliver 56.25M at the beginning of the cycle (Hahnel, 1999, p. 118, footnote 3). They can, however, export the remaining 50M at the end of the cycle out of the 250M that they produce. The initial import of 56.25M (on credit) will just be enough (with the 50M they already have) to enable southern countries to produce 1062.5C. They will use the remaining 50M imported at the end of the cycle (when they deliver their 62.5C) to replace their 50M of capital stock. In "new interpretation" terms the north is exporting $106.25 \times 0.125 = 128$ units of labor to the south, which is, in turn, exporting $62.5 \times 0.2125 = 128$ units of labor to the north.

14 As under "free trade," deliveries and payments have to be properly sequenced for this regime to work.

15 China has followed the Southeast Asian model of development first pioneered by Japan, but is the mostpolitically repressive of the Southeast Asian countries. China's political repression and growing influence, especially on the more corrupted democracies like that of the United States, poses a serious long-run threat to global democratic (including democratic socialist) development but this topic is beyond the scope of this paper, see (Fingleton 2008; Mann 2007). Similarly the more advanced social democratic Nordic countries, as opposed to the more christian democratic Germany, are better representatives of successful UE nations on most quality of life and public good indicators, though I use a larger "Christian democratic" country, Germany, as the representative UE example (Hill 2010; Huber and Stephens 2001).

16 UE economies with excessive surpluses are also a problem for the global economy. Sustainable global development requires more balanced global trade, at least among advanced countries, such as prevailed during the "Golden Age" 1945–1972 period of rapid global GDP and trade growth under the "BrettonWoods" managed trade regime. An exception to this would be modest UE country surpluses corresponding to manageable DC deficits financed through "global Marshall Plan" grants and long-term loans that would increase the pace of DC economic development (Baiman 2006; Marglin and Schor 1992).

17 In the U.S. progress in pursuing the economic policies above is probably dependent on progress in addressing deeper institutional problems of our "rentier society" (not just economy) including: a) ending "corporate personhood" (Hartmann 2010); b) enacting "industrial democracy" laws like Europe's "co-determination" laws (Hill 2010); c) creating a quasi socialized financial sector that serves the real economy like the German landesbaken, or regional community banks noted above; d) implementing an expansive "industrial policy" including public-private partnerships for education and training and applied sectoral research and development institutes like the German Fraunhofer institutes (Helper et al. 2012); e) reforming U.S. political democracy (that is now so corrupt that it has become in effect a plutocracy rather than a democracy) through measures such as: public campaign finance, strict regulation of lobbying and lobbyists, more

open media access and robust public media, one-person one-vote laws (changing the Senate), proportional representation and weighted, cumulative or "second choice" voting, measures to increase voting and reliable vote counting (Hill 2010); and f) measures to drastically reduce wealth and income inequality such as much higher minimum wage laws and maximum wage laws, and steeply progressive income (like the Eisenhower era 92 percent bracket – that would erase our current deficit if just applied to the upper 10 percent (Baiman 2011a) and wealth taxes.

References

AFL-CIO (2004) AFL-CIO Section 301 petition against China. American Federation of Labor and Congress of Industrial Organizations (AFL-CIO).

Amin, S. (1976) *Unequal development* (New York: Monthly Review Press).

Amsden, A. H. (1989) *Asia's next giant* (New York: Oxford University Press).

Baiman, R. (2010) The infeasibility of free trade in classical theory: Ricardo's comparative advantage parable has no solution, *Review of Political Economy* 22(3), 419–37.

Baran, P. (1968) *The political economy of growth* (New York: Monthly Review Press).

Brailovsky, V. (1981) Industrialization and oil in Mexico: a long term perspective. In *Oil or industry*, ed. T. Barker and V. Brailovsky (London: Academic Press).

Brandt Commission (1983) North-South (1983) and Common crisis (1983). Available from http://www.Brandt21Forum.info.

De Janvery, A. and Kramer, F. (1979) The limits of unequal exchange, *Review of Radical Political Economics* 11(4) (Winter), 3–15.

Devine, J. and Dymski, G. (1989) Roemer's theory of capitalist exploitation: the contradictions of Walrasian Marxism. *Review of Radical Political Economics* 21(3), 13–17.

Duménil, G. and Lévy, D. (2000) The conservation of value: a rejoinder to Alan Freeman, *Review of Radical Political Economics* 31(1), 119–45.

Eatwell, J. (1996) Unemployment on a world scale. In *Global unemployment: loss of jobs in the '90s*, ed. J. Eatwell (Armonk, NY: M. E. Sharpe).

Emmanuel, A. (1972) *Unequal exchange: a study of the imperialism of trade* (New York: Monthly Review Press).

Fanon, F. ([1963]1966) *The wretched of the earth*, trans. C. Farrington (New York: Grove Press).

Fine, B. and Saad-Filho, A. (1984) *Marx's capital* (New York: Pluto Press).

Foley, D. (1986) *Understanding capital: Marx's economic theory* (Cambridge: Harvard University Press).

——— (2000) Recent developments in the labor theory of value, *Review of Radical Political Economics* 32(1), 1–39.

Frank, A. G. (1978) *Dependent accumulation and underdevelopment* (New York: Monthly Review Press).

Furtado, C. (1970) *Obstacles to development in Latin America* (Garden City, NY: Anchor Books).

Greider, W. (1997) *One world ready or not: the manic logic of global capitalism* (New York: Simon & Schuster).

Hahnel, R. (1999) *Panic rules* (Boston: South End Press).

Hobson, J. A. ([1902]1948) *Imperialism* (London: Allen and Unwin).

Kay, C. (1975) *Development and underdevelopment: a Marxian analysis* (New York: St. Martin's Press).

Lenin, V. ([1916]1969) *Imperialism, the highest stage of capitalism* (New York: International Publishers).

Li, M. (2005) The rise of China and the demise of the capitalist world economy: exploring historical possibilities in the 21st century, *Science and Society* 69(3) (Summer), 420–48.

Mandel, E. (1975) *Late capitalism* (London: New Left Books).

Marglin, S. A. (1984) *Growth, distribution, and prices* (Cambridge: Harvard University Press).

Nell, E. (1980) Value and capital in Marxist economics. *Public Interest*, 15th anniversary issue: The crises in economic theory.

—— (1999) *Transformational growth* (New York: Cambridge University Press).

Nkrumah, K. (1965) *Neo-colonialism: the last stage of imperialism* (London: Thomas Nelson and Sons).

Paley, T. (1998) *Plenty of nothing* (Princeton, NJ: Princeton University Press).

Pieper, U. and Taylor, L. (1998) The IMF, the World Bank, and neoliberalism. In *Globalization and progressive economic policy*, ed. D. Baker, G. Epstein, and R. Pollin (New York: Cambridge University Press).

Piketty, T. and Saez, E. (2001) *Income inequality in the United States 1913–1998*. National Bureau of Economic Research, Working Paper 8467.

Prebisch, R. (1971) *Change and development—Latin America's great task*; report submitted to the Inter-American Development Bank (New York: Praeger Publishing).

Roemer, J. (1982) *A general theory of exploitation and class* (Cambridge, MA: Harvard University Press).

—— (1988) *Free to lose* (Cambridge, MA: Harvard University Press).

——, ed. (1986) *Analytical Marxism* (Cambridge: Cambridge University Press).

Ros, J. and Lustig, N. C. (2000) *Trade and financial liberalization with volatile capital inflows: macroeconomic consequences and social impacts in Mexico during the 1990s*. Center for Economic Policy Analysis Working Paper no. 18, February.

Schweickart, D. (2002) *After capitalism* (New York: Rowman & Littlefield).

Shaikh, A. (1974) Laws of production and laws of algebra: the humbug production function, *The Review of Economics and Statistics* LVI (1), 115–20.

—— (1979) Foreign trade and the law of value: Part I, *Science and Society* 43(3) (Fall), 281–302.

—— (1980) Foreign trade and the law of value: Parts I & II, *Science and Society* 44(1) (Spring), 27–57.

—— (1995) Free trade, unemployment, and economic policy. In *Unemployment*, ed. J. Eatwell (Armonk, NY: M. E. Sharpe).

Singer, H. W. (1998) Beyond the terms of trade: convergence/divergence and creative/uncreative destruction, *Zagreb International Review of Economics and Business* 1(1) (Spring), 13–25.

Stein, H., ed. (1996) *Asian industrialization and Africa: studies in policy alternatives to structural adjustment* (New York: Palgrave Macmillan).

Stiglitz, J. (2002) *Globalization and its discontents* (New York: W.W. Norton & Company).

—— (2004) The broken promise of NAFTA. *New York Times*, January 6.

Stretton, H. (1999) *Economics: a new introduction* (Sterling, VA: Pluto Press).

Sweezy, P. (1942) *The theory of capitalist development* (New York: Monthly Review Press).

Taylor, L., ed. (1990) *Socially relevant policy analysis* (Cambridge, MA: MIT Press).

Weeks, J. (1982) *Capital and exploitation* (Princeton, NJ: Princeton University Press).

Weisbrot, M. and Baker, D. (2002) *The relative impact of trade liberalization on developing countries* (Washington, DC: Center for Economic and Policy Research).

World Bank (1999) *Global development finance* (Washington, DC: World Bank).

6 Unequal exchange and the rentier economy[1]

1 Introduction

Detailed analysis of Bureau of Economic Analysis (BEA) methodology and data strongly suggests that U.S. GDP is overvalued on the output side. The ability to generate income without producing real value-added output is a key characteristic of a "rentier[2] economy." Broader indicators include a massive increase in financial activity and "finance, insurance, and real estate" (FIRE), declining manufacturing share, declining real investment in plant and equipment, increased outsourcing of production and rising trade deficits, declining employment and real wage growth, rising profits, growing inequality, and increasing aggregate demand dependency on private (household and business) and public sector debt. Indirectly, rentier interests also support low taxes and low public spending which lead to poor public health and public education outcomes. Based on these indicators, relative to other advanced countries like Germany, the U.S. has since the mid-1970s increasingly become a "rentier economy." Grafting a schematic "rentier economy" onto a simple "free trade unequal exchange" model from Baiman (2006) highlights the labor exchange, inequality, and efficiency characteristics of rentier (U.S.), unequal exchange (German), and developing country (China) economies. Reviving the U.S. economy and rebalancing the world economy will require major public policy measures to gradually reduce rentier activity and rebuild a more traditional advanced unequal exchange economy. Possible options include: a) maintaining a large public deficit to fund existing public services and income support programs and support aggregate demand, b) greatly expanding the public sector by implementing a large-scale federal jobs program funded through financial transactions tax to support living wage social service, infrastructure, and green technology jobs, and c) reducing and eventually eliminating the "structural" trade deficit using industrial and managed trade policies to rebalance U.S. and world trade which would allow the economy to overcome its current long-term rentier dependency on public or private debt.

2 Fictitious value-added output in U.S. GDP

Recent data strongly suggest that U.S. GDP is overvalued on the output side. Evidence for this comes from the BEA's "imputed" output methodology for calculating value added (Basu & Foley, 2011; Foley, 2011), and from the total factor productivity methodology used by the BEA to estimate value added in manufacturing (Houseman, 2007). In both cases increased value-added on the income side is erroneously presumed to equal increased value-added output.[3] The most suspect examples of these imputations or estimations are the FIRE sector (NAICS 52) and the computers and electronics product manufacturing (C&E) sector (NAICS 334). BEA data show that the value-added GDP share of FIRE increased from 14.7% of GDP in 1973 to 21.1% of GDP in 2010, a 44% increase in share (which tends to change very slowly over time) over 37 years.[4] Similarly, according to BEA data, the C&E sector supposedly increased its value-added by 260.5% from 2000 to 2008, comprising 80% of all growth in U.S. manufacturing output despite comprising only 9% of level output (Ezell & Atkinson, 2011).

2.1 Imputed output in financial services

Basu and Foley (2011, p. 29) note that:

> The U.S. national income accounts, however, treat incomes generated in the financial sector as arising from the production of a fictitious imputed input, "financial services", the value of which is measured by the incomes generated in the sector. Thus when a computer manufacturer pays bonuses to its executives, the payments have no impact on measured value added in the sector; they shift income from residual profits to compensation of employees. On the other hand, when a financial institution pays bonuses to its employees, measured value added in the sector increases.

One can conclude that as far as the national income accounts go, financial services are able to add value by adding income. The added income, whether from brokers' fees or direct traders' income, is financial gambling revenue that is related to increased trading and rising asset price bubbles. Not surprisingly as it is unrelated to increases in real output, Basu and Foley also show that this income accrual is increasingly disconnected with employment increases over successive U.S. business cycles.

Lest one assume that most trading revenue is zero sum, so that for every capital gain converted to fictitious income gain there will be a corresponding capital loss converted to income loss, two points are in order.

First, when overall trading volume, and value, rapidly increases, gains clearly exceed losses. In this regard, Taylor (2010, p. 18) includes several graphs displaying the roughly 100% real increase in housing prices (above the GDP deflator) from 1983 to 2007 and an even greater increase in real household debt, and Crotty (2008) provides data on a vast array of key indicators documenting the "secular rise in the absolute and relative size of U.S. financial markets" from the 1980s through 2007:

U.S. credit market debt was 168% of GDP in 1981 and over 350% in 2007. Financial assets were less than five times larger than U.S. GDP in 1980, but over ten times as large in 2007. The notional value of all derivative contracts rose from about three times global GDP in 1999 to over 11 times global GDP in 2007. The notional value of credit default swap derivatives rose from about $6 trillion in December 2004 to $62 trillion three years later. In the U.S. the share of corporate profits generated in the financial sector grew from 10% in the early 1940s to 40% in 2006.

(Economist, 2008)

Second, one might ask, what about the crash? Doesn't this run-up in capital gains reverse itself during the (inevitable) crash? Here again Crotty (2008) has compiled data showing that:

> World Bank research identified over 117 system banking crises between 1970 and the early 2000s (Capiro and Klingebiel, 2003). And time and again they were rescued by Central Bank intervention through monetary policy and increasingly large lenders of last resort bailouts. . . . Thus the large financial gains of the boom were private, but losses in the crisis were socialized.

Closer to home, on July 20, 2009, former Special Inspector General for the U.S. Treasury's TARP (Troubled Asset Relief Program), Neil Barofsky, estimated the cost of the Wall Street bailout, including aid offered by the Federal Reserve, to be $23.7 trillion, and this is before the Fed's recent program of "quantitative easing" (Kopecki & Dodge, 2009).

The point is clear. Income from financial trading or gambling does not reflect currently produced output but rather increased and more volatile asset prices. During asset bubbles capital gains are converted to fictitious "income." When the bubble crashes, much of the private "income" is ratified and preserved by socializing the losses. The rationale that financial markets "spread risk" and produce more efficient resource allocation is belied by the empirical evidence that shows increased risk, concentration of risk, more volatile princes, and (certainly since the 2007 recession) grossly inefficient misallocation of resources (Crotty, 2008). Financial services in other words are able to book capital gains as current income which through current NIPA (National Income and Product Accounts) practice technically becomes "value-added output" but with no real value added to output.[5]

2.2 Fictitious value-added increases from outsourcing

The other source of fictitious value-added is tied to increased markups in production that result from outsourcing to low-cost offshore production platforms. The story here is a bit more complex. It goes back to a Neoclassical assumption that the decomposition of "total factor productivity" growth into wage share times real wage growth plus profit share times profit rate growth provides a correct allocation of the real sources of "total factor productivity" growth. The assumption here is that factor incomes correctly reflect relative factor contributions to overall productivity increases.

In fact, Anwar Shaikh long ago demonstrated that the fact that this kind of specification *can* reflect a "marginal productivity" theory of income distribution from a "Cobb-Douglas"-like production function does not mean that it *does* reflect marginal productivity income distribution (Shaikh, 1974). Rather, Shaikh showed that the decomposition above can be derived from a basic accounting identity that reflects the necessary distribution of output growth to labor and capital income. Since the identity can be derived without making any assumptions regarding the relative contribution of labor and capital to total productivity growth, the decomposition using real wage and profit growth is meaningless with regard to measuring the relative contributions and proper shares of labor and capital to productivity growth.[6]

As this fact, which directly shows that the methodology used by the Bureau of Labor Statistics (BLS) to estimate value-added is in error (see equation 5 below), appears to be generally unknown, or in any case ignored, by mainstream (Neoclassical) economists, it is worth providing a clear and succinct proof based on a longer and more extensively annotated derivation produced by Taylor (2004, pp. 52–61):

Let P be overall prices, X output, L labor, K capital, w nominal wage, ω real wage, and r profit rate, and let "hats" symbolize growth rates so that:

$$\hat{x} = \frac{d(\ln x)}{dt} = \frac{\dot{x}}{x}$$

Then since output must equal income:

$$PX = wL + rPK$$

So that:

$$\text{Ln } P + \text{Ln } X = \text{Ln } (wL + rPK)$$

Or by taking a derivative and noting that : $\hat{w} = \hat{\omega} + \hat{P}$

$$\hat{P} + \hat{X} = \frac{wL}{PX}\left(\frac{\dot{w}}{w} + \frac{\dot{L}}{L}\right) + \frac{rPK}{PX}\left(\frac{\dot{r}}{r} + \frac{\dot{P}}{P} + \frac{\dot{K}}{K}\right) = \psi\left(\hat{w} + \hat{L}\right) + (1-\psi)\left(\hat{r} + \hat{P} + \hat{K}\right)$$

$$= \psi\left(\hat{\omega} + \hat{P} + \hat{L}\right) + (1-\psi)\left(\hat{r} + \hat{P} + \hat{K}\right)$$

So that after subtracting $\hat{P}$ from both sides and rearranging:

(1) $\hat{X} = \psi\,\hat{\omega} + (1-\psi)\hat{r} + \psi\,\hat{L} + (1-\psi)\hat{K}$

But by definition:

$$(2) \quad \hat{X} = \psi \left(\hat{L} + \left(\hat{X} - \hat{L} \right) \right) + (1 - \psi) \left(\hat{K} + \left(\hat{X} - \hat{K} \right) \right)$$

So that growth in "total factor productivity" growth or the "surplus" contribution to $\hat{X}$ after taking into account the growth in labor and capital (the LHS term in (3) below) will be equal to share weighted real wage and profit rate growth from (1) and (2) above:

$$(3) \quad \hat{X} - \psi \hat{L} - (1 - \psi) \hat{K} = \psi \hat{\omega} + (1 - \psi) \hat{r} = \psi \left(\hat{X} - \hat{L} \right) + (1 - \psi) \left(\hat{X} - \hat{K} \right)$$

where $\left(\hat{X} - \hat{L} \right)$ and $\left(\hat{X} - \hat{K} \right)$ are the growth rates of labor productivity $\dfrac{X}{L}$ and capital productivity $\dfrac{X}{K}$ respectively. The key point here is that there is no need to assume that relative real wage and profit rate growth have any relationship at all to the relative contributions of labor productivity and capital productivity to total factor productivity growth, as the equalities in (3) can be derived without any assumptions that link labor productivity growth to real wage growth or capital productivity to profit rate growth.

How does this relate to fictitious value-added rentier income?

Houseman (2007) investigates this "measurement" issue in detail. She notes that the BLS uses a KLEMS – capital (K), labor (L), energy (E), materials (M), and services (S) – method to measure multifactor productivity in manufacturing. KLEMS is computed as (Houseman, 2007, equation (3), p. 66):

$$(4) \quad In\left(\frac{A_t}{A_{t-1}} \right) = In\left(\frac{Q_t}{Q_{t-1}} \right) - \left[w_k \left(In\left(\frac{K_t}{K_{t-1}} \right) \right) + w_l \left(In\left(\frac{L_t}{L_{t-1}} \right) \right) + \right.$$
$$\left. w_{ip} \left(In\left(\frac{IP_t}{IP_{t-1}} \right) \right) \right]$$

where $In\left(\dfrac{A_t}{A_{t-1}} \right)$ is the percent change in multifactor productivity from time $t-1$ to time t, and similarly the terms from left to right represent percent changes in output (Q), capital (K), labor (L), and intermediate purchases (IP), weighted by their average share in production costs in adjoining periods t and $t-1$: w_k, w_l, and w_{IP}. After rearrangement (4) becomes:

$$(5) \quad In\left(\frac{Q_t}{Q_{t-1}} \right) - \left[w_k \left(In\left(\frac{K_t}{K_{t-1}} \right) \right) + w_l \left(In\left(\frac{L_t}{L_{t-1}} \right) \right) \right]$$
$$= In\left(\frac{A_t}{A_{t-1}} \right) + w_{ip} \left(In\left(\frac{IP_t}{IP_{t-1}} \right) \right)$$

The reader will recognize that equation (5) is the same as the first equality (from the left) in (3) with $w_{ip}\left(ln\left(\dfrac{IP_t}{IP_{t-1}}\right)\right)$ representing the additional contribution of intermediate purchases to *total* multifactor productivity growth (including the contribution of the intermediate purchases) on the LHS of the equality, embedding the Neoclassical assumption that growth (or decline) in factor *incomes or costs* (real wages, profits, or IP costs) provide an accurate method of allocating the relative contribution of different factors to overall productivity (and value-added) *output* growth.[7]

The problem here is that if an increasing share of production is outsourced to lower-cost producers so that the intermediate purchases no longer contribute to *domestic* multifactor productivity growth and w_{IP} declines due to lower-cost production of these intermediate goods, the value-added contribution of the outsourced IP in (5) to *total* multifactor productivity growth is presumed to decline. This means that value-added growth of the remaining production, assuming the finished product is sold at the same price or at a reduced price that does not fully pass-through cost savings, is automatically assumed to increase *even if the remaining labor and capital costs for producing the remaining parts of the product remain exactly as they were before*. $ln\left(\dfrac{A_t}{A_{t-1}}\right)$, or *domestic* multifactor productivity growth, must increase if the LHS remains the same, or does not decline by the same amount as $w_{ip}\left(ln\left(\dfrac{IP_t}{IP_{t-1}}\right)\right)$. Outsourcing is thus assumed to increase U.S.-produced value-added when in actuality there is no increase in value-added from U.S. production at all (after subtracting the lost U.S. value-added from additional non-US intermediate materials production).[8]

Presto! – as with booking fictitious value-added output from financial trading, here we are booking fictitious value-added from low-cost outsourcing. Again some might argue that over time perfect competition will force a full price pass-through of cost savings from outsourcing, thus eliminating the fictitious value-added. But the 260.5% increase in computers and electronics (NAICS 334) value-added output, accounting for 80% of U.S. manufacturing output growth from 2000 to 2008 in spite of comprising only a 9% level share of manufacturing output, when according to the BEA, computer and electronic parts grew by just 20% in current dollars and employment in the sector declined from 1.78 million to 1.09 million, and 90% of all electronics R&D now takes place in Asia, suggests otherwise (Ezell & Atkinson, 2011, p. 18).

3 The rentier economic model

Finally, we should note that rentierism through outsourcing and financialization are tied together. From 2000 to 2009, U.S. multinationals that collectively employ roughly a fifth of all American workers cut their workforces in the U.S. by 2.9 million while increasing employment overseas by 2.4 million, according to U.S. Commerce Department data (Wessel, 2011). Except for a brief period in the late

1990s outside of residential construction, U.S. investment has been stagnant or declining since the late 1960s (Beitel, 2009). At the same time, government data show that the wage share of value-added (that is supposedly produced in the U.S.) has persistently trended downward since 1980, falling by over 10% since 1983, even as the consumption share of value-added rose from about 95% in 1983 to about 105% in 2007, while the household debt to income ratio rose from about 25% in 1972 (the year of peak U.S. real hourly earnings for non-supervisory workers – \$9.27 in 1972 compared to \$8.91 in 2010 in 1982–4 dollars[9]) to about 170% by 2007 and profit rates (net of interest and taxes) increased or held steady at rates well above 1954 to 1980 rates (Taylor, 2010, pp. 58, 209). As Ivanova (2011) notes, "credit financing surpassed labor income as the key sustainer of consumer demand in the U.S. during the bubble years" (p. 19).

Data for six quarters after official recession end dates for the five most recent post-war recessions from 1975 to 2011 show a large trend decline in aggregate wage and salary share of National Income growth (from 38% to 1%) and trend increase in profit share of National Income growth (from 32% to 88%) (Sum et al., 2011).[10] Much of this profit of U.S.-based multinationals is from foreign affiliates: 48.6% in 2006 compared to just 17% in 1977 and 27% in 1994 – Business Roundtable and United States Council Foundation data cited in Meyerson (2011, p. 3). This cash is not going into real investment, but rather, as Ivanova notes: "the nation's biggest companies deriving a significant share of their income abroad are awash in cash, but either hoarding it, distributing it to shareholders, or investing it in financial assets (such as their own stock); they are not using it to expand or improve their domestic capital base" (Ivanova, 2011, p. 23).

The rentier economic model is clear. Income is generated without producing corresponding output through capital gains from financial bubbles and outsourcing of production, while holding wages down and using profits to generate more output-less income by further inflating domestic financial assets, and through consumer and home equity lending to maintain domestic demand and markups on domestic sales. The BEA has not been making a "mistake." The national accounts need to equate income to value-added output so that when there is no output to match the income, fictitious services and manufacturing value-added needs to be "imputed" to get the accounts to match.

But though it generates enormous amounts of income for rentiers at the very top of the income scale (78.2% of all increased family income in the U.S. from 1973 to 2008 went to the top 1% of families and *negative* 20.6% to the bottom 90% (Baiman, 2011a)), a rentier economy ultimately causes overall economic decline as is clear from the trend real wage decline since 1972. This can be seen in broader perspective by comparing "rentier economies" to more traditional advanced "unequal exchange" economies with larger manufacturing shares, more competitive exports, higher wages, more social spending and better quality-of-life indicators in key areas of health care and education.

World economic progress does not occur in a uniform fashion. Traditionally the richest countries are those with the most productive, advanced, and diversified manufacturing (or high-value-added traded good) capacities (Reinert, 2007).[11]

These countries are able to trade less labor for more labor from less productive countries through a process of "unequal exchange" that is especially pronounced under "free trade" (Baiman, 2006). But this implicit "exploitation" is how the world economy evolves. Overall productivity improves though most of the benefit initially accrues to leading economies.

Rentier economies, on the other hand, are able to "create" income without producing advanced manufacturing output in exchange. This does not advance world economic progress, but simply extracts labor from other countries without exchanging anything in return. In a more just world, economic development would be balanced so that all countries would have sectors of expertise and unequal exchange that would allow them to expend equal labor and advance world productivity at roughly similar rates. Policy measures can and should be employed to reduce the extremes of poverty and wealth produced by unequal exchange across nations (Baiman, 2006). But "rentier economics" is worse than global inequality from traditional "unequal exchange." Like capitalists who make no real investments, rentier economies do not advance world productive capacity and thus have no justification.

Moreover, rentier economics inevitably generates a persistent trade deficit as some of the income that doesn't correspond to output (especially the part that is lent to households for home equity and consumer credit) leads to disproportionate demand for goods that are no longer produced domestically and to the inevitable private "bubble" or public "deficit" macroeconomics that has characterized the U.S. since the 1980s. These result from the macroeconomic accounting identity:

Public Deficit + Private Deficit = Trade Deficit

The current push to reduce the public deficit ignores this identity and the fact that if the structural U.S. trade position is unchanged, unless a new (unsustainable) private deficit "bubble" emerges (as occurred in the late 90s, the last time the federal deficit was eliminated) to replace the spending injection that will be lost if the public deficit is cut, *cutting the public deficit will cause the economy to shrink* (thereby reducing the trade deficit through "non-structural" economic contraction) (Baiman, 2010b; Godly et al., 2008).

Thus the rentier economy lies at the heart of the increasing inequality, lack of real investment and job and wage growth, and increasing foreign trade deficit that characterize recent U.S. macroeconomic trends. The fact that such economies ultimately immiserate themselves may be a form of "ultimate" justice. In any case, both for reasons of "Hegelian justice" and our own self-interest, the U.S. needs to radically transform itself away from a rentier paradigm and toward a more traditional unequal exchange advanced economy.

4 Stylized characteristics of "rentier" versus "unequal exchange" advanced economies

The following figures document some of the stylized characteristics of "rentier" versus "unequal exchange" advanced economies. The most democratic of these unequal exchange economies are advanced social democracies with generous public sector spending that in some cases approaches 50% of GDP (see Figure 6.6 below). High progressive taxes and generous public spending ensure high levels of employment (these "workfare" societies have the highest labor force participation rates in the world[12]) and that the benefits of unequal exchange are broadly distributed. Other policies such as "co-determination" require all large companies to have significant shares of representatives of labor on their boards to ensure that national corporations are not run for exclusive rentier benefit (short-term returns for investors and upper management) but rather in the long-term interests of local and national economy, and financial sectors that support "high-road" investment in long-term development and high-value-added production (in Germany these are the "Landesbanken," or German public banks that play a central role in the Mittelstand, the small and medium-size enterprises that constitute the backbone of the German economy[13]) (Hill, 2010). As productivity in goods production increases, a larger share of employment must shift to the production of services. As the most important of these services are inherently "public goods" that cannot be privatized or efficiently commodified on a for-profit basis, a larger and larger share of GDP must be withdrawn from the market and provided on the basis of need rather than income (Baiman, 2010a).

Table 6.1 and Figures 6.1–6.6 show that in this OECD sample of countries and relative to other advanced countries, the U.S. has among the lowest real wages (Table 6.1), smallest value-added in industry (even with fictitious manufacturing value-added included) (Figure 6.1), highest FIRE value-added (Figure 6.2), lowest levels of investment in plant and equipment (Figure 6.3), and not coincidentally the largest trade deficit (Figure 6.4). They also show that the U.S. has (relative to other advanced countries) among the smallest tax revenue shares (Figure 6.5) and lowest level of public social expenditure (Figure 6.6). The latter is an indirect result of the rentier interest in low taxes and the privatization of public services to expand the scope of profitable private financialization of the economy.

Finally, in this context, Figure 6.7 (from Xing & Detert, 2010) is instructive. It estimates the production cost of an iPhone in 2009 at $178.96 and notes that most of it is actually produced in Japan, Germany, and S. Korea, with assembly

Table 6.1 Gross hourly wages

Gross wage in national currency 2004	Exchange rate to dollar 6/30/2004	Dollar wage	% US Wage	
327.192	6.103	$53.61	153.5%	Denmark
317.101	6.938	$45.70	130.8%	Norway
34.088	0.821085	$41.52	118.8%	Germany
4205.596	109.43	$38.43	110.0%	Japan
29.449	0.821085	$35.87	102.7%	Finland
		$34.93	100.0%	US
251.282	7.525	$33.39	95.6%	Sweden

Source: OECD data Historic exchange rates: http://www.x-rates.com/cgi-bin/hlookup.cgi

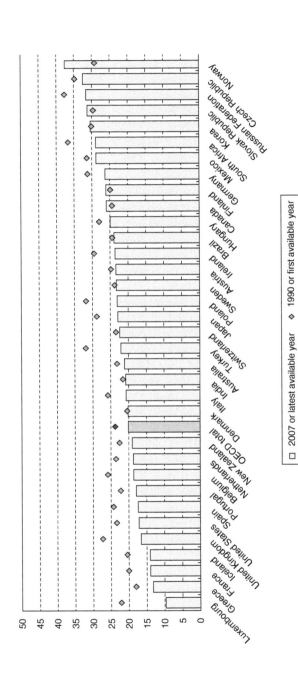

Figure 6.1 Value added in industry

As a percentage of total value added

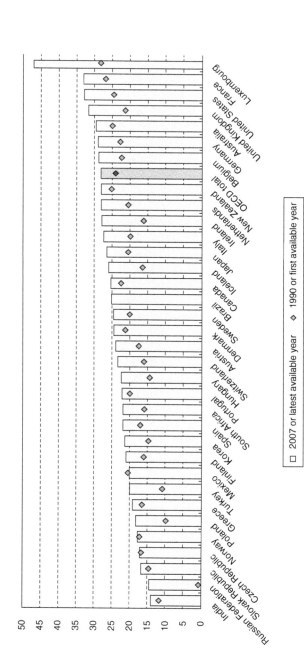

Figure 6.2 Value added in banks, insurance, real estate, and other business services

As a percentage of total value added

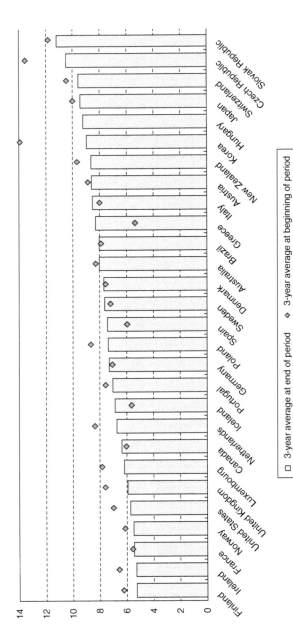

Figure 6.3 Gross fixed capital formation in machinery and equipment

As a percentage of GDP

Legend:
□ 3-year average at end of period
◇ 3-year average at beginning of period

Countries (left to right): Finland, Ireland, France, Norway, United States, United Kingdom, Luxembourg, Canada, Netherlands, Iceland, Portugal, Germany, Poland, Spain, Sweden, Denmark, Australia, Brazil, Greece, Italy, Austria, New Zealand, Korea, Hungary, Japan, Switzerland, Czech Republic, Slovak Republic

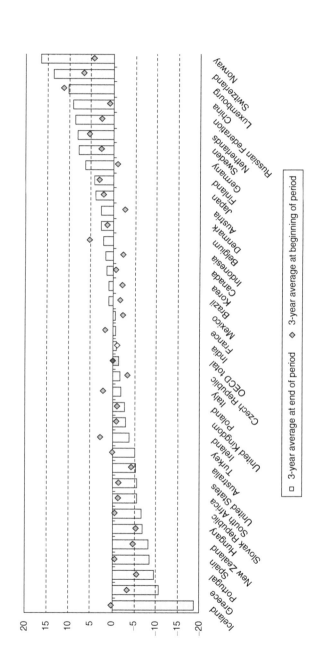

Figure 6.4 Current account balance of payments

As a percentage of GDP, average

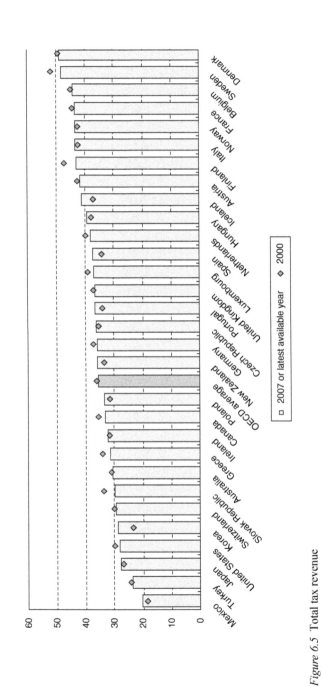

Figure 6.5 Total tax revenue

As a percentage of GDP

□ 2007 or latest available year   ◆ 2000

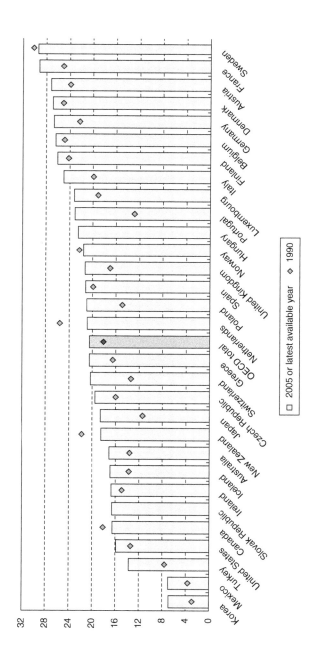

Figure 6.6 Public social expenditure

As a percentage of GDP

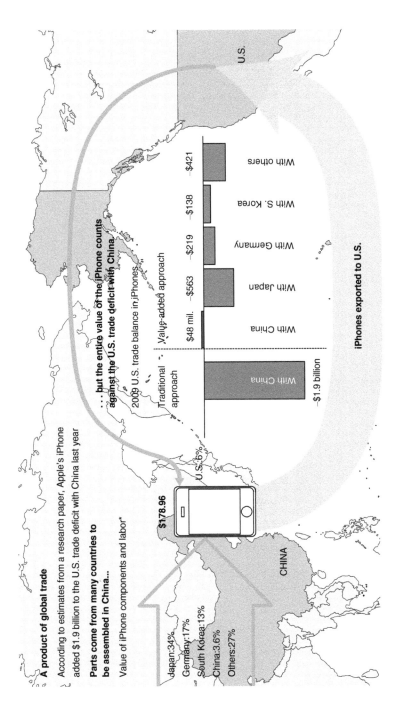

A product of global trade

According to estimates from a research paper, Apple's iPhone added $1.9 billion to the U.S. trade deficit with China last year

Parts come from many countries to be assembled in China...

Value of iPhone components and labor*

Japan:34%
Germany:17%
South Korea:13%
China:3.6%
Others:27%

$178.96

U.S.:6%

CHINA

... but the entire value of the iPhone counts against the U.S. trade deficit with China

2009 U.S. trade balance in iPhones

Value-added approach

$48 mil.   -$563   -$219   -$138   -$421

With China   With Japan   With Germany   With S. Korea   With others

Traditional approach

With China

-$1.9 billion

iPhones exported to U.S.

U.S.

Figure 6.7 Value of iPhone components and labor by country of origin

Figures don't add up to 100% due to rounding. Figures are estimates

Source: Xing, Y., and N. Detert 2010. How the iPhone Widens the United States Trade Deficit with the People's Republic of China. ADBI Working Paper 257. Tokyo: Asian Development Bank Institute.

in China, and some contribution by "others" including the U.S. This graph shows that much of the U.S. trade deficit on an iconic high-technology product ostensibly produced by a "U.S." company is actually with Germany, our paradigmatic "unequal exchange" high-wage, and high social spending, social-democratic economy.

These "stylized" facts will inform the simplified "unequal exchange," "rentier," and "developing country" world economic model below.

5 A simple rentier, unequal exchange, and developing country world trade model

Baiman (2006) uses a simple didactic model proposed by Hahnel (1999) that is an expanded version of a model first proposed by Roemer (1982), to show the impact of north–south "autarky," "free trade," "fair trade," "global Marshall Plan," and "developmental trade" on static and dynamic global inequality, efficiency, and economic development, using tools of "Roemerian" or "analytical Marxist" ("labor theory of value without a labor theory of prices") analysis. The following includes: a) a concise review of the Baiman (2006) unequal exchange north–south free trade model, and b) an update of this model to a three-country model with the addition of a "rentier economy" (RE), and with the "north" relabeled as an "unequal exchange" (UE) economy and the "south" relabeled as a "developing country" (DC).

5.1 A north–south unequal exchange "free trade" model

Baiman (2006), following Hahnel (1999, Appendix B) and Roemer (1982), postulates a world divided between north (the center) and south (the periphery) in which there are three technologies of production, two goods, one form of "labor" (L), and a subsistence utility function for both northern and southern populations. The two goods are a consumption good called "corn" (C) and a capital good called "machines" (M). The three linear fixed-coefficient technologies with single periods of production include: a labor-intensive consumption goods sector, a capital-intensive consumption goods sector, and an even more capital-intensive capital goods sector, defined as follows:

1) 5 units of labor + 0 machines yields 10 units of corn
2) 2 units of labor + 1 machine yields 10 units of corn
3) 1 unit of labor + 2 machines yields 10 machines

The model further postulates that:

a) Each northern and southern country has 1,000 workers who need 1,000 units of C per period. With its 1,000 workers each country can provide up to 1,000 units of "labor" per production cycle.
b) The workers of all countries desire to work as little as possible, or utilize as few units of labor as possible, to produce this subsistence consumption.

c)   Northern countries have an initial capital stock of two hundred machines.
d)   Southern countries have a capital stock of only fifty machines.
e)   There are more southern (capital-poor) countries than northern (capital-rich) countries.

In the absence of trade, under "autarky," northern and southern countries produce their 1,000 units of corn using these technologies at minimal cost with their own available machines and labor. Northern countries have plenty of machines and can therefore produce all of their corn using the more efficient technology. They will use 200L and 100M to produce 1000C and with technology 3, 12.5L and 25M to produce 125M, thus replacing the 100M plus 25M machines used up in every production cycle, leaving 75M unused. The "efficiency" or L/C ration for northern countries under autarky will therefore be 200L plus 12.5L, equaling 212.5L divided by 1000C or 0.2125.

Under "autarky" through technology 2, southern countries, on the other hand, will use 80L and 40M to produce 400C, and through technology 3 use 5L and 10M to produce 50M, replacing the 40M and 10M used up in each cycle of production. Because southern countries have only 50M, they will have to use the inefficient technology 1: through which 300L will produce 600C, to produce the rest of their needed corn. The efficiency ratio for southern countries under autarky will therefore by 80L plus 5L plus 300L, or 385L divided by 1000C, or 0.385. The "inequality" ratio of northern to southern countries under autarky will thus be 0.385/0.2125=1.81, indicating that southern countries have to expend 1.81 times more labor to produce their 1000C than northern countries.

Without loss of generality (to make the system balance and highlight the most important features of these models) we can assume single "representative" northern and southern countries. In this case total labor for representative northern and southern countries under autarky to produce 2000C for necessary consumption will therefore be 212.5L plus 385L or 597.5L for an overall L/C or efficiency ratio of 0.29875 (597.5/2000).

In a free trade regime, all countries will attempt to maximize their gain, or save as much labor time as possible, by producing and trading corn and machines. Northern countries have excess machines to sell. They will clearly gain from selling them for any amount of corn that will cover their opportunity cost (in corn) of replacing them. From technology 3: $0.1L + 0.2M = M$. Solving this for M shows that countries that have 0.2 spare machines can produce an additional M, including replacement of the existing stock of machines used up, by expending 0.125L. On the other hand, from technology 2: $0.2L + 0.1M = C$. Substituting in $M = 0.125L$ and solving for L gives $L = (1/0.2125)C$, so that every unit of labor used in producing replacement machines instead of corn could have been used to produce 1/0.2125 units of corn – again including replacement of machines used up, this time with a smaller 0.02M stock of initial available machines. This implies that for northern countries each M has an opportunity cost of 0.125 x (1/0.2125), or about 0.5882C. In other words, as long as they retain sufficient machines to reproduce their capital stock of machines and additional needed corn, northern countries will benefit from trading their extra machines for any amount of corn greater than about 0.5882C.

As is noted above, under autarky southern countries would have used up all of their need for machines to produce corn and replacement machines and would thus be forced under autarky to produce six hundred units of corn using the inefficient labor-intensive technology. On the other hand, if they could import more machines from the north they could produce corn more efficiently (with less labor). From technology 3 we have: 2L + 0M = 4C. But with an imported machine that does not need replacement, using technology 2 we have: 2L + 1M = 10C, indicating that it would be worth it for southern countries to pay up to 6C per imported machine. This therefore becomes the price that southern countries will have to pay for machines imported from northern countries. Given condition (f), southern countries will bid up the price of the scarce machines from the north to a level that is insignificantly (for the purposes of our description of the model) below 6C. Given that their opportunity cost for reproducing machines is only about 0.5882C, under "free trade" northern countries will thus be happy to trade their excess machines for 6C. Labor time minimization and subsistence production therefore lead to the trading and production pattern described in Table 6.2 below.[14]

By allowing for full utilization of machines, or capital, free trade increases the efficiency of the global economy relative to autarky. Using the same two-country normalization, only 40 + 385 = 425 labor units are necessary to produce 2,000 units for an efficiency ratio of 0.2125 L/C for both countries combined. The free trade regime is thus over 28% more efficient in terms of labor time saved than autarky (1 − 0.2125/0.29875 = 0.288). However, this increased efficiency comes at a price. Under free trade, northern countries need only forty units of labor to produce 1000C for an efficiency rate of only 0.04 L/C and a saving of 172.5 units of labor from the 212.5L that they would have to use under autarky. In contrast, *southern countries save no labor at all* as they continue to use 385 units of labor to produce their 1000C at the same L/C rate of 0.385. "Free trade" in an international capitalist system with a "class monopoly" by the northern countries over the means of production allocates *all* of the efficiency trading gains to the north, just as "free markets" under domestic capitalism with a class monopoly by capitalists over the means of production allocates all efficiency gains to capital (with surplus labor and in the absence of countervailing power by unions and the state) (Roemer, 1982). This, of course, results in a dramatic increase in inequality (of work effort) to 0.385/0.04 = 9.625, indicating that southern countries have to work 9.625 times more than northern countries for their 1000C rather than only 1.81 times more under autarky.[15] Moreover, as Hahnel (1999) points out, to the extent that the efficiency of the capital using technologies 2 and 3 improves relative to the labor-intensive technology 1 – a likely occurrence under the normal process of technological change – free trade will *increase* global inequality even as global efficiency improves, and this is true regardless of whether the technological improvement is output-increasing, labor-saving, or machine-saving. This is even clearer in the modified Hahnel model of Table 6.2, as this model implies

Table 6.2 Traditional "unequal exchange" based on "free trade" between the north and south

	Technology	L	M(input)	C	M(output)
North	2	20	10	100	
	3	20	40		200
Exports			150		
Total Production			200	100	
Imports				900	
Total Use		40	50	1000	Price = 6
South	2	380	190	1900	
	3	5	10		50
Exports				900	
Total Production			50	1900	
Imports			150		
Total Use		385	200	1000	Price = 6

that any efficiency improvements in technologies 2 and 3 relative to technology 1 will be completely captured by the northern countries through an increase in the international price of corn relative to machines, even as the labor cost of machines may go down.

Of course, in the real world "northern" countries do not have an absolute monopoly on capital and advanced production techniques and eventually technologies "trickle down" and world production capacity increases with the "unequal exchange" northern countries leading the way. Baiman (2006) outlines policy options including "a global Marshall Plan" and "developmental (or "solidarity") trade," rather than "free trade," that can and should be used to reduce global inequality and unequal development.

5.2 A "rentier economy," "unequal exchange economy," and "developing country" free trade model

Our concern in this chapter is not focused on showing how under free trade the "north" exploits the "south" while developing the world economy. Though the extreme global poverty and increasing inequality that result from free trade schematically described in Table 6.2 can and should be addressed through national and global policy measures as outlined in Baiman (2006), this is, as noted above, the age-old story of uneven capitalist development.

To expand the unequal exchange model of Table 6.2 to include rentier economies, we need to add a fictitious "product" D representing a "claim on output" – specifically one unit of "D" is a claim on output equaling one unit of C, and introduce another "rentier technology" that "produces" these claims on output "D" without producing any real value-added output. We also expand the definition of "machines" to include high-value-added "intermediate goods" for reasons that will become clear below. As before, "corn" represents "final consumer goods," so that the list of technologies and their outputs is now:

1) 5 units of labor + 0 machines yields 10 units of corn
2) 2 units of labor + 1 machine yields 10 units of corn
3) 1 unit of labor + 2 machines yields 10 machines
4) 1 unit of labor yields 100 D claims on output (with exchange value equal to a unit of corn) but no actual output

We also change the assumptions a) through e) in Section 5.1 by relaxing assumption b) to include "saving" or producing more than is necessary for current consumption, and adding a "rentier economy" (RE) as another economy in addition to the traditional "unequal exchange" (UE) economy (substituting for "northern") and "developing country" (DC) economy (substituting for "southern"). We also increase the "initial endowments" of machines for UE and DC economies by 50% equal to the magnitude of our expansion of world economic demand. As noted in Table 6.3 below, the U.S., Germany, and China are selected as "representative" RE, UE, and DC economies, though China is well on its way to developing advanced manufacturing capability (Baiman, 2010a).[16]
So the list of assumptions is now:

a) Each RE, UE, and DC country has 1,000 workers who need 1,000 units of C per period. With its 1,000 workers each country can provide up to 1,000 units of "labor" per production cycle.
b) Workers in UE and DC countries work to satisfy global demand for their output in the most efficient way (the least amount of labor) possible. Demand for their output includes their own domestic demand of 1000 C each plus another 500 C each of demand from the RE economy. What they don't currently consume, they save as claims D on future world output (or on present or future real wealth).
c) Unequal exchange countries have an initial capital stock of three hundred machines.
d) Developing countries have a capital stock of only seventy-five machines.
e) Rentier countries have no capital stock.
f) There are more southern (capital-poor) countries than northern (capital-rich) countries.
g) There are an even smaller number of rentier countries that have the ability to "produce" internationally recognized claims on output (D) without producing any real output or "value-added" (goods and services with "use value" that is of benefit to humans).

Table 6.3 below shows how the introduction of a rentier economy changes the traditional unequal exchange-based global economy. Rentier economies "freeload" on the labor of the rest of the world as they force the non-rentier economies to expend more labor to satisfy claims on output (D) by the rentier economy. This, and the fact that the "rentier technology" is extremely "productive" in terms of claims on output per worker, means that global productivity (output per labor) becomes less efficient and global income inequality increases. In our example the "rentier" technology 4) is ten times as productive in terms of direct output per worker (one worker generates 100 D in every production cycle) as the capital goods production technology 2 (one worker and two machines produce ten machines) and does not require any machines (think hedge fund managers). Specifically, the 9.625 labor per unit of corn inequality ratio between north and south (577.5/60 = 9.625) between unequal exchange (UE) and developing economies (DC) remains the same, but both UE and DC countries have to expend 50% more labor to produce an extra 500 units of corn each to satisfy the 1000 D claim on output "produced" by the rentier economy (RE). This means overall global productivity declines from 0.1925 (=385/2000 from Figure 6.2) units of labor per unit of corn to 0.2158 (10+60+577.5=647.5 divided by 3000 from Figure 6.3) units of labor per unit of corn as "freeloading" reduces global productivity.

In Table 6.3, as in Table 6.2, UE and DC countries maintain balanced trade with each other. However, the RE runs a persistent trade deficit of 1000 C per production cycle (all of its consumption needs) as it has nothing to sell in exchange for the corn it extracts from the rest of the world. As it cannot satisfy these claims through domestic production, a trade deficit is necessary for its economic reproduction. This trade deficit stems directly from its rentier "production" of claims on output (D) with no corresponding output; for example, through borrowing from the rest of the world by selling U.S. Treasury Bonds that generate an inflow of funds on capital account that offsets the current account deficit in "real" currently produced goods and services (e.g. corn).

Table 6.3 Global "free trade" with a rentier economy (U.S.), unequal exchange economy (Germany), and developing economy (China)

	Technology L	M (input)	C	M (output)	D (claims on output in terms of C)
Rentier Economy (U.S.)					
	4	10			1000
Export					1000
Import			1000		
Total Use		10	1000		
					D/C price = 1
Unequal Exchange Economy (Germany)	2	20	10	100	
	3	20	40		200
Exports			150		

	Technology	L	M (input)	C	M (output)	D (Claims on output in terms of C)
Total Production			200	100		
Imports				900		
Total Use		40	50	1000		
					C/M Price=6	
Developing Country (China)	2	380	190	1900		
	3	5	10		50	
Exports				900		
Total Production			50	1900		
Imports			150			
Total Use		385	200	1000		
				C/C Price=1		

	Technology	L	M (input)	C	M (output)	D (Claims on output in terms of C)
Rentier Economy (U.S.)						
	4	10				1000
Export of D						1000
Import of C				1000		Price C/D=1
Total Use		10		1000		
Unequal Exchange Economy (Germany)	2	30	15	150		1.5
	3	30	60		300	
Exports of M for C			225			Price C/M=6
Total Production				150	300	
Imports of C for M				1350		
Total Use		60	75	1500		
Imports (Accumulation) of D						500
Exports of C for D				500		
Developing Country (China)	2	570	285	2850		1.5
	3	7.5	15		75	
Exports of C for M				1350		

(continued)

Table 6.3 (continued)

	Technology L	M (input)	C	M (output)	D (claims on output in terms of C)
Total Production		75	2850		
Imports of M for C		225			
Total Use	577.5	300	1500		
Imports (Accumulation) of D					500
Exports for D				500	
	647.5				
	0.215833				

In return for the corn that the RE receives, it provides "claims on output" D that are accumulated by the other countries. In Table 6.3 these claims (or imports) are (arbitrarily – without loss of generality) equally divided between the UE and DC economies. Both UE and DC economies export finished goods to the RE economy which does not produce anything, and therefore has no need for intermediate or capital goods (M). As shown in Figure 6.7 above, much of the apparent U.S. RE trade deficit with DC like China is actually with advanced UE economies like Japan and Germany. Splitting RE imports equally between DC and UE economies reflects this, though a share of the "corn" finished good exports from the UE economy to the RE economy is likely to be high-value-added finished goods assembled in a DC economy and then re-exported to the RE economy.

These claims D represent foreign exchange reserves accumulated by UE economies and DC that have oriented their economies toward producing more than what they need for immediate consumption. This accumulation of reserves or wealth gives UE and DC countries that are able to do this greater opportunity for future domestic or foreign real investment, and correspondingly this gradual accumulation of liabilities increases the debt of the RE country to the rest of the world.[17]

The one caveat in this regard is that as long as this debt is denominated in D claims of which the RE country is the monopoly issuer, the RE debt to the rest of the world can be reduced simply by issuing more D. But doing this would risk a confidence crisis by the rest of the world in the exchange value of the D claims on output and put the RE country's continued ability to function as a rentier economy in jeopardy.

The RE has to expend less labor than the UE and DC economies to satisfy its basic needs of 1000 C per cycle (10, versus 40 and 285 – for 1000 C only). The ten workers who have jobs in the RE are thus able to obtain very high incomes. In the absence of steeply progressive taxation and large-scale social spending, the other

990 workers must either find work "servicing" the needs of the very high-income rentier workers for whatever they can get, or borrow income, or starve. Rentierism thus extends to the domestic economy as well as to the international economy, as has been noted above.

To achieve broad-based prosperity, UE economies must also have progressive taxes and large public sectors. UE economies appear better able to spread economic prosperity as they depend on continuous reinvestment, and productivity-enhancing educational and health care systems that allow them to maintain a productive and continuously improving traded goods sector that includes a larger share of the population.

What a deal! It looks like the RE economy has made it to Nirvana. Living off of others' labor sounds like a great situation. Kick back and relax (or trade a bit and watch your "investments" grow) – for those of us living in the premier RE economy, what's the problem?

The problem has been outlined above. All income growth in rentier economies goes to the very top-income earners who derive their income from rentier activities (rentier income from finance or from multinationals generating high returns from fictitious markup value-added production). Employment and income for other (non-financial activities) declines, leaving the bottom 90% of the population worse off (real family income for the bottom 90% in the U.S. declined by 6.4% from 1973 to 2008 even as per-family income for the top 1% grew by 175.6%, for the top 0.1% by 354.3%, and for the top 0.01% by 544.8% (Baiman, 2011a). As income (for the bottom 90%) declines, the economy becomes more dependent on private or public deficits to maintain past living standards. As investment and ability to produce real (not fictitious) value-added declines, the economy becomes dependent on imported goods paid for with IOUs to the rest of the world. Eventually domestic private sector borrowing bubbles crash and need to be replaced by massive deficit spending on the public side, and even with this large injection the economy is stagnant with job growth flat and wages and salaries declining.

Political ignorance, greed, and ineptitude make things worse. A fiction arises that the economic malaise is due to the public deficit! Ignorant and corrupt politicians wage a campaign to restrain the government's ability to deficit spend and try to block (by fanatically insisting that rentiers' obscene incomes should be sheltered from any additional taxation) any effort that would use the unique ability to make claims on the labor of the rest of world benefit the broad RE public, as opposed to the rentiers who believe that public spending threatens their financial investments. Perhaps they understand (per the deficit linkage above) that reducing the public deficit will cause more economic decline and immiseration for most Americans, or maybe they don't, but in any case the lobbyists and influence peddlers do not care, for the U.S. economy today is run to benefit the upper 1% of rentiers whose incomes have less and less relationship to how the rest of the economy is doing (Meyerson, 2011). Financial sector and multinational profits went up 40% in the seven quarters since the end of the recession, even as wage and salary income declined (Sum et al., 2011).

This is the problem with the rentier economy. It no longer functions as an economy for the betterment of the nation and the world, but rather as a vehicle for the enrichment of the very highest-income earners. In fact, like the famous "Dutch disease" problem, the ability to make such fabulous incomes so quickly with so little work causes the most capable and (potentially) productive individuals to expend their talents on financial gambling and rent seeking rather than invention and innovation to lift world productivity and economic capacity. Both human and physical capital are disinvested from productive sectors, including the funding of public infrastructure and goods and services, as the rentier class accumulates ever more economic and political power and forces more and more domestic public and private disinvestment to increase rents. The RE economy is a massively failed economy, as should be clear from over three decades of real wage decline in the U.S. and precipitous and accelerated loss of productive capacity (Baiman, 2010a).

6 Policy conclusions

What is to be done?[18]

a) Failed rentier economies like the U.S. need to exploit their rentier capacity for public (rather than private rentier) benefit. This means they need to maintain and increase federal deficit spending to fund existing public services and income support programs both at the federal and state and local levels. Rentier economies are sick and failed economies. They require federal deficit spending to prevent further short-term economic decline. Of course, these economies cannot continue to run large federal deficits forever – the world will lose faith in their currencies (e.g. the dollar in the U.S., or the pound in the U.K.) at some point and they will lose the ability to exploit their rentier capacity. However, the point that has to be stressed is that under current conditions these countries need a large amount of deficit spending to keep their economies going, and that maintaining a deficit to support critical public services and transfers is better than blowing up (and then bailing out) another unsustainable private deficit run-up, the benefit of which will mostly accrue to rentiers.

b) Rentier economies don't need to "shrink the size of their public sectors" (what the underlying "deficit" or "austerity" debates are all about). They need to dramatically increase it. In fact, they need to vastly expand taxing and spending to reorient their economies away from an RE and back to a UE configuration. This could be done, for example, through large-scale federal jobs programs that expand public and private sector living wage employment in a) social services, b) infrastructure, and c) new green technologies (Baiman, 2011b). Future economic prosperity for these economies is dependent on a large-scale revival of public jobs programs, industrial policy, and major changes in trade policy. The most successful UE economies in the world use their advanced traded goods production capacities to generously fund large public sectors – at up to 50% of GDP, that ensures that the benefits of UE are broadly spread to the entire nation (Baiman, 2010a; Hill, 2010). Rentier economies have the more difficult task of rebuilding a UE economy *and* vastly expanding and enhancing our public sector.

c) As they exploit their greatest remaining "economic" asset (rentierism), these economies need to shrink and eventually eliminate their rentier sectors. A straightforward way to do both (exploit and gradually eliminate) is to impose a financial transaction tax on all financial trading (the EU parliament has already recommended this) worldwide. It is indicative of the degree of economic distortion of the RE economy that, just for the U.S., this one tax has the potential to raise up to $1 trillion a year and fund up to 25 million living wage jobs over five years (Barclay, 2010; Baiman, 2011b). This should be immensely politically popular, would directly repress rentier activity, and if used for a productive jobs program, it would directly redevelop the UE side of the economy. Gradually, as these economies change their self-destructive and misguided "free trade" policies (designed for financial and multinational outsource rentierism) and are able to again produce competitive exports, then we can reduce federal deficit without causing more unemployment and shrink financial sectors to the point where FTT revenue will not be so large.[19] Recognizing that world trade cannot be sustainably managed (even under the most idealistic – and unrealistic – assumptions) on "autopilot" "free market" principles or exchange-rate "price signals," and that a politically constructed world trading system needs to be put in place to replace the highly successful Bretton-Woods regime, will be the first step in reducing and eventually eliminating "outsourcing rentierism" and implementing a global trading system that benefits public rather than rentier interests (Baiman, 2010c, 2011b). At this point these countries will be able to rely on more stable broad-based steeply progressive income and wealth taxes to fund a much larger and more generous public sector that will also provide high-value-added (in the real human use value sense) and well-paid "human service" (broadly defined) employment to the ever larger share of the workforce not engaged in high-value-added traded goods production (Baiman, 2010a).

Notes

1 This is a slightly edited reprint of a paper originally published in the *Review of Political Economy*, December 2014, 46(4), 536–57.
2 "Rentiers" are persons who derive most of their income from "rents." "Rent" is income derived from ownership of land or financial investment that is *deducted* from "profit" that the land or physical capital produces. Classic examples include rental payments to landlords and interest payments to creditors. Classical and modern economists have often derided "rental" income as unproductive and undeserved. Keynes, for example, famously advocated the "euthanasia of the rentier." Keynes wrote in the *General Theory*: "Now, though this state of affairs would be quite compatible with some measure of individualism, yet it would mean the euthanasia of the rentier, and, consequently, the euthanasia of the cumulative oppressive power of the capitalist to exploit the scarcity-value of capital. . . . But whilst there may be intrinsic reasons for the scarcity of land,

there are no intrinsic reasons for the scarcity of capital. . . . I see, therefore, the rentier aspect of capitalism as a transitional phase which will disappear when it has done its work" (Keynes, 1936, Chap. 24).

3 BEA (2007) provides a summary of the BEA "National Income and Product Accounts" (NIPA) methodology including the imputation of value-added for financial services.

4 Author's calculations from BEA GDP value-added by industry data downloaded July 12, 2011.

5 Needless to say we are talking about the broad array of mostly trading products that has characterized the financial explosion of the last few decades – see data below. There are still some financial products that provide real use value, for example by hedging and pooling risk (some options and insurance), though often even in these cases directly socializing the risk (for example through government price supports and national health systems) is more efficient than commodifying the risk in private financial products – see, for example, Newman (2009). The problem in a rentier economy is captured in Keynes' famous quote that: "Speculators may do no harm as bubbles on a steady stream of enterprise. But the position is serious when enterprise becomes the bubble on a whirlpool of speculation. When the capital development of a country becomes a by-product of the activities of a casino, the job is likely to be ill-done" (Keynes, 1936).

6 Ultimately, of course, as noted by Marx and Ricardo, the source of all production that has value for humans is human labor so that the "contribution" of capital is really just an indirect contribution of the labor that produced the capital. In the "direct" growth accounting exercise that follows, we ignore this. However, this point becomes important in the unequal exchange used in this chapter, and in Chapter 5.

7 Note that the expression $ln\left(\dfrac{X_t}{X_{t-1}}\right)$ for any variable X is an approximation of: $\dfrac{d(\ln x)}{dt} = \hat{x}$.

8 Other factors cited in the literature as also causing an artificial inflation of manufacturing value-added are: a) since 1997 very large presumed "quality improvements" especially in computers and electronics that reflect rapid increases in "quality" rather than increased output, and b) since 1980 increased use of "temporary help services" in U.S. manufacturing which artificially inflates manufacturing labor productivity as these workers do not count as manufacturing workers (Helper et al., 2012). Both may serve to "mask" or offset increases in rentier income in the national accounts with fictitious "qualitative productivity" increases on the output side, though the latter would be a transfer of income to rentiers from domestic workers rather than from foreign workers and suppliers.

9 BLS data downloaded July 25, 2011.

10 The recession of 1991Q1 to 1992Q2 when profit share of National Income growth declined by 1% and wage and salary share rose by 50% is the only outlier to this trend in Sum's data.

11 Reinert (2007) shows how support of diverse centers of manufacturing activity has been recognized as key to economic development for over seven centuries through the numerous works of economic thinkers in the "other canon" completely ignored by the current Neoclassical economic orthodoxy.

12 OECD Fact Book, 2009, 2007 data on "Share of persons of working age 16 to 64 in employment." BLS data indicate that U.S. labor force participation dropped by more than 4% during the recession and (as of this writing – July 2011) has stayed at this depressed level since the official end of the recession in June 2009.

13 I thank Peter Dorman for this information.

14 The "maximal" number of machines that any northern country can produce for export while still retaining enough machines to replace its stock of 200M is 160M. Given this constraint, there are actually two minimum labor 40L solutions for northern countries. Northern countries may also export all 160M at 6C each and produce their remaining 40C needs using technology 1 with 20L. Since both solutions give the same northern-country efficiency results and the former (the solution described in Table 6.1) allows for a one-to-one southern-country trading match, we have selected it, without loss of generality. Even so, as there are more southern than northern countries, some southern countries will be importing fewer than 150 machines.

15 In "new interpretation" terms, the "money equivalent of labor time," or MELT, is $2000/425 = 4.7059$ (Foley, 2000), or conversely, the labor required to produce a unit of corn is $425/2000 = 0.2125$. Since $1L + 2M = 10$ M, the labor required to produce a machine is 0.125. Thus the north exports $0.125 \times 150 = 18.75$ units of labor to the south but receives $0.2125 \times 900 = 191.25$ labor units from the south. Note that $385 - 191.25 + 18.75 = 212.5$ which is the labor that northern countries expend under autarky.

16 China has followed the Southeast Asian model of development first pioneered by Japan, but is the most politically repressive of the Southeast Asian countries. China's political repression and growing influence, especially on the more corrupted democracies like that of the U.S., pose a serious long-run threat to global democratic (including democratic socialist) development, but this topic is beyond the scope of this chapter. See Fingleton (2009), Mann (2007). Similarly, the more advanced social democratic Nordic countries, as opposed to the more Christian democratic Germany, are better representatives of successful UE nations on most quality-of-life and public good indicators, though we use a larger "Christian democratic" country, Germany, as our representative UE example (Hill, 2010; Huber & Stephens, 2001).

17 UE economies with excessive surpluses are also a problem for the global economy. Sustainable global development requires more balanced global trade, at least among advanced countries, such as prevailed during the "Golden Age" 1945–72 period of rapid global GDP and trade growth under the "Bretton-Woods" managed trade regime. An exception to this would be modest UE country surpluses corresponding to manageable DC deficits financed through "global Marshall Plan" grants and long-term loans that would increase the pace of DC economic development (Baiman, 2006; Marglin & Schor, 1992).

18 Progress in pursuing the economic policies outlined in what follows is probably dependent on progress in addressing deeper institutional problems of our "rentier society" (not just economy) including: a) ending "corporate personhood" (Hartmann, 2010), b) enacting "industrial democracy" laws like Europe's "co-determination" laws (Hill, 2010), c) creating a quasi-socialized financial sector that serves the real economy like the German Landesbaken, or Regional Community Banks noted above, d) expanded "industrial policy" including public–private partnerships for education and training and applied sectoral research and development institutes (Helper et al., 2012), e) reforming U.S. political democracy that is now so corrupt that it has become in effect a plutocracy rather than democracy, through campaigning for public finance, media access and robust public media, and one-person one-vote laws (changing the Senate) and some form of proportional representation (Hill, 2010), and f) measures to drastically reduce wealth and income inequality such as much higher minimum wage and maximum wage laws, and steeply progressive income taxes (like the Eisenhower era 92% bracket – that would erase our current deficit if just applied to the upper 10% (Baiman, 2011a)) and wealth taxes.

19 Contrary to received wisdom, when studied carefully, Ricardian comparative advantage is an argument for *managed* trade. "Free trade" in the Ricardian parable is overdetermined and unsustainable (Baiman, 2010c), even under most ideal (and unrealistic) assumptions.

References

Baiman, R. (2006) Unequal exchange without a labor theory of prices: on the need for a global Marshall Plan and a solidarity trading regime, *Review of Radical Political Economics*, Winter 38(1), 71–89.

—— (2010a) Toward a new political economy for the U.S., *Review of Radical Political Economics*, 42(3), or Chicago Political Economy Group at: http://www.cpegonline.org/workingpapers/CPEGWP2010-1.pdf.

—— (2010b) The links between the three types of national deficits, CPEG, June, at: http://www.cpegonline.org/multimedia/DeficitLinkages.ppt.

—— (2010c) The infeasibility of free trade in classical theory: Ricardo's comparative advantage parable has no solution, *Review of Political Economy*, July 22(3), 419–37.

—— (2011a) Eisenhower era income tax rates on the upper 10% of families would immediately erase the federal deficit, CPEG Working Paper 2011–12, or: http://www.cpegonline.org/workingpapers/CPEGWP2011-2.pdf.

—— (2011b) Self-adjusting "free trade": a generally mathematically impossible outcome. Submitted for publication, available from author.

Barclay, B. (2010) Found money: the case for a financial transactions tax," *Dissent Magazine*, 57(3), or Chicago Political Economy Group at: http://www.cpegonline.org/workingpapers/CPEGWP2010-2.pdf.

Basu, D. and Foley, D. (2011) Dynamics of output and employment in the U.S. economy, SCEPA Working Paper 2011–14.

Beitel, K. (2009) The rate of profit and the problem of stagnant investment: a structural analysis of barriers to accumulation and the spectre of protracted crisis, *Historical Materialism*, 17, 66–100.

Bureau of Economic Analysis (2007) An introduction to the national income and product accounts, Sept., or: http://www.bea.gov/scb/pdf/national/nipa/methpap/mpi1_0907.pdf.

Caprio, G. and Klingebeil, D. (2003) Episodes of systemic and borderline financial crises, World Bank, January.

Chicago Political Economy Group (CPEG) (2009) Ron Baiman, Bill Barclay, Sidney Hollander, Joe Persky, Elce Redmond, Mel Rothenberg, a permanent jobs program for the U.S.: economic restructuring to meet human needs, http://www.cpegonline.org/reports/jobs.pdf. Updated version with additional author Haydar Kurban in *Review of Black Political Economy*, 39, 29–41.

Crotty, J. (2008) Structural causes of the global financial crises: a critical assessment of the "new financial architecture", September, PERI, Working Paper Series, No. 180.

Economist (2008) What went wrong, May 19, or: http://www.economist.com/node/10881318.

Ezell, S. and Atkinson, R. (2011) The case for a national manufacturing strategy, April, Information Technology & Innovation Foundation, or: http://www.itif.org/files/2011-national-manufacturing-strategy.pdf.

Fingleton, E. (2009) *In the Jaws of the Dragon: America's Fate in the Coming Era of Chinese Dominance* (New York: St. Martin's Press).

Fletcher, I. (2009) *Free Trade Doesn't Work: Why America Needs a Tariff* (Washington, DC: U.S. Business and Industry Council).

Foley, D. (2000) Recent developments in the labor theory of value, *Review of Radical Political Economics* 32(1), 1–39.

—— (2011) The political economy of U.S. output and employment 2001–2010, Presentation to conference of the "Institute for New Economic Thinking," April 8–10, Bretton Woods, NH.

Godley, W., Papadimitriou, D. B., and Zezza, G. (2008) Prospects for the United States and the world: a crisis that conventional remedies cannot resolve, The Levy Institute of Bard College, Strategic Analysis, Dec. or: http://www.levyinstitute.org/pubs/sa_dec_08.pdf.

Hahnel, R. (1999) *Panic Rules* (Boston: South End Press).

Hartmann, T. (2010) *Unequal Protection: How Corporations Became "People" and How You can Fight Back*, 2nd Edition (San Francisco, CA: Barrett-Koehler Publishers).

Helper, S., Krueger, T., and Wial, H. (2012) Why does manufacturing matter? Which manufacturing matters? A policy framework, Washington D.C.: Brookings, February 2012, or: http://www.brookings.edu/~/media/research/files/papers/2012/2/22%20manufacturing%20 helper%20krueger%20wial/0222_manufacturing_helper_krueger_wial.pdf.

Hill, S. (2010) *Europe's Promise: Why the European Way is the Best Hope in an Insecure Age* (Berkeley, CA: Univ. of California Press).

Houseman, S. (2007) Outsourcing, offshoring and productivity measurement in United States manufacturing, *International Labor Review*, 146(1–2).

Huber, E. and Stephens, J. (2001) *Development and Crisis of the Welfare State: Parties and Policies in Global Markets* (Chicago, IL, Univ. of Chicago Press).

Ivanova, M. (2011) Marx, Minsky, and the great recession, *Review of Radical Political Economics*, 45(1), 59–75.

Keynes, J. M. (1936) *The General Theory of Employment Interest and Money* (London: Palgrave Macmillan).

Kopecki, D. and Dodge, C. (2009) U.S. rescue may reach $23.7trilllion, Barofsky says (Update 3), Bloomberg News, July 20, or: http://www.bloomberg.com/apps/news?pid= newsarchive&sid=aY0tX8UysIaM.

Mann, J. (2007) *The China Fantasy: How Our Leaders Explain Away Chinese Repression* (New York: Viking Penguin).

Marglin, S. and Schor, J. (1992) *The Golden Age of Capitalism: Reinventing the Post-War Experience* (Oxford: Clarendon Press).

Meyerson, H. (2011) Business is booming: America's leading corporations have found a way to thrive even if the American economy doesn't recover. This is very, very bad news, *American Prospect*, January 28, or: http://prospect.org/cs/articles?article=business_is_booming.

Newman, S. (2009) Financialization and changes in the social relations along commodity chains: the case of coffee, *Review of Radical Political Economics*, 41(4), 539–59.

Reinert, E. (2007) *How Rich Countries Got Rich and Why Poor Countries Stay Poor* (New York: Public Affairs).

Roemer, J. (1982) *Free to Lose* (Cambridge, MA: Harvard University Press).

Shaikh, A. (1974) Laws of production and laws of algebra: the humbug production function, *The Review of Economics and Statistics*, 56(1), February, 115–20.

Sum, A., Khatiwada, I., McLaughlin, J., and Palma, S. (2011) The "jobless and wageless" recovery from the great recession of 2007–2009: the magnitude and sources of economic growth through 2011 and their impacts on workers, profits, and stock values, May, Center for Labor Market Research.

Taylor, L. (2004) *Reconstructing Macroeconomics: Structuralist Proposals and Critiques of the Mainstream* (Cambridge, MA: Harvard University Press).

—— (2010) *Maynard's Revenge: The Collapse of Free Market Macroeconomics* (Cambridge, MA: Harvard University Press).

Wessel, D. (2011) Big U.S. firms shift hiring abroad: work forces shrink at home, sharpening debate on economic impact of globalization, April 19. *Wall Street Journal*.

Xing, Y. and Detert, N. (2010) How the iPhone widens the United States trade deficit with the People's Republic of China, ADBI Working Paper 257.

Part III

Globalization that supports human and planetary well-being

Are simple and highly abstract trade models like the basic free trade (FT) and unequal exchange (UE) models of Chapters 2–6 at all useful? We all know that in the real world both trade and investment are much more complex phenomena than that described in either of these models. While deconstructing Ricardian comparative advantage and Meade's Neoclassical free trade equilibrium, and demonstrating the mathematical *infeasibility* of free trade under the most idealistic pro-free trade assumptions, is certainly important as these doctrines provide the foundations for both academic and real-world policy support for free trade, can anything of *practical* policy value be derived from the simple, and in many ways equally unrealistic though at least logically consistent, unequal exchange models of Chapters 5 and 6?

Not surprisingly, my answer is yes!

Part III comprises two chapters that broadly address international trade policy in the U.S. and the world.

Chapter 7 shows that the U.S. economy faces a fundamental structural and institutional crisis that requires major changes in economic policy and far-reaching programs including: a) a federally funded *permanent living wage jobs program* mostly funded through transactions taxes on finance; b) emergency measures to cap and gradually *reduce the U.S. trade deficit*; and c) a transparent and coherent *"industrial policy"* to increase high-value-added, competitive manufacturing exports. The chapter forcefully argues for "non-predatory" trade and industrial policies that move the U.S. and world economies toward sustainable and balanced trade and development.

Chapter 8 concludes the book by offering practical policy options for an international trade and finance regime that would support sustainable and broad-based *global* prosperity. It shows how the simple models of Parts I and II point to managed and fair trade policy options that directly contradict FT ideology and practice. It grounds these models on a "demand and cost model" (DCM) meme that is posed as an alternative to the standard "supply and demand model" (SDM) meme of introductory economics. The FT model of Part I is shown to be an international version of SDM, and the UE model of Part II an extension of DCM. Based on these building blocks, policies to support more equitable and sustainable international trade in the practical near-term, and longer-term ideal goals, are proposed for the global economy.

7   Toward a new political economy for the U.S.

1 Introduction[1]

For at least three decades, the U.S. economy has failed to produce an adequate number of well-paid jobs (CPEG, 2009). Current efforts to "jolt" or "stimulate" the economy, while laudable, are inadequate for the task of creating an economy that works for the vast majority of Americans. As of October 2009 the U.S. economy faced a gap of 10.9 million jobs to make up for job losses and new labor force entrants since the start of the Great Recession in December 2007. Just filling this gap will require the creation of 583,000 jobs every month continuously for two years.[2] Addressing the economy's longer-term failure will require the creation of many more jobs.

In manufacturing, the situation is even direr. Since the 2001 recession the U.S. has lost 42,400 factories including 36% of plants employing more than 1,000 workers (which declined from 1,479 to 947) and 38% of factories employing between 500 and 999 workers which declined from 3,198 to 1,972. An additional 90,000 factories are now at risk of going out of business (McCormick, 2010). Manufacturing full-time equivalent employment (FTE) has declined from 18.6 million in 1987 (19.1% of all FTE) to 12 million in 2008 (10.3% of all FTE).[3] Moreover, this is not just a result of productivity improvements as manufacturing value-added as a percentage of GDP has declined from about 17% to 12% over the 1987 to 2007 period.[4] Particularly in the last ten years, the U.S. economy has lost critical capacity and technological leadership in key high-tech and emerging green technology sectors (McCormick, 2010).

Economics students know that there are four major categories of national expenditure that make up GDP: a) consumption, b) investment, c) government spending, and d) exports minus imports. Aggregate consumption in the U.S. is not likely to grow quickly unless employment and incomes increase. Adequate employment generating private domestic investment was not occurring before 2007 and is even less likely now. The U.S. has been running a trade deficit for decades and, as will be documented below, this is unlikely to change soon without a revival of U.S. manufacturing. The only feasible way to restructure and revive the U.S. economy for long-term and sustainable job growth at this point is through a massive publicly funded *permanent high-quality* jobs program accompanied by far-reaching trade and industrial policies. Given continued rapid productivity advances in manufacturing, and in some but not all service sectors, many of these jobs will be in the service sector.

Across advanced mixed economies, we find that the level and conditions of employment in the service sector are dependent on the kinds of services that are dominant and how they are funded and provided. In more "liberal" (in the classic sense) economies like those of the U.S. and U.K., industrial policy and service sector growth has been oriented toward for-profit services, propelling massive private investment and employment in retail and financial services.[5] In social democratic economies service sector growth and industrial policy has been focused on public, non-profit, and highly regulated private provision of health care, education, and human services based on generous public funding that in some cases approaches 50% of GDP – see Figure 7.1 below.

Since the beginning of the current "Great Recession" the Chicago Political Economy Group (CPEG) has been calling for the U.S. to vastly expand publicly pro-vided, well-paid, and professionalized "human" service employment and provision, and eliminate and reduce economic incentives that lead to financial and low-end (non-"human") service sector job growth. This goal, shared by other commentators such as Kuttner in *Obama's Challenge* (2008), is at the core of our indepen-dently arrived-at proposal: "A Permanent Jobs Program for the U.S.: Economic Restructuring to Meet Human Needs" (CPEG, 2009); see: www.cpegonline.org.

This program is based on the following premises:

1) The U.S. economy has not been generating an adequate number of well-paid jobs for many decades.
2) As manufacturing employment declines due to productivity increases and globali-zation of production, productive work will increasingly be in the service sector.
3) Moreover, as for-profit service sector work, for example in retail, warehous-ing, and distribution, also becomes more efficient, productive service sector work will increasingly be in largely publicly funded non-commodifiable areas like health care, education, and human services, which are best pro-vided through direct state provision or non-profit providers funded directly or indirectly by the state.

	2006
U.S.	28.00%
Australia	30.60%
Canada	33.30%
U.K.	37.10%
Italy	42.10%
France	44.20%
Denmark	49.10%
Sweden	49.10%

Figure 7.1 Tax revenues as a percent of GDP

Source: OECD Revenue Statistics 1965–2007 2008 Edition

4) This inevitable "socialization" of the economy requires a fundamental and long-term restructuring effort that must be led by major increases in progressive public taxing and spending that move the U.S. closer to a social democratic configuration like that of the most successful northern and western European advanced economies which typically have a much larger share of their economies tied to public funding.

5) To support high-quality education, health care, and human service, these jobs must be professionalized and well paid. As these jobs will inevitably make up an increasing share of all jobs, they need to be good jobs if we are to sustain an equitable and vibrant economy.

6) The growth of a large and productive public services economy must be complemented by an internationally competitive export sector that will allow the U.S. to finance necessary imports. Without a viable export sector, public service sector growth will lead to a large increase in the already unsustainable trade deficit that the U.S. has been running since the 1970s.

7) In the foreseeable future a large share of exports will be tradable goods (as opposed to services), i.e. manufacturing exports. Thus, to sustain an advanced public sector service economy, we will need to be able to produce an adequate output of high-value-added and competitive manufactured tradable goods, as countries like Denmark or Sweden are able to do, to support our imports.

8) We need to reinvigorate the U.S. manufacturing sector so that it regains the ability to sustain necessary imports for an advanced economy. This suggests that in the short term we need to increase manufacturing employment that as noted above has dropped by almost 50% in the last two decades.

9) None of this necessary long-term restructuring can occur without large-scale, radical public policy efforts. In the following we outline a proposed set of public policies that would begin to move the U.S. economy toward a sustainable and prosperous future.

The U.S. economy thus needs both radical *restructuring* to increase publicly funded productive service employment and *revitalization* to increase production of high-value-added internationally competitive tradable goods that can be exported to pay for necessary imports. As many of these exports will, for the foreseeable future, be manufactured *goods*, a core high-skilled high-value-added manufacturing capability must be maintained and/or recreated. These policies must both reverse the alarming growth of *inequality* in income and wealth that underlies the increasing corruption of democratic politics in the U.S. and the inability of the economy to sustainably increase overall prosperity.

Policies necessary to accomplish these goals are:

A) A large-scale and permanent federal *jobs program.*

B) A *trade policy* that openly breaks with the fundamentally misguided and historically and mathematically erroneous "free trade" doctrine of the last half century.

C) A complementary *industrial policy* that recognizes the "evolutionary economics" or Schumpeterian imperative of continuously generating, and maintaining as long as possible, a sufficient number of "retainable industries" adequate to balance necessary imports to sustain an advanced economy.

2 Permanent jobs program for the U.S.: economic restructuring to meet human needs

The following is an outline of a permanent federal jobs program that has been proposed by the Chicago Political Economy Group (CPEG) since the beginning of the current recession (Baiman, 2010a). Details of the full program including funding and taxing estimates can be accessed at www.cpegonline.org.

The program proposes that the federal government support the creation of 5 million new high-quality jobs each year, or 17.5 million new jobs over five years in three broad areas:

(1) Investment in *public infrastructure* such as transportation, educational and health care facilities, and parks.
(2) Current *social services*, which will include a major upgrading of pay and working conditions of human service jobs such as those in child, elder, and health care.
(3) Industries of the future, particularly the areas of energy, agriculture, and other broadly defined *"green" technologies*.

The jobs that the program creates and supports are necessary for the economic and social development of the U.S. economy. These are not short-term stop-gap or make-work jobs. They should pay good wages equal to the median wage today. In 2008Q3, according to the BLS, this was $18/hr or $37,440 per year. Including various other items discussed in detail below, this implies a cost of $175 billion for each cohort, so that by the fifth year of the program, assuming no further need for Keynesian stimulus through deficit financing, the cost would be $867.5 billion. Thirty-five percent more funding is built into the proposal for administrative costs and to account for the fact that some of the jobs created would be managerial and supervisory jobs paying more than $18/hr (CPEG, 2009, p. 9). Workers in these jobs should have the same rights as others, including the right to assert increased control over their workplace by associating together into unions, taking advantage of the opportunity offered by the Employee Free Choice Act. The CPEG proposal does not include social safety net spending, assistance for state and local governments, or "job creation tax credits."

Moreover, just as the program expands access to good jobs, its funding mechanisms restructure the economy away from finance and financial schemes and toward productive activities. CPEG proposes to finance these jobs largely through *taxes on financial transactions*. In 1996 the World Bank estimated that worldwide such a tax would raise $25 billion/day or $832 billion annually. In the U.S. in 2008, using only stock transactions on registered exchanges, the tax would have generated (for one side only, if both buyer and seller pay the amount doubles) $175.2 billion. When transactions in various derivative markets and the off-exchange bond market are included, the revenues generated, even discounting the likely reduction in trading, would be sufficient to finance most if not all of our jobs program. An estimate of $600 billion does not seem unreasonable for a 0.25% tax on both buyers and sellers.[6] Many of these incomes and much of this wealth have come from employment in trading, regulatory arbitrage, or other activities carried on within the finance industry. These taxes can be seen as a modest down-payment on what the financial sector owes the rest of us in return for the decision to rescue companies and individuals who led the country into the great recession.

The Economic Policy Institute (EPI) has recently also proposed a jobs program funded largely through financial transactions taxes (EPI, 2009). However, the EPI proposal is significantly smaller and of shorter duration than the CPEG proposal. EPI proposes the creation of 4.6 to 6 million jobs over a three-year period at a first year cost of $400 billion. The program would be funded through a financial transactions tax of 0.5% that would take effect three years after the implementation of the jobs program and continue for ten years. EPI estimates that this would raise $113–$226 billion.

Roughly 2 million of the jobs created in the proposal would be tied to expanded safety net funding and federal assistance to state government (EPI, 2009, p. 22). These are both laudable and necessary goals but the jobs created would be temporary, as would be the 239,000 tied to school modernization. These leaves about 2.4 to 8 million direct public service jobs and jobs created by the "job creation tax credit" whose duration may or may not be long term. EPI does not address wages, benefits, or working conditions for these jobs.

Fundamentally, the EPI proposal appears to be premised on the notion that the U.S. economy is fundamentally sound, but needs a short-term boost to get it back on track to creating well-paid, mostly private sector jobs. The CPEG proposal is based on the premise that the U.S. economy has not created a sufficient number of well-paying jobs for many decades (well before the current crises) and is unlikely to do so in the future absent a permanent and large-scale restructuring of the U.S. economy that has to be led by public sector jobs creation.

3 Rebalancing world trade to create a sustainable U.S. and world economy

The myth that "free trade" is a sustainable world trade solution is as debilitating as the myth of a "private sector" job creation solution to the current crises. In fact, the cornerstone of the free trade doctrine, Ricardo's theory of comparative advantage, has been shown to be mathematically overdetermined and infeasible (Baiman, 2010a). Comparative advantage demonstrates static gains from *managed trade*, not free trade. For Ricardo's parable to work England must impose a tariff or quota on Portuguese wine. A similar demand-side analysis of a general world trading model that satisfies Marshall-Lerner and other assumptions proves that even under the most idealized Neoclassical conditions, "free trade" is mathematically unstable and thus an economically infeasible outcome (Baiman, 2010b).

Period	Total Census Basis (1)	End-Use Commodity Category (billions of 2.5 dollars)						
		Foods, Feeds, & Beverages (2)	Industrial Supplied	Capital Goods	Automotive Vehicles, etc.	Consumer Goods	Other Goods	Residual (3)
2007	−$734.7	−$5.5	−$239.8	−$15.9	−$136.7	−$324.9	−$16.0	$4.0

(1) Detailed data are presented on a Census basis. The information needed to convert to a BOP basis is not available.
(2) Includes petroleum and petroleum Products.
(3) The "residual" represents the difference between total Census Basis exports or imports and the sum of the components. For additional information, see www.census.gov/foreign-trade/aip/priceadj.html.

Figure 7.2 U.S. 2007 trade balance in goods

In a masterful new book Fletcher (2009) looks at the history, policy, and theory of U.S. and world free trade. Worldwide "free trade" tends to increase global inequality.[7] Fletcher notes that according to the World Bank the entire net decline of the number of people living in poverty in the world since 1981 has been in China. Elsewhere their number increased (World Bank, 2008, p. 10). Free trade has also produced an unsustainable U.S. trade deficit. Fletcher points out that over the last two decades the U.S. has bought over $6 trillion (about $20,000 per American) more from the world than it has sold back to it and that our annual trade deficit, which until the recession was about 5% of the GDP, was the largest of any country since Italy in 1924. Moreover, even before the 2008 recession the U.S. had not generated any net new manufacturing or service jobs in internationally traded sectors (Fletcher, 2009, p. 2).

In 2007 (before the recession) the U.S. had a trade deficit in every single goods category; see Figure 7.2.

Moreover, this deficit in goods exports is not made up by taking out Petroleum products; see Figure 7.3.

In 2007, the U.S. had $129.6 million service and $90.8 million income receipts and surpluses; see Figure 7.4 below. This was hardly enough to make up for our deficit in current account.

The United States has even been running a deficit in "high technology" since 2002. Chinese imports are half of our deficit in manufactured goods and over 100% of our

Trade Balance (Billions of 2000 dollars)				
Period	Total Census Basis (1)	Petroleum	Non-petroleum	Residual (2)
2007	−$654.8	−$121.1	−$545.2	$11.5

(1) Detailed data presented on a Census Basis. The information to convert to a BOP basis is not available.
(2) The "residual" represents the difference between total exports or imports, and the sum of the components in the table.

Figure 7.3 U.S. 2007 trade balance excluding petroleum

		Exports	Imports	Net
1	**Exports of goods and services and income receipts**	**$2,462,099**	**–$3,072,675**	**–$610,576**
2	Exports of goods and services	$1,643,168	–$2,344,590	–$701,422
3	Goods, balance of payments basis2	$1,138,384	–$1,969,375	–$830,991
4	Services3	$504,784	–$375,215	$129,569
5	Transfers under U.S. military agency sales contracts4	$25,436	–$32,820	–$7,384
6	Travel	$97,050	–$76,354	$20,696
7	Passenger fares	$25,636	–$28,437	–$2,801
8	Other transportation	$51,550	–$67,100	–$15,550
9	Royalties and license fees5	$83,824	–$24,656	$59,168
10	Other private services5	$220,077	–$141,664	$78,413
11	U.S. government miscellaneous services	$1,212	–$4,184	–$2,972
12	Income receipts	$818,931	–$728,085	$90,941
13	Income receipts on U.S. –owned assets abroad	$815,960	–$718,019	&97,941
14	Direct investment receipts	$363,247	–$126,532	$236,715
15	Other private receipts	$450,480	–$427,159	$23,321
16	U.S. government receipts	$2,233	–$164,328	–$162,095
17	Compensation of employees	$2,971	–$10,066	–$7,095

Figure 7.4 2007 U.S. current account in services (millions of current dollars)

deficit in technology (there is a U.S. surplus with the rest of the world in these goods). More generally, in 1989 only 30% of Chinese imports competed with high-wage industries in the U.S., but by 1999 that figure had risen to 50% (Fletcher, 2009, pp. 70–1).

McCormick (2010) provides detailed documentation of the demise or drastic decline, particularly over the last decade, of U.S. capacity across high-tech and emerging green technology sectors including: printed circuit boards, photovoltaic cells, wind energy, cell phones, steel production, and machine tools. McCormick notes that in 2007 Georgia Tech's bi-annual "High Tech Indicators" study found that the U.S. peaked in 1999 at 95.4 (on a scale of 100) and had fallen to 76.1. China technological standing moved from 22.5 in 1996 to 82.7 in 2007, higher than the U.S. for the first time since the index was created two decades ago.[8]

Gomory and Baumol (2000), building on earlier work by Krugman and others, have simulated the impact of capturing path-dependent, dynamic, "retainable industries" that enjoy oligopolistic rent or "unequal exchange" due to scale or other barriers to entry. Their work suggests that without an industrial policy to encourage the growth of these kinds of industries, U.S. trade deficits that are not fundamentally due to low-wage competition will not be overcome. Moreover, without a trade policy a permanent jobs program will further increase these unsustainable trade deficits. We are not therefore likely to be able to sustain a jobs program without a trade policy.

Greider (2009) and Gomory and Baumol (2000) point out that in social democratic countries labor, community, and other local stakeholders have institutional power that enables them to often block significant disinvestment or offshoring of high-value-added high-wage employment. In contrast, U.S.-based multinationals are often driven by short-term returns with no concern for the long-term impact of investment or outsourcing decisions in their home country where many of them no longer produce or design the bulk of their products. The U.S. must thus rely on macro policy. Greider suggests using Article 12 of the WTO, under which countries that run persistent and unsustainable trade deficits may apply emergency tariffs as a remedy. Under this plan the U.S. would invoke this Article to cap and gradually reduce its trade deficits. Revenue from these tariffs would be used to support raising real wages and consumption in the poorest low-income developing countries. This strategy is similar to that advocated by Schweickart (2002), Palley (1998), and Baiman (2006), where it is called "solidarity trade policy." These payments might complement payments to developing countries to offset carbon emissions reductions under carbon cap and trade schemes.

An alternative or complementary "natural strategic tariff" or flat tariff approach with progressivity sustaining cuts in other taxes is proposed by Fletcher (2009). This would avoid the political problems of trying to design industry-specific tariffs but would have the effect of subsidizing emerging dynamic manufacturing sectors with rapidly declining cost curves that are more likely to turn into "retainable industries" without generating (at say a 30% level) comparable cost advantages for more mature "commodity" industries that are not in the U.S. interest to retain.

A composite solution might be a natural strategic tariff adequate to cap and gradually reduce U.S. deficits, invoked through WTO Article 12, the proceeds of which would be rebated for progressivity neutralization in the U.S. and to the poorest developing countries to support economic and environmental upgrading. Warren Buffett has proposed that exporters be given a $1 certificate for every dollar that they export and that importers be required to purchase these certificates for every dollar that they import (Fletcher, 2009). This would result in a flat tariff on importers and flat subsidy for exporters but no public revenue. Another alternative is to acknowledge that self-regulating free trade is impossible and instead to use global diplomatic leverage and trade sanctions to force major surplus "trade predator" countries to appreciate their currencies and/or cut back on mercantilist policies until world trade comes into approximate balance.[9]

4 Industrial policy to maintain U.S. prosperity

As should be clear from the discussion above, it is likely to be difficult, if not impossible, to ultimately solve the U.S. trade problem through legislation alone. An industrial policy will be necessary. Such a policy needs to follow the historic pathways described by Norwegian economist Eric Reinert's ground-breaking book on the neglected institutionalist "other canon" of economic thought and policy history (Reinert, 2007). We need to find a way to incubate "good industries" that can be retained and that function as dynamic drivers of further development.[10]

Industrial policy suggestions include changing the federal corporate tax code to provide tax deductions for domestic value-added production and tax penalties for offshore production. The tax can be implemented in a gradual fashion over some number of years to allow a transition to domestic production (Greider, 2009, Chap. 7). However, such a change in tax code, including new transactions taxes as proposed in the jobs program, can only be the start of a comprehensive industrial policy for the U.S. Pollin and Baker (2009) offer some initial suggestions for a U.S. industrial policy centered on public and transportation infrastructure, and clean energy.

5 Conclusion

The small bore "stimulus" or "jolt" rhetoric coming out of Washington needs to end. The U.S. economy faces a fundamental structural and institutional crisis that requires major changes in economic policy and far-reaching programs including: a) A federally funded *living wage jobs program* mostly funded through transactions taxes on finance, b) Emergency measures to cap and gradually *reduce the U.S. trade deficit*, and c) A transparent and coherent *"industrial policy"* to increase high-value-added, competitive manufacturing exports.

The goal should be to support "non-predatory" trade and industrial policies that move the U.S. and world economies toward sustainable and balanced trade and development. This will require an explicit eschewal of the "neoliberal" or "Neoclassical" economic policies that have generated enormous concentrations of wealth, especially for finance capital, and economic growth in selected countries, but increased poverty and inequality for workers and the unemployed throughout most of the world.

Notes

1 This is a reprint of a paper originally published in the *Review of Radical Political Economics*, September 2010, 42(3), 353–62.
2 AFL-CIO 2010 Jobs Initiative. See: http://www.aflcio.org/issues/jobseconomy/jobs/jobsinitiative.cfm#gap.
3 BEA data on full-time equivalent employment by sector. 1–2 million of this decline may be attributable to the shift from SIC to NAICS codes over this period but the decline is still very large.
4 Federal Reserve Bank of St. Louis data cited in McCormick (2010, p. A4).
5 This has increasingly dominated a long-standing "implicit" and unacknowledged Pentagon-based industrial policy in the U.S. – see Pollin and Baker (2009); Ruttan (2006). In the U.K. large-scale deindustrialization and macro policy benefiting the "City" at the expense of the larger economy began under Margaret Thatcher – see Harvey (2005).
6 For detailed documentation of CPEG transactions tax estimates see Barclay (2010), available on: www.cpegonline.org. Barclay's estimate of about $1 trillion is considerably higher than the $350 billion (both without repression) estimated by Baker et al. (2009). See Barclay (2010) for a detailed discussion of these differences.
7 One reason for this is that under free trade *all* efficiency gains from technological change accrue to developed nations; for a working-out of the underlying economic logic of this, see Baiman (2006).

8 Needless to say this finding sparked considerable debate. For a recent review see Porter et al. (2009). The authors conclude that while China's precise current standing in high tech may be debatable, "If not yet, then within not too many years, the United States will likely be supplanted by China as the leading technology-based economy" (p. 1).
9 The print edition of Kuttner (2010, p. A8) includes an informative table adopted from Peter Navarro that divides nationalist industrial and trade policies into "predatory," "ambiguous," and "sensible."
10 A simplified version of "developmental trade" with "unequal exchange" is modeled in Chapter 5.

References

Baiman, R. (2006) Unequal exchange without a labor theory of prices: on the need for a global Marshall Plan and a solidarity trading regime, *Review of Radical Political Economics* 38(1), 71–89.
—— (2010a) The infeasibility of free trade in classical theory: Ricardo's comparative advantage parable has no solution, *Review of Political Economy* 22(3), 419–37.
—— (2010b) Self-adjusting free trade: a generally mathematically impossible outcome. Unpublished paper submitted for publication.
Baker, D., Pollin, R., McArthur, T., and Sherman, M. (2009) *The potential revenue from financial transactions taxes*. PERI and CEPR.
Barclay, W. (2010) *A financial transactions tax: revenue potential and economic impact*. CPEG Working Paper 2010–12 available at www.cpegonline.org.
Chicago Political Economy Group (2009) *A permanent jobs program for the U.S.: economic restructuring to meet human needs*, at http://www.cpegonline.org/reports/jobs.pdf.
Economic Policy Institute (2009) *American jobs plan: a five point plan to stem the U.S. jobs crises*, at: http://epi.3cdn.net/c68c0d218e2750adb3_rwm6iz75b.pdf.
Fletcher, I. (2009) *Free Trade Doesn't Work* (Washington, D.C.: U.S. Business and Industry Council).
Gomory, R. and Baumol, W. (2000) *Global Trade and Conflicting National Interests* (Cambridge, MA: MIT Press).
Greider, W. (2009) *Come Home America* (Emmaus, PA: Rodale).
Harvey, D. (2005) *A Brief History of Neoliberalism* (Oxford: Oxford University Press).
Kuttner, R. (2008) *Obama's Challenge* (Chelsea, VT: Chelsea Green).
—— (2010) Playing ourselves for fools. *American Prospect*. Jan/Feb.
McCormick, R. (2010) The plight of American manufacturing. *American Prospect*. Jan/ Feb.
Palley, T. I. (1998) *Plenty of Nothing* (Princeton, NJ: Princeton University Press).
Pollin, R. and Baker, D. (2009) *Public investment, industrial policy and U.S. economic renewal*. Dec. PERI and CPER.
Porter, A. L., Niles, C., Newman, J., Roessner, D., Johnson, D., and Jin, X-Y. (2009) International high tech competitiveness: does China rank #1? *Technology Analysis and Strategic Management* 21(2), 173–93.
Reinert, E. S. (2007) *How Rich Countries Got Rich and Why Poor Countries Stay Poor* (Washington, DC: Public Affairs).
Ruttan, V. (2006) *Is War Necessary for Economic Growth?* (Oxford: Oxford University Press).
World Bank (2008) *World Development Indicators: Poverty Data Supplement* (Washington, DC: World Bank).
Schweickart, D. (2002) *After Capitalism* (Lanham, MD: Rowman & Littlefield).

8   There is no alternative to managed global trade

Just as Chapter 7 offered trade and industrial policy solutions for the U.S., this concluding chapter seeks to offer practical and policy options for an international trade and finance regime that would support sustainable and broad-based *global* prosperity. Specifically, this chapter shows how the simple models of Parts 1 and 2 point to managed and fair trade policy options that directly contradict free trade (FT) ideology and practice. It grounds these models on a "demand and cost model" (DCM) meme that is posed as an alternative to the standard "supply and demand model" (SDM) meme of introductory economics. The FT model of Part I is shown to be an international version of SDM, and the unequal exchange (UE) model of Part II an extension of DCM. Based on these building blocks, policies to support more equitable and sustainable international trade in the practical near term, and longer-term ideal goals, are proposed for the global economy.

Before entering into a deeper analysis of long-term managed trade goals based on the UE and DCM models, Section 1 will ground this discussion on a broadly realistic understanding of "stylized facts" that characterize the current state of global trade and finance, and Section 2 will outline some of the widely recognized practical failures of the current FT globalization regime now being pursued. Longer-term goals and principles for international trade and finance, supported by SDM and DCM analysis, and by the FT and UE models of Parts 1 and 2, are then addressed in Sections 3–7.

1 World trade and finance in the early twenty-first century

The following data points, or "stylized facts," are useful characterizations of modern global trade and finance.[1]

First, though more volatile, from 1985 to 2012, foreign direct investment (FDI) has grown faster than exports, or trade. This is in contrast to the late "Golden Age," or "Keynesian" 1975 to 1985 period when trade grew faster than FDI at almost double its rate of growth after this period (Stretton, 1999) (Marglin and Schor, 1992).[2] Moreover, directly contradicting FT ideology, the post 1985 FT era has been characterized by persistent large global trade imbalances with mostly developed country deficits and developing country surpluses. For example, in 2005–7 at 6% of GDP, the U.S. alone accounted for roughly half of the world's current account deficits, and China at 10% of GDP accounted for a large share of world surpluses.[3]

Second, much of this is related to an exponential growth in transnational corporations (TNCs). For example, in 2009 there were about 82,000 parent TNCs that controlled around 810,000 foreign affiliates and these were mostly not large vertically integrated hierarchies but international networks of various sizes.[4] This has led to a growth in intra-firm TNC trade that is estimated to comprise roughly *a third* of all global trade. Another estimate calculates that 90% of U.S. imports and exports flow through a U.S. TNC, and 50% of these between affiliates of the same TNC (Blonigen, 2006, p. 1).

Third, the most rapidly growing feature of modern economic "globalization" has been non-FDI financial capital flow which swamps not only the value of actual trade and FDI, but the entire world GDP many times over. For example, the notional value of derivatives trading was estimated in 2010 to be 1.2 quadrillion, at least twenty times the value of world GDP estimated at 50 to 60 trillion that year (Cohan, 2010). Some of the (non-derivative) capital flow is of course direct borrowing and investing that finances the growing and persistent trade imbalances, but the much larger share is a huge pool of speculative capital sloshing around the world at breakneck speed for trading on stocks, bonds, commodities, foreign exchange, financial and equity indices, and derivatives of all of the above.

Finally, both the FT and UE models presented in Chapters 2–6 assume that developed countries in the global "north" maintain a real capital stock and productivity advantage over developing countries in the global "south." While this is true in terms of standard measurements of the aggregate dollar-denominated market value of production per person employed,[5] it is increasingly not the case for particular traded goods industries that employ the latest and most productive product and process technologies in new plants in *developing countries*, thus often exploiting both wage *and* direct productivity advantages over older plants and technologies employed in developed countries.

2 Practical near-term reforms to the current international trade and finance regime

Dani Rodrick has famously asserted that there is an "inescapable trilemma" for world economy (Rodrick, 2007):

> democracy, national sovereignty and global economic integration are mutually incompatible: we can combine any two of the three, but never have all three simultaneously and in full.

Another leading mainstream commentator, Martin Wolf of the *Financial Times*, makes a similar point citing Rodrick in a recent column (Wolf, 2016):

Above all, if the legitimacy of our democratic political systems is to be maintained, economic policy must be orientated towards promoting the interests of the many not the few; in the first place would be the citizenry, to whom the politicians are accountable. If we fail to do this, the basis of our political order seems likely to founder. That would be good for no one. The marriage of liberal democracy with capitalism needs some nurturing. It must not be taken for granted.

While it is encouraging that leading Neoclassical (NC) economists and mainstream commentators have finally realized that capitalist globalization is not producing broad social benefits, their critique is too narrowly focused on the effort to impose *global capitalism* through FT.[6] Within this framework the only way that "national sovereignty" can be compatible with "global economic integration" is if nations support the FT version of "corporate managed trade" (CMT), in many cases against the national interest (see Section 8.3 below). But the truth is that the NC economic ideals of capitalism *in general* have *never* worked as a basis upon which to construct *democratic*, just and sustainable, and broadly prosperous economic development at *either* national or global levels (Baiman, 2016). The contradiction between democracy and capitalism is just *more glaring and obvious in a global context* with little to no democratic oversight and hugely disparate national standards that can be, and are, exploited for private gain in socially and environmentally destructive ways. As Rodrick points out, this understanding lay at the core of the Bretton-Woods agreement that reflected Keynes' view that global trade and finance should be *limited* to serving national economic purposes (Rodrick, 2007; Keynes, 1933).

Though markets, private property, and individual material incentives can be useful and important in driving economic development, they must be embedded, taxed, guided, and regulated if they are to produce sustainable, just, and broadbased prosperity. Just as the notion that national economies should be *based on* and *directed by* free markets fails as a *meme* for domestic economic development, it a fortiori cannot serve as an ideological *principle* for globalization. FT is just a version of capitalist "free market" ideology that is particularly dysfunctional in practice because of the lack of democratic global governance. The most successful markets have never been "free" but rather successfully structured by political institutions to produce broad-based prosperity (Polanyi, 1944; Baiman, 2016, Chap. 11). The recent effort to construct global FT, or free markets, has foundered, not because global capitalism is inherently distinct from its domestic version, but because markets in themselves do not necessarily produce social benefit, and global free markets, or FT, as shown by the UE models of Chapters 5 and 6, are particularly prone to producing exploitative and destructive economic and social outcomes.

Unmasking the guise of free market and free trade legitimacy serves many purposes. It makes clear that the massive global imbalances in trade, finance, wealth, and income have occurred because neoliberal economic policy has aided and abetted their occurrence. The sixty-two billionaires, who own more wealth than half of the planet, especially if they benefited from inherited wealth, do not "deserve" their fantastic rewards (Oxfam, 2016). Rather, we have constructed markets, and through mainstream NC economics legitimated this construction, that have produced a moral travesty (Baiman, 2016). This allocation of wealth serves no conceivable social purpose and is highly destructive of basic human dignity, democracy, and social and environmental stability and sustainability.[7] Though one can arguably imagine a case for rewarding self-made entrepreneurs with some level of unequal economic wealth and power to engage in Schumpeterian "creative destruction" of outsize long-term benefit to humanity and to the planet, market sanctioning of generational wealth accumulation through rentier returns cannot be justified, and in fact runs directly counter to even classic liberal ideology as Thomas Piketty (2014) has persuasively pointed out.

The same point applies to global imbalances among nations and excessively concentrated massive institutional financial imbalances. These are not "deserved" or "inevitable" market outcomes, but social products that can be eliminated, or mitigated, just as they have been sanctioned and supported through social policy. A world trading system where the U.S. persistently runs a deficit of over 0.5% of world GDP that is offset by persistent 0.1%–0.4% surpluses by countries such as China, Germany, Japan, and (until recently) oil exporters is not sustainable (Wolf, 2014; Flowers, 2014). Similarly, the massive growth and dominance of finance and extreme institutional concentration of financial capital documented in Chapter 6 is not sustainable. As shown in Chapter 6, both trends are linked and both exert destructive and undemocratic political and economic pressure in support of macroeconomic austerity that has trapped nations and workers around the world in unnecessary misery from lack of employment, health care, education, pensions, and human services brought on by starving public sectors to fund private and (other) public creditors. Unsustainable German surpluses have dramatically slowed macroeconomic growth in Europe, and as shown in Chapter 7, U.S. deficits have eviscerated the U.S. economy and distorted China's economy, even as U.S. capital and investment flow initially supported economic development in Europe and Asia.

What can be done about these immediate practical problems to put the global economy on a path to broadly shared sustainable development?

As has been repeatedly, and I hope conclusively, demonstrated in this book, there is no substitute for social choice in economic policy. Markets are not, and cannot be, replacements for the ever more urgent (given the threat of species extinction posed by global warming) development of global governance and collective action mechanisms. Though accountable and democratic social-choice mechanisms are hard to create and sustain and up to this point exist only in the most democratic nations and communities and to a very limited extent internationally, this is not an excuse to support a global oligarchy that overrides democracy at both the national and international level in the name of FT principles. Measures to reconstruct a new global trading system that supports national and international democracy and thereby limits the power and reach of global capitalism, as Bretton Woods did so successfully in the post-war years, are essential (Rodrick, 2007).

On the national level, we must do all we can to support the age-old struggle for democratic rights and freedoms so that this can continue at an accelerated pace, recognizing that cloaking imperialist military "realpolitik" in the language of support for democratic freedoms will not achieve this objective. Internationally we must jettison the now (after the 2008 financial crash) ideologically, if not institutionally, bankrupt and repudiated push for a neoliberal international trade and financial regime, and engage in pragmatic reforms of international trade and finance, and domestic economic policy, that reduce the imbalances described above. The record of the last few decades since the collapse of the Bretton-Woods trade and finance regime and the ascendancy of national and global free market and FT thinking and policy, and not coincidentally large and persistent global trade imbalances and global financial instability, have provided indisputable proof that global trade will *not* self-adjust toward a sustainable equilibrium, as is formally demonstrated (under the most ideal assumptions) in Chapter 4.

With regard to trade and finance, in the near term, most effective social-choice power continues to reside in nation states. As documented in Chapter 7 (see also Baiman, 2016, Chap. 11), most of the now developed nations of the world including the U.S. and U.K. in their prior history pursued a pragmatic approach to "free trade" that does not conform to the rhetorical FT doctrine espoused by the WTO and other international neoliberal economic bodies. As discussed in Chapter 7, the U.S. (and perhaps the U.K.) appear to be among the few major nations that have in modern history to this point (August 2016) *actually* followed free market principles, probably as much due to the political power of domestic finance and transnational corporations as genuine ideological belief. So a key, and hopefully imminent, immediate reform would be a U.S. (and UK) backing away from FT policies as described in Chapter 7.

The U.S., for example, is one of the only developed countries without a "value-added tax" (VAT) that effectively penalizes imports and subsidizes exports relative to domestic consumer products.[8] Similarly, the slowing of export-dependent growth in China will hopefully lead that country's leadership to allocate a greater share of output to labor and build up a domestic consumer market that will benefit its own citizens as well as the world economy. Likewise, one would hope that the German leadership will come to its senses and realize that enforcing macroeconomic austerity is not in Germany's long run economic or political interest, as the recent "Brexit" vote has shown.

More broadly, these practical changes in domestic policy could be enhanced through international efforts to create new "global Marshall fund"-like "green" sustainable development funds for southern Europe to save the EU, and for developing countries that do not have the leverage of a China, or an India, to force "developmental" UE as described in Chapter 5. As Wolf and many others including Keynes have pointed out, generosity by "winners" in international trade and finance has generally been much more successful at generating long-term prosperity and sustainable development than narrow efforts to collect on debts and reward rentiers (Wolf, 2016; Keynes, 1919). The impact of the Marshall Plan in anchoring U.S. post-war prosperity and democratic political stability in western

Europe and East Asia vindicates the wisdom of victor generosity in providing global credit and direct investment. As has been noted, Keynes was also a prescient advocate for structuring the international trade and finance regime so as to allow national governments maximum "self-sufficiency" in pursuing macroeconomic policies conducive to broad-based full employment and poverty reduction (Keynes, 1933). It is high time that national and global leaders recognize the wisdom of Keynes' expressly anti-free trade and capital flow views.

Finally, extreme individual and institutional imbalances of wealth and income need to be eliminated through confiscatory national and global inheritance and wealth taxes, as Piketty (2014, Part 4) has called for. And as discussed in Chapter 6, the excessive and concentrated power of finance and financial rentierism needs to be addressed through extensive financial regulation that reduces, or even eliminates as proposed in Iceland, the power of finance to create money, and take excessive risks and rewards with publicly guaranteed money (AFP, 2015). An immediate and relatively easy measure that would not, for example, require the construction of a comprehensive database on financial wealth would be the imposition of a stiff global financial transactions tax, to suppress the excessive risk and financial profits engendered by the enormous overhang of private and institutional financial speculation (Kay, 2015). For example, the yearly notional value of derivatives trading on the Chicago Mercantile Exchange in 2015 is almost one quadrillion, a thousand trillion, dollars, or over thirteen times world GDP.[9] A tiny tax on this pool of enormously risky bets and market manipulation strategies could generate trillions in desperately needed public revenue and reduce the excessive risks and instability generated by this kind of exorbitant financial gambling (Barclay, 2010; Lewis, 2014).

The popular backlash against the EU represented by Brexit was a direct result of the increasing neoliberal policy bent taken by EU leadership and the construction of an essentially unworkable macroeconomic system that prescribed "free" factor flows before, and increasingly as a substitute for, the construction of a single democratic community with the ability to structure EU economic policy to further broad-based public benefit rather than enhancing the power of private capital and its beneficiaries (Weisbrot, 2016). To be fair, the choice was not a simple one, and many, including myself, would have preferred an internal democratization of EU policies as an advance toward more globalized social choice, but in any case the backlash against the pro-market pro-private finance decisions of the recent EU leadership cannot be denied. FT, even with labor mobility, cannot be democratically sustained in the long run.

3 The relationship between FT and the supply and demand model (SDM), and UE and the demand and cost model (DCM)

The simple FT and UE trade models of Chapters 4–6 are important as stories, or "memes," that present diametrically opposed views of the global economy.[10] The FT analysis presented (and refuted) in Chapters 2–4 conforms to the NC view that the economy is fundamentally composed of individual agents acting rationally in their own interests in competitive markets that force accountability and make this self-interest benefit the common good. In other words, FT is a version of the "methodological individualism rational acting" (MIRA) form of analysis common to NC economics (Baiman, 2016, Chap. 3; Taylor, 2004, Chap. 2).

Like, and based on, the supply and demand model (SDM) which is pervasive in mainstream introductory economics, FT assumes that under the right conditions, global trade is a *self-adjusting system that maximizes social benefit for actors (in the simple-model countries) who act rationally in their own self-interest*. But as is shown in Baiman (2016), the "perfectly competitive free market" (PCFM) SDM is fundamentally flawed, as is the related NC definition of "market efficiency." FT is an international trade version of the SDM and its supposed "efficiency" and "normalcy" is thus based on the same ghostlike artificial constructions as the SDM that purport to demonstrate the optimality of relying on MIRA and free markets to determine international flows of trade and finance.

The simple textbook FT doctrine is based on the premise that there exists a market-derived (from individual business choices) supply, or export curve, that coupled with a similarly market-derived (from individuals and businesses) demand, or import, curve results in an equilibrium price and quantity supplied and demanded of a traded good or service, after taking into account exchange rates (that are themselves assumed to be "floating" or set by market-determined offer and bid curves for domestic and (each separate convertible) foreign currency). Though we have shown, in Chapter 4, that this FT "meme" as an idealized description of a global trade equilibrium is not feasible, as the viewpoint that it represents is dominant within NC economics, it is important to further deconstruct it by linking it to the SDM meme of introductory economics, which is even more removed from reality and forms the bedrock pillar of NC economic indoctrination more generally.

Before discussing how the UE models of Chapters 5 and 6 provide alternative and more realistic memes for global trade and finance, it is useful to analyze in detail the ways in which SDM ideology presents a woefully false and unrealistic view of how the economy works, and present an alternative DCM meme that offers both a more realistic view of the underlying workings of a market economy and an alternative "micro-foundation" for a UE understanding of trade and finance, similar to the way in which the FT doctrine is built upon an understanding of the economy that presupposes the SDM meme.

4 The supply and demand model (SDM) meme

The introductory economics SDM meme is presented in Figure 8.1 below:

The fundamentally Walrasian[11] SDM story is presented in introductory texts as a description of the workings of Adam Smith's *invisible hand*. The latter is an automatic feedback dynamic story explaining how in competitive markets greater demand drives up prices and profits, stimulating increased investment that leads to greater supply. SDM supposedly supplies a rigorous foundation for the rhetorical message of objective market forces coordinating individual

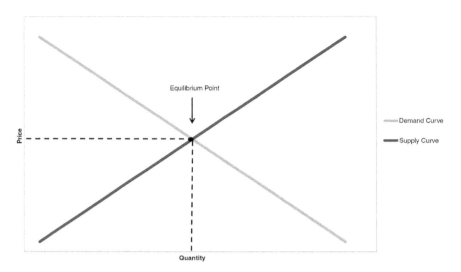

Figure 8.1 The supply and demand model (SDM)

self-interest and providing a beneficial and balanced social equilibrium through freely adjusting price signals.

Given exogenous technological and natural constraints (Baiman, 2016, Chap. 1), the SDM model shows that capitalist *market* economies *gravitate toward a social welfare-maximizing, stable, market-clearing equilibrium that is perfectly determined by natural conditions and individual choice,* as:

a)   "Objective" market forces are produced by aggregations of *agent* choices in such a way that no *individual* buyer or seller can significantly affect overall supply or demand curves. "Perfectly competitive free market" (PCFM) equilibrium prices and quantities are determined by *nature, technology,* and (almost as sacrosanct in liberal political thinking) "free and voluntary" *individual* agent *choices* in their own self-interest. These free market equilibrium prices *perfectly and deterministically* balance the objective and inviolate forces of supply and demand so that *quantity supplied* exactly equals *quantity demanded,* resulting in an equilibrium *clearing* of all markets. The SDM thus provides a scientific and objective solution to the central economic problem of "allocating scarce means to competing ends" that is *free and fair* as it properly reflects "consumer sovereignty" and individual choice.

b)   *Shifts* and *movements along* these curves not only generate unique, objective, and fair equilibrium prices and quantities, but the equilibrium so obtained is a "self-correcting" *stable equilibrium.* In the absence of supply or demand curve shifts, any movement away from equilibrium price or quantity will automatically generate price changes (or "price signals") that will induce individual producers and consumers to make choices based on their own self-interest that will return the system to (the prior existing) equilibrium. The SDM model thus includes a dynamic self-adjustment mechanism that moves the system toward its unique equilibrium position and sustains this equilibrium once it is obtained.

c)   Finally, as the SDM equilibrium generated by the individual self-interested agent choice subject only to (exogenous) constraints of nature and technology *maximizes social welfare*, the SDM is a modern and rigorous formalization of Adam Smith's "invisible hand" doctrine. The SDM thus provides "objective scientific" support for the cornerstone ideology of NC economics: that competitive markets will cause actions motivated by private self-interest to serve the public good. The SDM thus shows that PCFMs are optimally socially efficient.

Any more or less formal model ignores some aspects of reality, so it would serve little purpose to critique SDM for not *precisely* replicating reality. It is well known, for example, that SDM cannot determine distribution (*factor* markets play a role but can't set "initial endowments") and disregards *exogenously determined* (in the SDM model) *tastes, nature, and technology*.[12] The standard NC response to critiques of this approach is that factors influencing tastes, nature, and technology are outside of the sphere of economic science (Baiman, 2016, Chapters 1–4). NC's claim is that the proper way to address distribution, for example, is through a political reconfiguration of initial endowments (or wealth) that does not "interfere" with the efficient workings of the market as depicted by the SDM. The construct backing up this position is the "second fundamental theorem of welfare economics" that proves that a PCFM can provide any desired distributional outcome through an appropriate setting of initial endowments.[13] All of these SDM PCFM outcomes are said to be "pareto optimal" – a term that sounds like *optimal* but in fact is defined as a situation under which no agent can become better off through a voluntary market exchange with another agent – an outcome that is pretty much a tautological consequence of the workings of a PCFM defined as the result of individual agents trying to improve their welfare through voluntary market exchanges.

   In introductory and applied economic texts, the concepts of "consumer surplus" (CS) and "producer surplus" (PS) are employed to generate a more normative justification for PCFM and SDM equilibriums. CS is defined as the area under the demand curve for prices that consumers would have been willing to pay as opposed to what they actually paid at the (always by definition) lower *equilibrium* price level determined by a horizontal line through the intersection of the demand and supply curve. PS is defined as the (necessarily positive or zero) profit that equals the area above the supply curve and below the horizontal equilibrium price line. Standard NC introductory economic texts then explain that such an equilibrium maximizes the sum of consumer and producer surplus and that the imposition of any non-market price or quantity restriction will diminish this measure of overall social welfare.[14]

Any "government intervention" into the "free market" that artificially attempts to keep prices low (like rent control) or high (like agricultural price supports) will lead to shortages or surpluses and "dead weight" CS+PS loss relatively to the "pareto optimal" or welfare-maximizing (unconstrained) market equilibrium price and quantity, as shown in Figure 8.2 below.

Critiques of both the measure (why should the welfare derived from PS or profit be considered equivalent to welfare derived from CS?) and its units (why should a dollar of CS for an extremely wealthy individual like Donald Trump have the same "social welfare" value as a dollar of CS for an average-income person?) have been rigorously developed (Baiman, 2001, 2002; Granqvist & Lind, 2004; Baiman, 2016, Chaps. 9–10). Critiques of these supposedly objective scientific "principles of microeconomics" show that even a presumably more realistic modified SDM widely used by NC applied microeconomists (used, for example, to justify the disastrous deregulation of electricity in California) can be shown to rest on *basic assumptions* reflecting particular sets of *values*, such as the primacy of *efficiency* and *individual choice* over *equity* and *social choice*, and a mistaken belief that the former can be strictly and scientifically *separated* from the latter (Baiman, 2002).

For now it is important to demonstrate the complete (and not just approximate) lack of realism of the introductory textbook SDM which is, as has already been noted, a model that most students who have any formal exposure to economics at all never get beyond.

The standard introductory economics SDM model is dependent on *independent* supply and demand curves which in practice rarely exist. For example, if one asks a pizza producer how many pizzas they would *produce* at different possible sales prices (i.e. what would be their SDM model "supply curve" – which by

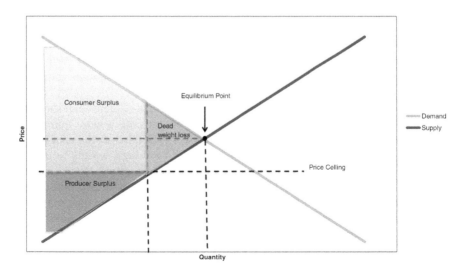

Figure 8.2 SDM consumer surplus and producer surplus dead weight loss

construct is a hypothetical "wish list" that is dependent on "received prices" over which an individual supplier has no influence), if there was a response at all, it would be: "Well, that depends on what I thought demand would be." But the answer to this *demand* question, by assumption, plays *no role* in the construction of the supply curve. The supply curve is supposed to give the number of pizzas a producer would produce based purely on *supply conditions* – that is, the cost of producing each additional pizza relative to a given price set by the market. This is based on the assumption that producers will be able to sell every pizza they can produce at the *market price* and that no individual producer could possibly produce enough pizzas to change the market price. As far as individual producers are concerned, the supply curve is supposed to reflect *infinite demand* at every price.

If this sounds hokey, it is. How many producers do you think construct (necessarily purely theoretical) supply curves to determine the *maximum* output they can produce profitably at any market-determined "given price," and produce this with the expectation that demand for their output at this price will be infinite? Such a producer wouldn't need to worry about demand. They would produce as much as they could, and bingo – it will be snapped up by the "infinite demand" that will be available at that price.

Moreover, what if, because of economies of scale for example, cost of production per unit *declines* as you produce more? The model obviously breaks down completely in this case, as every producer will produce an infinite supply. The whole "supply curve" hypothetical construction is premised on an assumption that *every* producer will experience increasing costs per unit as output increases, and that these incremental, or *marginal*, unit costs will increase fast enough that no producer will be able to obtain a large enough share of the market to influence prices (thus becoming an *oligopolist* or *monopolist* instead of a *"perfect competitor"*) before this happens. This is a nonsensical assumption in today's advanced economies in which most major sectors are dominated by giant, often multinational, firms whose reach and profitability are based on large-scale production, sourcing of inputs, and marketing.

Ask the same question of a hypothetical pizza *consumer*, and you are likely to get a fairly well-defined downward-sloping demand curve, provided that nearby pizza shops selling the same kind of pizza are available and that the consumer has a limited pizza budget, i.e. that *effective substitution* and *income constraint* conditions hold. The problem here is that though individual, and after adding them up *aggregate*, *demand* curves are a fairly well-defined theoretical construct, the existence of hypothetically independent upward-sloping *supply* curves for firms and for markets generally are *not*. In the short run, assuming some level of *normal* excess capacity, *variable average costs* (costs that vary with the amount of output produced) per unit produced are often relatively *constant* so that *average costs* (which includes the *fixed* overhead and set-up costs) per unit produced should *decline* as these fixed costs are defrayed over larger production runs (Lavoie, 2009, Chap. 2). Thus, total (variable and fixed) short-run average costs, which are by definition supposed to be based *exclusively* on cost-side factors, will generally either be *downward* sloping, or at the very least (if there are some offsetting increases in average costs for *unusually* high levels of production such as overtime pay) *flat*.[15]

When SDM is applied to the long run, a period of time over which plant and equipment (or "capital") can be expanded, there is even greater reason to believe that total average costs, for most industries, will decline as greater market power and economies of scale (larger plants lowering cost per unit output) and scope (franchising reducing joint overhead costs such as marketing and financing) reduce the costs of inputs and production. NC economic texts (i.e. almost all economics texts) are forced to resort to dubious claims that "administrative inefficiencies" stemming from large size will inevitably add sufficient costs per unit to offset all of the advantages of large-scale production, to justify a "U"-shaped long-run average cost curve assumption.[16]

This is a necessary assumption if PCFMs are to naturally evolve toward an optimally efficient production and pricing configuration at the bottom of a "U"-shaped long-run average total cost curve. But this is contrary to the actual experience of most advanced capitalist economies in which larger and larger firms achieve cost, marketing, and financial advantages, and effective oligopoly power over numerous industries and large market segments. Wal-Mart is just the latest example of the efficiencies of scale, including market (and political) power, that adhere to the largest and most concentrated units of capital. The "natural" tendency of capitalism in most cases is to evolve toward greater oligopoly a la Marx, rather than PCFM a la Adam Smith, in complete disregard of standard NC textbook microeconomic theory.[17]

In other words, though "diminishing marginal utility of consumption" which generates "U"-shaped indifference (convex) curves and downward-sloping demand curves (because consumers derive less and less satisfaction or "utility" as they purchase more of a commodity, they will increase their "quantity demanded" only if relative prices of the commodity decline) arguably makes some sense as describing one aspect of consumption behavior, "diminishing marginal productivity" which generates (eventually) upward-sloping (convex) supply curves (since average costs per unit increase, profit-maximizing suppliers will only produce more if sales prices increase) does *not* generally describe *any* characteristic of production.[18]

Rather, *diminishing marginal productivity* (DMP) is an ahistorical and *ideological artifact* based on "fixed" rather than "produced" means of production (Sraffa, 1960; Nell, 1996; Lee, 1998). It stems originally from Ricardo's analysis of rent on increasingly less fertile land and became a central principle after Alfred Marshall developed the now standard *increasing costs* SDM formulation, though Marshall himself was careful to specify that this was one possible type of industry cost configuration along with *decreasing cost* and *constant cost* possibilities (Marshall, 1890, Book IV, Chap. 13).

Both Ricardo and Marshall were analyzing nineteenth-century agricultural and manufacturing conditions with limited technology and excess capacity in manufacturing, often dependent on work teams whose output could not easily be expanded without loss of efficiency (Nell, 1998, Chaps. 1–2, 9). Of course, even in post-industrial twenty-first-century economies some sectors like agriculture, natural resource extraction, capital goods production, and *exchange* (rather than production) markets such as financial markets may have binding short-term supply constraints and consequent upward-sloping cost and/or supply curves. "Fictitious commodities" like labor that (like land) are *not produced for the market* may also, *when there are shortages*, exhibit upward-sloping and even backward-sloping supply curves.

However, most manufacturing and service sectors in advanced economies have excess capacity and *produced* or *slack* inputs (like labor for which an excess "reserve army" of unemployed generally exists) whose supply can be expanded without increasing (but possibly reducing overhead and fixed) costs per unit.

Why then is NC economics so wedded to the nineteenth-century DMP principle?

The answer, I think, is clear. Without short-run, or long-run, DMP, there can be no upward-sloping supple curve and price setting devolves to a markup on production costs. None of the aforementioned a)–c) SDM outcomes will occur.

5 The (mostly real) demand and cost model (DCM) story

The introductory economics DCM meme is presented in Figure 8.3 below:

As has been noted, though it is ubiquitous in economic texts, an independent supply curve does not exist for most of the economy. Rather, as is well known, supply curves exist only for firms in so-called "perfectly competitive" markets where normal production occurs where *upward*-sloping marginal costs both *exist* and *exceed* total average costs. These are the only cases where a supply curve (equal to the marginal cost curve) can exist. Approximate examples may occur in a few specialized

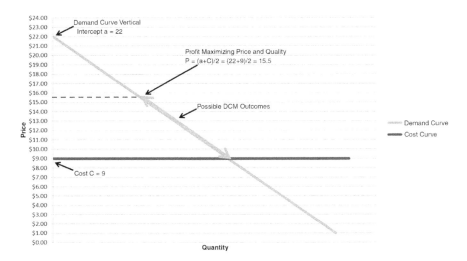

Figure 8.3 The demand and cost model (DCM)

markets, such as some agricultural or natural resource markets: where prices are set globally, individual producers are small relative to the global market and can sell as much as they can produce at the global market price, and incremental costs of production rise as production increases; and barter markets, such as financial trading markets, where equilibrium prices for offers and bids of financial products are reconciled. *With the exception of these special cases, in the rest of the production economy, firms set prices and levels of production based on costs and demand.*

The real demand and cost model (DCM) that characterizes most production markets in the economy is as follows.

Almost all firms have some *market power* in the sense that they face a downward-sloping demand curve. This implies that the amount of product they can sell depends on a price they have some power to set based on competitive conditions in their market and their long-run marketing and production strategy. "Monopolistically competitive" firms (in markets where a large number of firms compete but each firm has some price-setting power, for example in retail trade) may have only *local* market power with very limited price and quantity ranges based on their locational convenience to customers. "Oligopolistic" firms (in markets where a small number of firms have dominant market shares and determine price ranges and major product design for the entire industry, for example automobile or smartphone producers) may face demand curves with steeper slopes and more flexible price and quantity ranges that are still limited by competition. "Monopoly" firms (in markets with only one producer, for example regulated utilities or drug companies with patents) have complete (hopefully subject to some regulation) freedom to set prices and quantities (Allen et al., 2013, Chap. 7).

All firms also face average total cost curves which are generally flat or slightly downward sloping in their normal range of production (Lavoie, 2009, Chap. 2; Lee, 1998). If the firm is to stay in business these cost curves must be *below* the demand curve in normal production ranges.

How are prices and quantities set?

Firms will generally apply a "markup" over costs that will depend on how much they want to sell and on their long-term strategy. If they want to sacrifice short-term profits to increase market share over the long run, they will keep prices relatively low. If they want to maximize short-term profit and don't care about market share, they will keep prices high. For a useful "heuristic" introductory story, assume a linear downward-sloping demand curve:

$$P = a - bQ$$

where $a > 0$, $b > 0$ are both constant vertical intercept and slope parameters, and P and Q are price and quantity demanded along the demand curve. Assume also a constant average total cost = marginal cost curve: C that is lower than P in the normal range of production. Under these conditions short-term profit will be maximized when:[19]

$$P = (a + C)/2$$

An unregulated monopoly firm can maximize its short-term profit by setting its price at this level. For all other firms this will be an *upper bound on price* as any higher price will reduce both demand *and* profit. Firms will therefore set a price Q that is between (a + C)/2 and C, with a range of production Q between (a − C)/2b and (a- C)/b.[20] As noted, the exact price that firms set within this range will depend on competition and firm strategy. *The amount that firms produce, or "quantity supplied," will adjust to the level of demand at the price selected by the firm along the demand curve.*

As is evident from these examples, the *qualitative* prices and quantities outcomes of the DCM are the *same* as those of the SDM. But the DCM does *not precisely specify* how much, if any, price change will accompany quantity-supplied change when the demand curve shifts, and similarly whether, and if so how much, price or quantity-supplied change will occur when the cost curve shifts. Most importantly, the DCM suggests, and empirical data confirm, that market-clearing quantity supplied and demanded is fundamentally determined by *demand* conditions, most often by firms simply increasing or reducing output to match demand with no, or very little, change in price.[21] However, for intro-ductory textbook purposes, both models provide an explanation of the workings of demand and cost, or "supply," on price. Admittedly the DCM model does not offer as clean and unambiguous an answer, but *qualitatively* both at least point to the same possible outcomes in terms of price and quantity changes. Given that the DCM story offers a realistic approximation of reality, whereas the SDM is an utter fantasy that posits a curve that in most cases cannot be defined, why do introductory economics textbooks almost universally stick with the SDM? Yes, the SDM story is pedagogically simpler to explain, but it's also *patently untrue*, and the DCM model, though a bit more complex, is well within the reach of introductory students. If economics is to maintain its claim to be a "social *science*," shouldn't it be in the business of teaching about *reality* and not purveying *fairy tales*?

It is hard not to conclude that the major reason for the ubiquitous appear-ance of the SDM in economics textbooks is that it legitimates the PCFM ideology of NC economics (Baiman, 2016). Most critically, instead of show-ing that economic outcomes in capitalist market economies gravitate toward a social welfare-maximizing, stable, market-clearing equilibrium that is perfectly determined by natural conditions and individual choice, the DCM shows that price and quantity outcomes in market economies are *subjectively determined, socially embedded, mostly quantity choices, reflecting institu-tional and class power constrained by objective conditions that result in unstable and generally socially non-optimal equilibrium price and quantity outcomes*, as:

a) Equilibrium prices are *not precisely* determined as in a mechanical clock by objective (or exogenous to the model) forces of nature, technology, and indi-vidual agent choice, but rather are a product of *external social and market, and internal to the firm, institutional power and strategy*, that results in a *selection* of prices and quantities from a *range* determined by demand and cost conditions. Moreover, empirical studies show that firms mostly *change output levels in response to demand* with little change in price, and are unlikely to (given that almost all firms in advanced economies have some market power to set prices) fully "pass through" cost changes to consumers.[22] Markets are *embedded in* and *products of* society rather than a natural, or objective, apolitical technocratic mechanism to which society must adapt. Market equilibrium prices and quantities are thus *not perfectly determined* but rather *are selected from a range* given by demand and cost conditions resulting in active *firm adjustments* of *quantity supplied* to *quantity demanded* and occasional price changes. These "equilibrium" quantities and prices are thus not objective but *subjective* products of social governance, class power, and firm strategy that are only partially influenced by cost and individual consumer choices that are themselves constrained and molded by class, culture, and marketing (Hahnel and Albert, 1990).

b)   The equilibrium so obtained is *not* necessarily a "self-correcting" stable equilibrium as it results from *shifting demand curves* rather than *shifts along fixed* demand and supply curves. If multiple firms adjust output in the same direction, firm output decisions will impact income streams, causing shifts in demand curves that will lead to a *multiplied* reduction or increase in output, moving the market farther and farther away from its initial equilibrium position. The new equilibrium will clear product markets at the new lower or higher levels of "effective" (backed up by spending) quantity demanded (which, depending especially on income distribution, may have little relationship to actual or optimal levels of *social* output or *needs*), but this new equilibrium, like the old one, will *not* be stable or *clear* labor or capital markets. A "free" market equilibrium is thus fully compatible with high levels of unemployment, unused capacity, and unmet social and individual need that could be satisfied if social resources were fully employed.[23]

c)   Finally, for the reasons discussed above, and because the DCM equilibrium does *not* occur, as in the SDM, at the point of intersection of the supply and demand curves, as is shown in Figure 8.4 below, the DCM equilibrium is *not* generally welfare optimal in either the static NC "pareto optimal" sense or the more general Keynesian sense of fully employing underused resources.[24] Thus the DCM supports a post-Keynesian or Keleckian understanding of the modern capitalist market economy and fundamentally *undermines* Adam Smith's "invisible hand" doctrine, and with it "objective scientific" support for the Walrasian cornerstone ideology of NC economics.[25]

The *social choice* implications of DCM also differ in important ways from the *individual choice*-based SDM. In the DCM, individual producer choices are influenced by social and institutional factors and produce at quantity and price levels that clear product markets but do *not* maximize social welfare in the very narrow individual choice-based "pareto optimality" sense discussed above.

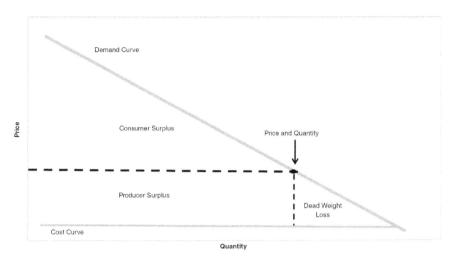

Figure 8.4 DCM consumer surplus and producer surplus dead weight loss

In the DCM, world social welfare and efficiency depend on *the degree of* com-petition in demand and cost markets, as these will determine how the relative incentives for *static* and *dynamic* efficiency gains are distributed. High demand and robust short-term price competition among producers will result in reduced prices and higher output in the short run, providing *static* efficiency gains, or increased quantity supply and demand, at lower prices with no changes in plant and equipment. Meanwhile, excessive "cut-throat" competition, for example between small firms with little market power, may prevent production units from obtaining a large enough scale and scope to support significant present and future cost reduction and product innovation, thereby impairing *dynamic* efficiency.[26]

6 FT and UE trade models highlight exchange vs. exploitation, analyses of globalization

The DCM model, and more advanced applied microeconomics "second-best" versions of it (Baiman, 2016, Part III), show *that there is no inherent normative value in market outcomes.* Rather, as Polanyi (1944) long ago pointed out, *mar-kets are embedded in society, and the degree to which they are socially beneficial or exploitative and destructive depends on how they are constructed, guided, and regulated, through social choices made by firms, governments, and in the case of international trade and finance, international trading regimes.*

This key insight is demonstrated again in the international trade context by the UE models of Chapters 5 and 6. Chapters 2–4 demonstrate that FT ideol-ogy as expressed in the Ricardian comparative advantage parable (Chapter 2) and Meade's NC FT solution (Chapter 3), and in the textbook free trade doctrine

(Chapter 3), are respectively mathematically inconsistent, inapplicable, and infeasible. The UE models of Chapters 5–6 demonstrate that FT, or trade and finance based on individual profit-maximizing, regulated through freely floating exchange rates and international MIRA-based market forces, is likely to be socially exploitative and harmful to long-term international political and economic progress.

The point is that "free market" prices are not an ideal goal that the global economy should be directed toward. To the contrary: FT prices are like to be highly exploitative and of benefit to corporations, individuals, and countries that can leverage market power and unequal exchange to their own benefit as demonstrated in the UE models of Chapters 3 and 4. Though these simple models are constructed in terms of hypothetical "southern," "northern," and "rentier" (in Chap. 6) countries, their unequal exchange outcomes are equally applicable to the real current global trade world of massive FDI, intra-TNC, and rentier capital flow, described in Section 1 above. The exchanges described in the model can, without loss of generality, be applied to any trading agents with unequal power (described in the model as unequal ownership of capital stock) that can negotiate an unequal exchange with an agent with less market power. The agents can be corporations, individuals, or countries. The source of the market power can reside in superior technology and public or private capital stock or infrastructure (though the model focuses on private capital stock) or other sources of market power such as the privileged monopolistic or oligopolistic network, marketing, and supplier relationships employed by TNCs or localized production agglomerations within countries or regions (Dicken, 2015, Chaps. 2–8).

The UE model highlights the most important aspect of global (and domestic) "exchange": its dependence on *market power*. "Free markets" allow TNCs, individuals, and countries that have the power to force unequal exchange to do so. And the UE model shows that market power is regenerative and cumulative. Over time, in the absence of exogenous changes, the gap between economic agents that have power and those that do not *increases* in direct contradiction to NC "convergence" ideology. Note in particular the way in which the UE model of Chap. 5 shows that, in the idealized setting of the model, *all* of the benefits of trade accrue to the "north" and technological progress *increases* the north–south gap over time. Furthermore, the UE model of Chap. 6 shows how "rentierism," or the ability to extract value (measured in the simple UE models as labor value) without producing useful real goods or services through rentier financial power, further exacerbates global inequality and undermines sustainable long-term economic growth and development in both the "rentier" economy and its trading partners, capturing the implications of the last, or fourth, "stylized fact" of global trade and finance of Section 1.

"Free markets" do not produce "natural" or "socially efficient" equilibrium prices and quantities, but simply transfer and reflect unequal market power relationships. *Market outcomes can be relatively exploitative (unequal or producing greater inequality and exploitation) or socially beneficial (relatively equal or moving toward greater equality and fairness), depending on how the markets are structured within or between nations.* Similarly, markets can produce beneficial and sustainable short and long-run innovation or suppress technological and organization progress, depending on how they're structured. For example, Europe and Asia enjoy much higher-quality and more affordable broadband access than the U.S. in spite of the fact that most of the original technological innovation occurred in the U.S., because relatively unregulated telecom markets in the U.S. (and many other countries) are dominated by oligopolies and monopolies that can extract rentier profits with less investment in broad-based infrastructure and public service (Miller, 2014). The U.S. health care system is an even more egregious example of how relatively unregulated for-profit markets can produce terribly inefficient and wasteful outcomes, especially when compared with the highly successful single-payer Canadian health care system that is regulated to induce competition over *quality* and not rentier profit extraction (Davis et al., 2014).

None of these points of course are particularly new, but they bear repeating in the international trade and finance context. For example, the role that private international ratings agencies and capital markets have come to assume in local, state, national, and international economic policy, coupled with the ever increasing power of private finance and "independent" central banks whose governance and policies largely reflect the interests and priorities of private finance, is a clear case of financial sector dominance over democratically elected governments and quasi- accountable international bodies, in spite of the abundant evidence of rampant corruption and illegality within international and domestic finance (Douglas-Bowers, 2011; Vitali et al., 2011; Hong, 2016).

7 Conclusion: long-terms goals to support a more just and sustainable global trade regime

In a sense, the case against FT is almost banal. Anyone who recognizes that reliance on PCFM cannot substitute for social policy should, in principle, recognize that the notion that FT should serve as the backbone and guiding principle of international trade and finance is a non-sequitur. There is no principled argument for FT unless one believes that there is some inherent normative value to "free market" outcomes, as NC "core theory" stridently but unsuccessfully attempts to prove and introductory economics texts work mightily to disseminate (Baiman, 2016). If one does not accept this, there is no argument for FT.

However, it is useful to specifically lay out the case against free markets, or FT, in the international context. While Part I of this book demonstrates that the FT doctrine is, from multiple vantage points, inconsistent, inapplicable, and infeasible, the basic UE model employed in Part II and the DCM summarized in this chapter and at greater length in Baiman (2016, Chap. 5) offer simple frameworks for making a (high level and abstract but) principled case for managed international trade and finance. This argument can be made as part of a general need to:

a)   construct global markets that work to generate sufficient, but not excessively large, profit markups that produce both short and long-term broad-based and sustainable human well-being

b)   demonstrate that prices and particularly the wage component of costs of production are largely determined socially and do not reflect "inherent" or "objective" efficiency costs, and design rules that *reduce international unequal exchange* by raising rather than lowering global labor and social and environmental production standards

c)   show that international trade and finance, like their domestic counterparts, are fundamentally based on governance, or social choices, made by agents with the power to establish and enforce the rules, so that the choice is not whether international trade should be based on "free trade" so "managed trade," but rather by whom and for what purpose are global trade rules being put in place.

In this sense, the real issue is whether to continue to support "corporate managed trade" disguised as "free trade" based on rules designed by and managed for the benefit of transnational corporations and their agents, or establish a global "democratic managed trade" regime constructed and enforced by democratically accountable representatives to fairly and sustainably benefit all of humanity and the planet.

7.1 Constructing international markets that work

The importance of this aspect of global social policy should be uncontroversial as it follows the basic (NC and radical economics) view that to produce public benefits, markets must be sufficiently *competitive* to keep prices low for consumers in the short run, but not so competitive that they do not support dynamic investment and robust product and process competition in the long run. This is, or should be, a widely accepted role of public policy. Ensuring the former is arguably the only role for public policy in NC theory; see Baiman (2016, Chapters 9 and 10).

In the radical and UE context of this book, the issue is one of creating markets that constrain the gap between costs and markups so as to ensure adequate but not excessively large or small profits for producers. In the DCM model of Figure 8.3, the key policy objective is to enforce a socially beneficial gap between the cost line and the price and quantities demanded on the demand curve *selected* by firms. As noted in Section 4, very low markups produce lower prices and more consumer surplus and benefit in the short term, but may reduce potential future "dynamic efficiency" gains from reinvesting firm profits in new products and processes. Conversely, high markups and profits may signal a lack of competition and wasteful and socially destructive rentier exploitation of excessive market power. Just as with national policy, but even more so in the international context where the stakes and inequities of power are likely to be larger, a public policy regime is required to monitor, tax, and regulate markets to optimize markup levels.

A radical or post-Keynesian (PK) DCM view, in contrast to the false SDM picture, highlights the fact that there is no inherent value to standalone or "free" market prices and quantities, like billion-dollar returns to hedge fund managers or oil companies. More generally, *no private person or company inherently "deserves"* *a particular income or profit from the market.* Rather, markets are social constructs whose outcomes need to be constantly evaluated and adjusted through taxes, subsidies, social planning, and other regulation, to produce social benefits. Flows of income and wealth should be subject to constant review to continuously adjust market rules as necessary, and publicly fund increasing shares of economic activity (see Chapters 5–7), to improve broad social benefits from prices, income and investment streams, and wealth accumulations.

7.2 Reducing international unequal exchange

At a deeper level, the UE models of Chapters 5 and 6 show that unregulated FT produces unequal exchange or a transfer of labor from those countries (or individuals or corporations) with a weaker market position to those who have more power in the market. The models further show that in the absence of "non-market" effects, technological progress is likely to increase unequal exchange and thus economic and social inequality between and within nations. "Non-market" effects would apply, for example, to the industrial and managed trade policies that are employed by East Asian countries and accepted and supported by the U.S. (through open trade policies) as part of "cold war" political strategy.

Since gaps in wages, environmental and social regulation, and taxes are typically much larger internationally than domestically, the importance of an international trade and finance regime that *reduces unequal exchange* and economic and social inequality between nations is even greater in global trade than in most domestic contexts. This is particularly the case given the stylized facts of Section 1 showing that modern international trade and finance is *dominated by* FDI and portfolio capital flows, and inter- and intra-TNC trade – trends that are generally motivated by efforts to capture profit by *exploiting UE* between nations and are largely successful at doing so. This shows that international trade is driven by UE and *absolute advantage*, not equal exchange and *comparative advantage*.

In the DCM context, the issue is: where is the cost curve set in Figure 8.3?

And the underlying answer highlighted by the UE models is that, especially when production processes and technologies are comparable per the fourth stylized fact in 7.1, cost curves are largely social and national outcomes. Because of this NC absolute or relative "purchasing power parity" (PPP) "law of one price" underlying "fundamental" price rules ignore the fact that global prices are functions of national costs and especially labor costs, that are largely determined by social, economic, and political conditions such as minimum wage laws and relative labor union rights and power, and environmental, zoning, and tax and subsidy laws, and their enforcement (Eiteman et al., 2016, Chap. 6). The fact that, as shown in the UE models, FT will level down prices and production costs to their lowest possible level and set this as the global price does not mean that this is a socially optimal, "naturally efficient," or "just" price as this price is not produced by an "objective" SDM. Rather, per the DCM and UE models, costs of production, and prices, reflect the social, political, and economic conditions of the location, or locations, of production.

For example, the fact that (in January 2015) a "Big Mac" cost 12.2% more in Denmark than it did in the U.S. does *not* imply, as suggested by PPP FT doctrine, that the Danish Krone is overvalued.[27] It more likely reflects the fact that due to strong unions Danish fast food workers (in Sept. 2014) made an average of $20.70 an hour, and had pension, paid holidays, sick days, and regular pre-assigned working hours, compared with about $9 an hour, and generally none of these benefits, in the U.S. (Greenberg, 2014). International trade should *not* be a means of reducing prices to the lowest international level, for example the $1.36 PPP cost of a Big Mac in Russia (based on a 2015 sample of thirteen countries and the Euro area).[28] Ideally, an international trade regime would *raise* international standards, allowing countries like Denmark to impose tariffs on imported goods and services with lower local production costs due to lower social and environmental standards, and rebate this revenue to these countries to support a gradual rising of social and environmental standards as suggested in Chapters 5–7.

In this sense, standard measures of market "efficiency" cost of production, especially in the global context, often do not reflect the real costs, or *truly* greater efficiency or quality in production, but simply different social and environmental standards. In extreme cases, like that of the U.S., highly profitable companies in a large low-wage service sector that is not tolerated in most western European economies not only pay wages and benefits that are below a minimal "living wage" for most workers, but offset, or "externalize," the costs of basic needs like health care, day care, shelter, and food for their workers onto the public sector, to which they often also pay low or negative taxes due to special corporate subsidies (Jacobs, 2015). Low-cost companies that do not pay the real costs of reproducing their workers shown in Chapters 5 and are *not* "efficient" in any true sense. *Prices in any given market should reflect, or at least over time move toward, the social costs of living in that market.* As shown in Chapters 5 and 6 making profit by arbitraging living standards does not improve global production efficiency but sets up a race to the bottom with most of the benefits accrued by TNCs who do not generally "pass through" the full cost benefits of low-wage production. A meaningful global trading regime should as much as possible, over time, reduce this kind of UE arbitrage, rather than expand and support it for the benefit of TNCs and their agents and owners, as FT regimes have done.

Policies that are necessary to reduce UE (in the absence of fortuitous non-market political power by agents with otherwise less market power) are described in Chapters 5–7. Basically these require trade and finance regimes to level-up the prices of weaker market powers so as to raise rather than lower global social standards as FT regimes do. Though they sound like utopian wishful thinking, there is no inherent reason why "equal exchange" coffee trading regimes, and "Marshall Plan"-like efforts to generate developmental trade, cannot be extended to other forms of trade and finance. At the very least, eliminating FT-inspired prohibitions against "non-market" trading between nations would allow individual countries to institute tariff regimes, as described in Chap. 7, that induce a leveling-up of international standards and serve to protect and enhance social and economic democracy on a bilateral basis.

Ideally, this underlying social cost of production aspect of international trade and finance should be governed by the following principles, all derived from the UE analysis of Chapters 5 and 6 (the term "social costs" refers to the total real cost of labor, taxes, and regulation that reflects existing exchange rates):

a) Prices in any society should reflect the true social costs of that society.
b) Societies with higher social costs have the right to impose tariffs on goods and services produced in lower-social-cost societies up to a level that equalizes these costs to producers in both societies, and rebate these revenues to support broad-based increases of social costs and (if relevant) productivity in lower-standard societies.
c) When, for political reasons or to support economic development, a higher-social-cost society subsidizes production in a lower-social-cost society by not imposing tariffs at this level, the burden of these subsidies should be shared by *all* producers and workers in the higher-social-cost society, and not just by directly affected domestic producers and workers.
d) Only tariffs on trade between societies with comparable social costs, or tariffs that exceed levels that can be justified based on b) above, should be considered "predatory" and not permitted.
e) Developing country "infant industry" protective tariffs should be permitted and encouraged, along with other global development initiatives including massive grants to support green development, job creation, and sustainable real wage growth. Subject to c) these should include "productivity pricing offsets" that take into account generally lower developing country productivity when applying social-standard raising tariffs as in b) above.

Of course these policies, and those enumerated in earlier sections, all depend on national, international, and corporate governance, and this brings us to the final and most basic point.

7.3 Corporate managed trade (CMT) or democratic managed trade (DMT)?

All markets, including international markets, are social constructs. The real question is who, and for what ends, are they being constructed?

As should be painfully obvious to all at this point, modern "trade" agreements are mostly *not about trade, but about global political economic governance.* For example, reportedly only five of the twenty-nine sections of the proposed (but kept largely secret from the public) "Trans-Pacific Partnership" (TPP) that would establish international trade and finance rules for about 40% of the world's economy address trade. The remaining sections deal with rules regulating (or preventing regulation of), for example, the internet; local investment content requirements; hospital, banking, and transportation; patent rights for pharmaceuticals and media production; and most tellingly, as in almost all FT agreements since the 1994 "North America Free Trade Agreement" (NAFTA), an "investor state dispute settlement" mechanism that allows private TNCs to sue governments for losses of expected profits that are deemed to be the result of public action. These TPP "[t]ribunals would have final say over any disputes with no right of appeal to domestic courts" (Public Citizen, 2015).

Moreover, almost all of the tribunal members and negotiators who have been and would be charged with drafting and enforcing the TPP (including representatives of about 600 private TNCs) are and would be corporate lawyers and lobbyists, and the agreement has been negotiated in the utmost secrecy with not even U.S. congressmen allowed to take notes or copy any parts of the agreement and share it with the public. What we know of the TPP has largely been from unauthorized sources such as Wikileaks (Goodman and Assange, 2015).

It could not be clearer that these supposed "trade agreements" are really highly unpopular global governance agreements that are designed to override national democratic governance and lock into place a form of private TNC corporate governance in international treaties that would be very difficult to change for years to come. This is a form of private *dictatorship* over global economic policy, orchestrated through brute class power by TNCs and allied or complicit public officials who have been ideologically captured by neoliberal or Neoclassical FT ideology. These agreements are a direct anti-democratic usurpation of global economic and political power by capital through TNCs, which should themselves also be democratized, as they have been to some extent through "co-determination" laws and other measures in western Europe (Hill, 2010), and their allies.

The major reason the fiction can be maintained that these agreements are not corporate takeovers of democratic rights is that the FT and free market doctrines are based on the mythical notion that the economic sphere is "private" and that private economic agents have no real social power, as they are simply responding to objective and efficient market forces (Baiman, 2016, Chap. 3). Showing the real UE nature of international trade and finance lays bare the fact that multinational organizations that are under the sway of and administered by powerful TNCs and their agents, and likeminded (and often "on leave" from TNC employment) government officials, are making social choices that affect the destinies of millions of people and indeed the planetary survival of the human species, purely in their own interest and generally without even the pretense of subscribing to the basic economic principle that all those seriously affected should have an equal "voice," or democratic representation, in making them.

Our lives, our planet, our future is at stake. FT is not only bad economics, it has become an ideology that undermines basic democracy. Global democracy *has* become increasingly necessary, but it should not be fictionally turned over to "market forces" and then in reality usurped by private TNCs, rentiers, and "international agencies" and central banks that largely cater to their own interests. This must stop and be reversed, and this can only happen if FT ideology is shown for the utter sham that it is. I hope this book will serve as a contribution to the unveiling of "free trade" ideology, one of the greatest, most persistent, and most destructive doctrinal myths of NC economics.

Notes

1 Much of this is from Chapter 1 of Peter Dicken's excellent book; *Global Shift: Mapping the Changing Contours of the World Economy*, 7th Edition, 2015, NY: Guilford Press.
2 See WTO (2006, Chart II.1).
3 Op. cit. (Dicken, 2015, p. 20).
4 Op. cit.
5 For example, World Bank Data (downloaded 8/8/2016) indicate that in terms of 2011 "purchasing power parity" dollars, GDP per person employed in China, Germany, and the U.S. respectively in 2015 was $29,138, $84,971, and $111,455; see: http://data.worldbank.org/data-catalog/world-development-indicators.
6 Statements from Lawrence Summers, a former leader and key implementer of the NC economic effort to impose the "Washington Consensus" neoliberal FT model on the global economy, also suggest serious remorse, or at least second thoughts regarding the FT project (Summers, 2016):

> "What is needed is a responsible nationalism – an approach where it is understood that countries are expected to pursue their citizens' economic welfare as a primary objective but where their ability to harm the interests of citizens elsewhere is circumscribed. International agreements would be judged not by how much is harmonized or by how many barriers are torn down but whether citizens are empowered."

> As do comments from another leading NC economist and former erstwhile supporter and implementer (with now broadly recognized disastrous results) of "shock therapy" following standard free market doctrine, who has recently been having second thoughts about FT (Sachs, 2011):
> "The simple fact is that globalization has not only hit the unskilled hard but has also proved a bonanza for the global super-rich. They have been able to invest in new and highly profitable projects in emerging economies. Meanwhile, as Warren Buffett argued this week, they have been able to convince their home governments to cut tax rates on profits and high incomes in the name of global tax competition."

7 See, for example, the political agenda of the billionaire Koch brothers in the U.S. (Goldenberg, 2015).
8 For example, Germany's VAT is 19%, see: http://www.cfe-eutax.org/taxation/VAT-taxation/germany (downloaded 8/15/2016) . A VAT or "Value Added Tax" is a type of sales tax that is usually applied to a wide range of goods and services. In order to not put domestic producers at a disadvantage it is also is levied on the prices of imported goods and services and subtracted from the price of exports.
9 http://www.cpegonline.org/2016/06/20/cpeg-to-illinois-legislature-lasalle-street-tax-now/.
10 A "meme" is defined as ""an idea, behavior, or style that spreads from person to person within a culture" in the Miriam Webster dictionary. A meme carries cultural ideas, symbols, or practices by transmitting them through popular culture. The term was first popularized by the British evolutionary biologist Richard Dawkins in *The Selfish Gene* (1976).
11 For a more advanced discussion of the difference between "Walrasian" and post-Keynesian or "Ricardian" theories of growth and value, or output and pricing, see Nell (1967), reprinted in Nell (1992, Chap. 2).
12 For an advanced discussion the role of *tastes, nature, and technology* in the NC model, see Marglin (1984, Chap. 2). For theoretical proofs and discussions of how endogenizing these factors undermines the "fundamental theorems of welfare economics," see Hahnel and Albert (1990).

13 See any intermediate or advanced standard NC microeconomics textbook, for example Mansfield (1994).
14 See, for example, the popular Mankiw (2008). For a simple critique of CS methodology, see Hill and Myatt (2010, Chap. 4). For in-depth critiques of CS and PS, see Baiman (2016, Part III).
15 Piero Sraffa first raised (a variant of) this critique of the textbook Marshallian micro-economics story in Sraffa (1926). It has been reiterated by generations of "Sraffians" and "post-Keynesians" and other non-NC economists ever since with little apparent impact on NC microeconomic theory. For a comprehensive treatment of this NC attach-ment to "household production" as opposed to "industrial production," see Nell (1998).
16 See any introductory or intermediate economics or microeconomics text, for example Mansfield (1994).
17 The fundamentally ideological NC "U"-shaped cost curve assumption should not be confused with the post-Keynesian "Penrose effect" that assumes that attempts to increase *growth* will eventually result in a decline in the *profit rate* that underlies the post-Keynesian long-run theory of the firm (Penrose, 1959; Lavoie, 2009, Chap. 2). The Penrose effect is a *dynamic* effect which does not stipulate rising costs as firm output increases at any given point in time.
18 For an outline of a more comprehensive and realistic theory of consumer behavior, see Lavoie (2009, Section 2.1).
19 Total revenue (TR) = $aQ - bQ^2$, so that marginal revenue (MR) = $a - 2bQ$. As MC = C is below P = $a - bQ$, MR will intersect C from above at the short-term profit-maximizing point where MR = MC. At this point $a - 2bQ = C$, so that Q = $(a - C)/2b$. (Note that $a - C > 0$ by assumption that the demand curve is above the cost curve in usual production range.) This implies that the profit-maximizing price is P = $a - b(a - C)/2b = (a + C)/2$.
20 Op. cit. When P = $(a + C)/2$, then Q = $(a - C)/2b$. When P = $a - bQ = C$, then Q = $(a - C)/b$.
21 See, for example, Hill and Myatt (2010, p. 57), who note that in a survey of a represen-tative sample of 200 non-agricultural firms in the U.S. (Blinder et al., 1998): a) almost all of the firms in the sample were "price-makers" (as in the DCM) rather than "price takers" (as in the SDM), and b) though prices were periodically reviewed, they were not determined instantaneously by supply and demand as (p. 298):
    "the median number of price changes for a typical product in a typical year is just 1.4 and almost half of all prices change no more than once annually. Among firms reporting regular price reviews, annual reviews were by far the most common. At the other end of the spectrum, only about 10 percent of all prices change as often as once a week, and about 7 percent of all firms schedule price reviews at least weekly."
22 Ibid.
23 This was one of Keynes' (1936) central points (Baiman, 2016, Chap. 6).
24 In the latter part of this text we will show that more advanced, widely used, "applied microeconomic" generalizations of the SDM can be similarly shown to be social wel-fare *reducing* rather than optimizing.
25 See schools of economic thought discussion in Baiman (2016, Chap. 3).
26 Joseph Schumpeter (1942) of the "Austrian school" was a particular advocate of the importance of *dynamic* efficiency or "creative destruction" and the relative unimpor-tance of *static* allocation efficiency at one point in time.
27 Eiteman et al., 2016, Exhibit 6.1, p. 149.
28 Op. cit. Eiteman et al. (2016).

References

AFP (2015) Iceland looks at ending boom and bust with radical money plan, March 31. *The Telegraph*: http://www.telegraph.co.uk/finance/economics/11507810/Iceland-looks-at-ending-boom-and-bust-with-radical-money-plan.html.

Allen, B. W., Doherty, N. A., Weigelt, K., and Mansfield, E. (2013) *Managerial Economics: Theory, Applications, and Cases*, 8th Ed. (New York: W.W. Norton).

Baiman, R. (2016) *The Morality of Radical Economics: Ghost Curve Ideology and the Value Neutral Aspect of Neoclassical Economics* (New York: Palgrave).

—— (2001) Why equity cannot be separated from efficiency: the welfare economics of progressive social pricing, *Review of Radical Political Economics* 33, 203–21.

—— (2002) Why equity cannot be separated from efficiency II: when should social pricing be progressive, *Review of Radical Political Economics* 34, 311–17.

Barclay, B. (2010) A financial transactions tax: revenue potential and economic impact, Chicago Political Economy Group (CPEG) Working Paper 2010–12: http://www.cpe gonline.org/workingpapers/CPEGWP2010-2.pdf.

Blinder, A. S., Canetti, E., Lebow, D., and Rudd, J. B. (1998) *Asking about Prices: A new Approach to Understanding Price Stickiness* (New York: Russell Sage Foundation).

Blonigen, B. A. (2006) Foreign direct investment behavior of multinational corporations, *NBER Reporter: Research Summary*, Winter.

Chang, H-J. (2008) *Bad Samaritans: The Myth of Free Trade and the Secret History of Capitalism* (New York: Bloomsbury).

Cohan, P. (2010) Big risk: $1.2 quadrillion derivatives market dwarfs world GDP, *AOL News*, June 9: http://www.aol.com/article/2010/06/09/risk-quadrillion-derivatives-market-gdp/19509184/.

Davis, K., Stremikis, K., Squires, D., and Schoen, C. (2014) *Mirror, Mirror, on the Wall: How the Performance of the U.S. Health Care System Compares Internationally*, June (New York: Commonwealth Fund).

Dawkins, R. (1976) *The Selfish Gene* (Oxford: Oxford University Press).

Douglas-Bowers, D. (2011) Worldwide recession and the credit rating agencies: what is their impact on the global economy? Nov. 1. Montreal: Global Research: http://www.globalresearch.ca/worldwide-recession-and-the-credit-rating-agencies-what-is-their-impact-on-the-global-economy/27397.

Dicken, P. (2015) *Global Shift: Mapping the Changing Contours of the World Economy*, 7th Edition (New York: Guilford Press).

Eiteman, D. K., Stonehill, A. R., and Moffett, M. H. (2016) *Multinational Business Finance*, 14th Ed. (Boston: Pearson).

Fingleton, E. (2009) *In the Jaws of the Dragon: America's Fate in the Coming Era of Chinese Dominance* (New York: St. Martin's).

Flowers, A. (2014) Martin Wolf's grand theory of global financial disorder, Sep. 11, *FiveThirtyEight*:http://fivethirtyeight.com/datalab/martin-wolfs-grand-theory-of-global-financial-disorder/.

Goldenberg, S. (2015) Work of prominent climate change denier was funded by energy industry, Feb. 21. *The Guardian*: https://www.theguardian.com/environment/2015/feb/21/climate-change-denier-willie-soon-funded-energy-industry.

Goodman, A. and Assange, J. (2015) Julian Assange on the Trans-Pacific Partnership: secretive deal isn't about trade, but corporate control, May 27, *Democracy Now*: http://www.democracynow.org/2015/5/27/julian_assange_on_the_trans_pacific.

Granqvist, R. and Lind, H. (2004) Excess Burden of an income tax: what do mainstream economists really measure?" *Review of Radical Political Economics* 37(4), Fall, 453–70.

Greenberg, J. (2014) Can you make $45,000 per year at McDonald's in Denmark?, Sept. 3, PunditFact:http://www.politifact.com/punditfact/statements/2014/sep/03/other-98/can-you-make-45000year-mcdonalds-denmark/.

Hahnel, R. and Albert, M. (1990) *Quiet Revolution in Welfare Economics* (Princeton: Princeton University Press).

Harris, G. (2014) Borrowed time on disappearing land facing rising seas, Bangladesh confronts the consequences of climate change, March 28, *New York Times*: http://www.nytimes.com/2014/03/29/world/asia/facing-rising-seas-bangladesh-confronts-the-consequences-of-climate-change.html.

Hill, S. (2010) *Europe's Promise: Why the European Way is the Best Hope in an Insecure Age* (Berkeley, CA: University of California Press).

Hill, R. and Myatt, T. (2010) *The Economics Anti-Textbook: A Critical Thinkers Guide to Micro-Economics* (Halifax and London: Fernwood Publishing and Zed Books).

Hong, N. (2016) Banks dealt blow in Libor lawsuits: appeals court restores private suits against Bank of America, J.P. Morgan Chase, Citigroup and others, May 2, *Wall Street Journal*: http://www.wsj.com/articles/civil-antitrust-lawsuits-reinstated-against-16-banks-in-libor-case-1464022330.

Jacobs, K. (2015) Americans are spending $153 billion a year to subsidize McDonald's and Wal-Mart's low wage workers, Aug. 15, *The Washington Post*: https://www.washingtonpost.com/posteverything/wp/2015/04/15/we-are-spending-153-billion-a-year-to-subsidize-mcdonalds-and-walmarts-low-wage-workers/?utm_term=.0d2f14fd818e.

Kay, J. (2015) *Other People's Money: The Real Business of Finance* (New York: Public Affairs).

Keynes, J. M. (1919) *The Economic Consequences of the Peace* (London: Macmillan).

—— (1933) National self-sufficiency, *The Yale Review* 22(4), 755–69.

—— (1936) *The General Theory of Employment, Interest, and Money* (Cambridge: Cambridge University Press).

Lavoie, M. (2009) *Introduction to Post-Keynesian Economics* (New York: Palgrave Macmillan).

Lee, F. (1998) *Post Keynesian Price Theory* (Cambridge: Cambridge University Press).

Lewis, M. (2014) *Flash Boys: A Wall Street Revolt* (New York: W. W. Norton & Company).

Mankiw, N. G. (2008) *Principles of Macroeconomics*, 5th Ed. (Independence, KY: South-Western).

Mansfield, E. (1994) *Microeconomics: Theory and Applications*, 8th Ed. (New York: W. W. Norton and Co.).

Marglin, S. (1984) *Growth, Distribution, and Prices* (Cambridge, MA: Harvard University Press).

Marglin, S. and Schor, J. (1992) *The Golden Age of Capitalism: Reinterpreting the Post-War Experience* (Oxford: Clarendon Press).

Marshall, A. (1890) *Principles of Economics* (London: Macmillan and Co.).

Miller, C. C. (2014) Why the U.S. has fallen behind in internet speed and affordability, Oct. 30, *New York Times*: http://www.nytimes.com/2014/10/31/upshot/why-the-us-has-fallen-behind-in-internet-speed-and-affordability.html?_r=2.

Nell, E. J. (1967) Theories of growth and theories of value, *Economic Development and Cultural Change* 16(1), 15–26.

—— (1992) *Transformational Growth and Effective Demand* (New York: New York University Press).

—— (1996) *Making Sense of a Changing Economy* (London: Routledge).

—— (1998) *Theory of Transformational Growth* (Cambridge: Cambridge University Press).

Oxfam (2016) An economy for the 1%: how privilege and power in the economy drive extreme inequality and how this can be stopped, Oxfam Briefing Paper. Jan. 18. Oxford, UK: http://policy-practice.oxfam.org.uk/publications/an-economy-for-the-1-how-privilege-and-power-in-the-economy-drive-extreme-inequ-592643.

Penrose, E. (1959) *The Theory of the Growth of the Firm* (Oxford: Oxford University Press).

Piketty, T. (2014) *Capital in the Twenty-First Century* (Cambridge, MA: The Belknap Press of Harvard University Press).

Polanyi, K. (1944) *The Great Transformation* (New York: Farrar & Rinehart).

Public Citizen (2015) Secret TPP text unveiled: it's worse than we thought, Nov. TPP Text Analysis: http://www.citizen.org/documents/analysis-tpp-text-november-2015.pdf.

Rodrick, D. (2007) The inescapable trilemma of the world economy," June 27, blog post accessed September 1, 2016 at: http://rodrik.typepad.com/dani_rodriks_weblog/2007/06/the-inescapable.html.

Sachs, J. (2011) Tripped up by globalization, August 18. *Financial Times*: http://www.ft.com/cms/s/0/2b9dab2e-c817-11e0-9501-00144feabdc0.html#axzz4J1l6HvoX.

Schumpeter, J. (1942) *Capitalism, Socialism, and Democracy* (New York: Harper & Row).

Sraffa, P. (1926) The law of returns under competitive conditions, *Economic Journal* 36, 535–50.

—— (1960) *Production of Commodities by Means of Commodities: Prelude to a Critique of Economic Theory* (Cambridge: Cambridge University Press).

Stiglitz, J. (2016) Beware of TPP's investor–state dispute settlement provision, March 28. *Roosevelt Forward: Rewrite the Rules*: http://rooseveltforward.org/beware-tpps-investor-state-dispute-settlement-provision/.

Stretton, H. (1999) *Economics: A New Introduction* (New York: Pluto Press).

Summers, L. (2016) Voters deserve responsible nationalism not reflex globalism, July 9, *Financial Times*: https://www.ft.com/content/15598db8-4456-11e6-9b66-0712b3873ae1.

Taylor, L. (2004) *Reconstructing Macroeconomics: Structuralist Proposals and Critiques of the Mainstream* (Cambridge, MA: Harvard University Press).

Vitali, S., Glattfelder, J. B., and Battiston, S. (2011) The network of global corporate control, *PLOS ONE*: http://journals.plos.org/plosone/article?id=10.1371/journal.pone.0025995#s3.

Weisbrot, M. (2016) "Brexit" might be the wake-up call Europe needs, June 21, *The Hill*: http://thehill.com/blogs/pundits-blog/international/284220-brexit-might-be-the-wake-up-call-europe-needs.

Wolf, M. (2014) *The Shifts and the Shocks: What We've Learned – and Have Still to Learn – From the Financial Crisis* (London: Penguin Books).

—— (2016) Capitalism and democracy, the strain is showing, August 30. *Financial Times*: http://www.ft.com/cms/s/0/e46e8c00-6b72-11e6-ae5b-a7cc5dd5a28c.html#axzz4J1l6HvoX.

World Trade Organization (WTO) (2006) *World Trade Developments in 2005* (Geneva: WTO).

Index

absolute advantage 55
administered trade 57
aggregate demand and supply 17
algebraic Heckscher-Ohlin model (AHO)
    6, 29, 30–3
Amin, S. 72
analytical Marxism 72–3, 87
Asia 153
autarky 10–11, 74–5, 108, 109

Baiman, R. 98, 99, 107, 110
balanced trade: comparative advantage 17,
    19, 21, 22, 26; exchange-rate based
    trading systems 52–5; impossibility
    of bilateral trade balances in three-
    country trade 55–9
banking crises 93
Barofsky, N. 93
Basu, D. 92
Baumol, W. 131, 132
Big Mac 156
bilateral trade balances: cannot be
    included in three-country trade 55–9;
    imbalances in a three-country free
    trade system 59–62
Brandt Commission 81
Bretton-Woods system 23, 63–4,
    65, 137
Brexit 139, 140
Buffett, W. 132
Bureau of Economic Analysis (BEA)
    91–2, 97

Canada 153
capital flows 136
capitalism 137
Chacholiades, M. 46, 47
Chicago Political Economy Group (CPEG)
    jobs program 126–7, 128–9

China 43, 47, 51, 83, 138, 139; repression
    86, 119; unequal exchange and the
    rentier economy 106, 107, 111,
    113–14; U.S. and technological
    standing of 130–1, 134
claims on output 110–15
classical theory *see* comparative advantage
co-determination 99
Colander, D. 23–4
community indifference curves 39
comparative advantage 2, 5–6, 9–28,
    54, 88, 119, 129; cross-price effects
    17, 18–20; fully specified constant
    elasticity model 20–2; simple own-
    price formalization 10–20, 26–7
competition: degree of 151; monopolistic
    148; perfect 30–1
computers and electronics manufacturing
    (C&E) sector 92, 96
constant elasticity version of comparative
    advantage 20–2
constant returns to scale 30–1
consumer surplus 143–4, 151
consumption 125
corporate managed trade (CMT) 137, 154,
    157–8
cost of living 156
costs: increasing 38–9; reducing
    international unequal exchange 155–7;
    social 156–7; total short-run average
    costs 145–6; U-shaped cost curve
    assumption 146, 160; unequal factor
    costs 30, 40, 41–4, 45
cross-price effects 17, 18–20
Crotty, J. 92, 93
currency appreciation 57
currency depreciation 57
current account balance 99, 103; U.S.
    130, 131

For Product Safety Concerns and Information please contact our EU
representative GPSR@taylorandfrancis.com
Taylor & Francis Verlag GmbH, Kaufingerstraße 24, 80331 München, Germany

www.ingramcontent.com/pod-product-compliance
Ingram Content Group UK Ltd.
Pitfield, Milton Keynes, MK11 3LW, UK
UKHW020949180425
457613UK00019B/607